Jossey-Bass Teacher

Jossey-Bass Teacher provides K–12 teachers with essential knowledge and tools to create a positive and lifelong impact on student learning. Trusted and experienced educational mentors offer practical clas[…] for improving teaching practice in a […]e educator to another, we want to be[…]aching. Jossey-Bass Teacher resource[…]nowledge and essential tools.

Essential knowled[…]methods from which teachers may d[…]cite their students. Connecting the[…]solid research base and time-tested n[…]ny of the most experienced and well-[…]

Essential tools save[…]e materials for in-class use. Our publi[…]ments, games, ready reference, and n[…]y lesson, or a daily plan. These essen[…]sive materials on topics that matter n[…]

Science Sleuths

Science Sleuths

60 Forensic Activities to Develop Critical Thinking and Inquiry Skills, Grades 4–8

Pam Walker and Elaine Wood

Published by Jossey-Bass
A Wiley Imprint
989 Market Street, San Francisco, CA 94103-1741 www.josseybass.com

Jossey-Bass books and products are available through most bookstores. To contact Jossey-Bass directly call our Customer Care Department within the U.S. at 800-956-7739, outside the U.S. at 317-572-3986, or fax 317-572-4002.
Jossey-Bass also publishes its books in a variety of electronic formats. Some content that appears in print may not be available in electronic books.

Library of Congress Cataloging-in-Publication Data
Walker, Pam, 1958-
Science sleuths : 60 forensic activities to develop critical thinking and inquiry skills, grades 4-8 / Pam Walker and Elaine Wood.
p. cm.
ISBN-13: 978-0-7879-7435-0 (pbk.)
ISBN-10: 0-7879-7435-8 (pbk.)
1. Forensic sciences—Problems, exercises, etc. 2. Forensic sciences—Study and teaching (Elementary)—Activity programs. 3. Forensic sciences—Study and teaching (Middle school)—Activity programs. I. Wood, Elaine, 1950- II. Title.
HV8073.W342 2007
363.25'6—dc22

2006017862

Printed in the United States of America
FIRST EDITION
PB Printing 10 9 8 7 6 5 4 3 2 1

Contents

CRIME SCENE DO NOT CROSS CRIME SCENE DO NOT CROSS CRIME SCENE DO NOT CROSS CRIME SCENE DO NOT CROSS CRIME SCENE DO NOT CROSS CRIME SCENE DO NOT CROSS

About the Authors

CRIME SCENE DO NOT CROSS CRIME SCENE DO NOT CROSS CRIME SCENE DO NOT CROSS CRIME SCENE DO NOT CROSS CRIME SCENE DO NOT CROSS CRIME SCENE DO NOT CROSS

Pam Walker has twenty-five years of experience in teaching science. She earned her B.S. from Georgia College and M.Ed. and Ed.S. from Georgia Southern University. Walker is the 2007 Georgia Teacher of the Year. **Elaine Wood** has spent thirteen years teaching science. She earned her A.B., M.S., and Ed.S. from West Georgia College. Both Walker and Wood teach science in Douglasville, Georgia. They are coauthors of several resource books, including *Hands-On General Science Activities with Real-Life Applications; Crime Scene Investigations, Real-Life Science Labs for Grades 6–12;* and *Crime Scene Investigations, Real-Life Science Activities for Elementary Grades.*

Preface

Media coverage has brought a once obscure branch of applied science, forensics, to front and center stage. With its newfound glamour and mass appeal, forensic science is an ideal vehicle for teaching the nature of science as well as basic science concepts. The influence of this hot television topic is obvious as millions of viewers vicariously help detectives and investigators solve grizzly crimes through scientific inquiry.

Forensic science is an excellent classroom tool that fosters interest in science in general. Besides teaching students to think like scientists, it also helps them understand, master, and apply science concepts. In addition, forensic science relies heavily on science process skills, manipulative skills, laboratory skills, and interpersonal skills, all emphasized by the National Science Education Standards.

Science Sleuths is a resource for teachers who want to improve their students' critical thinking skills and basic scientific knowledge. Forensic science, the application of science to processes of law, is an integrated field that naturally ties together concepts in math, biology, chemistry, physics, medicine, geology, and behavioral science with critical thinking and manipulative skills.

The activities and experiments in *Science Sleuths* vary widely, covering topics that range from techniques for sharpening observation skills to recipes for extracting DNA. In this book, students have the opportunity to develop and conduct many of their own original experiments, a skill that science teachers are using in the classroom. The book also teaches basic lab techniques with highly directed experiments.

Science Sleuths is filled with forensic science activities that can be completed without the use of specialized lab equipment. The text exposes students to problems, both real and fictitious, that need solutions. By focusing on skills related to critical thinking, the book helps students:

- Identify questions that can be answered through scientific investigation
- Design and carry out original experiments
- Collect and analyze data
- Explain scientific concepts and make predictions
- Make logical deductions and develop explanations based on evidence
- Share findings with others clearly and logically
- Integrate math and writing skill with science

Science Sleuths is a valuable resource for the traditional classroom and for home schoolers. The book ties a variety of science concepts to current events, making the material highly relevant. The six chapters in this book address using the power of observation, how to get and use information, earth science, physical science, biology, and critical thinking and problem solving. Every chapter contains ten activities, of which two are optional homework. Each student activity is prefaced with teacher information. Activities include a statement of goals or objectives, background information to familiarize students with the topic, a list of materials needed, a detailed procedure, and conclusion questions. A glossary is provided at the end of the book.

All activities in this book contain a Science Sleuth Activity Package that students should read. Most activities can be read and completed in less than one hour. However, depending on the maturity of the students, some experiments may require more time. Teachers should examine each activity carefully to be sure that it is appropriate for the maturity of their students involved.

Science Sleuths

Chapter One

Stop, Look, and Listen

Using the Five Senses in Forensic Science

The power of observation, using the senses to gather information, is a detective's most important tool. Observation is a fundamental skill and the basis for every thorough investigation in both forensics and science. Through systematic observation and documentation, detectives and scientists identify problems, collect evidence, and develop theories. In this chapter, students are encouraged to use their natural curiosity to learn how to become careful, methodical observers. The ability to observe depends on the five senses. These senses have natural limitations, and students find out how simple instruments and techniques can give them an edge in scientific thinking.

Activity 1.1: Trained Eyes

Teacher Briefing

In this activity, students begin to develop skills of systematic observation by looking closely at a familiar place. The activity allows you to choose between using your own classroom or exchanging classrooms for the day with another teacher so that the setting will be familiar to students but not exactly what they are used to. If you do exchange classrooms, make sure that you and the other teacher tell students to take any valuable items with them. Also be sure to let the principal and support staff know about your plan.

Activity Preparation

- Optional preparation: Gather this optional equipment:
  Magnifying glass
  Tweezers
  Envelopes to collect evidence
- Make arrangements to switch classrooms if you choose that option.
- If you have decided to use your own classroom, determine how you will divide it up into search areas and plan ahead what items you will change in each area at the end of the exercise. For example, you might add a new picture to the bulletin board, turn a desk at an angle, or erase something on the chalkboard.
- Make copies of Science Sleuth Activity Package.

First, Tell Your Students . . .

When detectives arrive at a crime scene, they quickly put their skills of observation to work. Observation is the first step in every investigation because the place where a crime occurred has a story to tell.

Smart detectives look at everything. That's why they often see things that others overlook. Here's a classic case in which keen observation solved a case. It happened almost a century ago, in 1910.

A midnight burglar broke into the home of Clarence Hiller, his wife, and four daughters. The perpetrator woke the family, scuffled with Mr. Hiller, and then escaped. The police were called, and detectives were quickly dispatched to the Hiller home. In spite of a thorough search, they turned up little evidence. However, one sharp-eyed detective noticed that the paint on the porch railing was still wet and found out from Mr. Hiller that he had painted it on the afternoon of the break-in.

A thorough check of all the railings revealed that the intruder had left four clear fingerprints in the fresh paint. Back then, fingerprints were not always collected for evidence as they are today. But the detectives collected them anyway, just in case they might be useful.

By coincidence, police in another part of town had arrested a man that same evening. Thomas Jennings was found wandering around a neighborhood, acting confused and lost. His clothes were torn and dirty, so officers suspected that he had been up to no good. Officers had Mr. Jennings sitting in the local jail by the time the detectives finished their investigation of the Hiller home. Jennings's fingerprints were compared to those from the porch railing and found to be a perfect match.

Good eyes—the kind that spot little pieces of evidence—are as essential in solving crimes today as they were in 1910. All detectives need good observation skills. Start training your eyes to see it all.

Activity Procedure

1. Distribute the Science Sleuth Activity Package, magnifying glasses, tweezers, and envelopes.
2. If you are switching classrooms, do this now.
3. Divide your students into groups, and give each group an area to search. For example, one group might search the chalkboards and displays, while others search in cabinets and bookcases. You can divide the student desks into different sections for searching. If you are using your own classroom, make sure that students search an area where they don't usually sit.
4. Tell students to follow the directions in the Science Sleuth Activity Package. Let them know that they'll be asked some questions later, so they need to observe carefully.
5. Give students a fixed amount of time, about ten minutes, to do their search.
6. If you are using your own classroom, have students stand in the back of the room and close their eyes while you make your planned changes in the room's environment.

Summary and Discussion

- If you use another teacher's classroom, ask students:

  How is it different from their own classroom?
  What is the other class studying?
  How many boys and how many girls are in the class? (The groups will need to collaborate on this answer.)
  Was anyone in the classroom eating recently?
- If you use your own classroom, ask students what they noticed about the classroom that was new to them.
- Systematic strategies help make searches more successful. Ask the students if they have any ideas about such strategies.

Name ______________________________ Date ______________________

Science Sleuth Activity Package: Trained Eyes

Background

When detectives arrive at a crime scene, they quickly put their skills of observation to work. Observation is the first step in every investigation because the place where a crime occurred has a story to tell. In a way, the crime scene is like a jigsaw puzzle that hasn't been put together. Pieces of the puzzle are lying around, right in front of your eyes. Some are stuck under other pieces, and some are turned upside down. With a little patience, you will be able to put each piece together to make a picture that can help solve the crime.

Wise detectives look at everything. That's why they often see things that others overlook. Observant eyes—the kind that spot little pieces of evidence—are essential in solving crimes. Like all other skills, you can develop your powers of observation by practice. In this investigation, you'll get a shot at observing with detective eyes.

Activity Directions

1. Join your group in the area that the teacher has assigned you to search. You may want to discuss with your group how to conduct the search, dividing up the space or the tasks.
2. Look at the area as a whole. Make notes or draw a picture of the main things that are in the area.

   ____

   ____

3. Now take a closer look. What was happening here most recently? Was a class working on a project? Was someone reading? Has anyone been eating? How can you tell?

   ____

   ____

4. What does this room say about the people who spend time here? Is there sports equipment in sight? A novel? A CD?

   ____

   ____

5. Now, get on your hands and knees and look closely at the floor. Peek under and behind the furniture. What has gotten lost back there? Are there any hairs or threads? What could they tell you?

   ____

   ____

6. Join your group, and review your findings as you prepare to answer the questions your teacher will ask.

Activity 1.2: Up Close and Personal

Teacher Briefing

This is an extension of the previous activity, with students learning to observe things about their personal clothing and their possessions. Students are paired to work with a partner. Depending on the age and maturity of your students, you will need to consider whether the pairs should be same-sex or not and what limits you should set on the search.

Activity Preparation

- Decide how you will pair students.
- Consider any limitations you want to put on the search.
- For each student, provide:

  Magnifying glass
  Tweezers
  Envelopes to collect evidence
  Plastic bag or newspapers
- Make copies of the Science Sleuth Activity Package.

First, Tell Your Students . . .

When detectives check out a scene, they *really* check it out. To find tiny clues, they get up close and personal with a magnifying glass.

One of the best places to discover clues with a magnifying glass is on clothing. Hairs, threads, and tiny specks of dirt will cling to clothes. These tiny messengers give a detective hints about where those clothes have been.

Some of the most important evidence in a case may not be out in plain view—it could be in a bag or a purse. The more that detectives can explore a crime scene, the more they can learn about what happened. A personal possession like a backpack, purse, suitcase, or wallet often holds clues that tell a detective something about its owner and that person's habits.

Activity Procedure

1. Distribute the Science Sleuth Activity Packages, magnifying glasses, tweezers, and envelopes.
2. Following your plan, assign the students to their partners.
3. Tell the students to inspect their clothes and shoes for possible evidence, following the guidelines in their Science Sleuth Activity Package. Depending on the age and maturity of your students, you may want them to inspect themselves rather than their partner.

4. Tell students that they are going to search each other's backpacks or purses. Give them a few minutes to place any personal items in their desk. You may also want them to place their wallet or any money or valuable items in the desk.
5. Now tell students to search each other's belongings, following the guidelines in their Science Sleuth Activity Package.

Summary and Discussion

- Ask students if they found anything surprising in their search of their own clothes and shoes. Were they able to identify the source of any threads or hairs on their clothes? How about stains on their shoes?
- Ask students what they found in their partner's backpack. Can they tell what their partner likes to eat? to read? to listen to? Were there any materials with dates showing where their partner had been or is planning to go?
- Ask students to imagine they are assigned a case involving a missing person. Where is the first place they would search for evidence? What kinds of things would they hope to find?
- Ask students to imagine that they searched a woman's purse and found three receipts issued on the same date. One receipt was for the purchase of gasoline in one town at 9:00 A.M., another receipt for lunch in a town two hundred miles to the north, and a third for a hotel located another two hundred miles down the road. What could they conclude about her activities? Student answers will vary but might suggest that the woman has traveled four hundred miles by car on this date and that she stopped for only one meal.
- During the 1997 robbery of a convenience store in Conroe, Texas, would-be thieves Michael and Lisa Morrison held up the store and then ran out with their pockets full of cash. They would have made a clean getaway except for one mistake: Mrs. Morrison left her purse at the store. What kind of useful information might the detectives find in her purse?

Name ________________________________ Date ________________________

Science Sleuth Activity Package: Up Close and Personal

Background

When detectives check out a scene, they *really* check it out. To find tiny clues, they get up close and personal with a magnifying glass.

One of the best places to discover clues with a magnifying glass is on clothing. Hairs, threads, and tiny specks of dirt cling to clothes. These tiny messengers give a detective hints about where those clothes have been. Use your magnifying glass to check out the clothes that you're wearing. See what they reveal about your activities today.

Some of the most important evidence in a case may not be out in plain view; it could be in a bag or purse, for example. The more detectives explore a crime scene, the more they learn about what happened there. A personal possession like a backpack, purse, suitcase, or wallet often holds clues that tell a detective something about its owner and that person's habits.

Activity Directions

1. Start at your feet and inspect your shoes. Look at the tops of them first, and then check out the soles. Do you see any soil? How about bits of plants? Where could they have come from? Use this space to make notes about what you see.

   ____

   ____

   ____

   ____

2. Inspect your clothing inch by inch. Look in the hems, cuffs, and pockets. Do you find any threads, hairs, or stains that might tell something about where you've been or what you've done? Make notes on what you find.

   ____

   ____

   ____

   ____

3. Review the list of things you found on your person. Can you explain where each clue came from?

   ____

   ____

   ____

   ____

Name ______________________________ Date ____________________

Science Sleuth Activity Package: Up Close and Personal, *Cont'd.*

4. Using the plastic bag or newspapers your teacher provided, spread out the contents of your partner's backpack. Make a list of the things you find.

   ___

   ___

   ___

   ___

5. Do you see any schoolwork? Does it tell you what classes your partner is taking?

   ___

   ___

   ___

   ___

6. Is there a calendar or notepad in the book bag where your partner writes down assignments and dates? Does it tell you where your partner has been or is going?

   ___

   ___

   ___

   ___

7. Is there any food in the bag?

   ___

   ___

   ___

   ___

8. Are there any clues in the bag to what your partner does for fun? Books? CDs?

   ___

   ___

   ___

   ___

Activity 1.3: Quick Draw

Teacher Briefing

This activity extends the observation skills students have been learning. Students are asked to visualize an imaginary crime scene, translate the verbal data they receive into a sketch, and draw conclusions about what happened based on what they see in their sketch.

Activity Preparation

- Provide students with art materials such as markers, colored pencils, and special paper.
- Make copies of the Science Sleuth Activity Package. Add a blank page to it where students can make their drawing.

First, Tell Your Students . . .

Crime scene sketches are important pieces of evidence in solving cases. A sketch helps investigators visualize items at the crime scene in proper perspective. Long after the crime scene is closed or released, an investigator can still see exactly where each item was located with respect to other items at the scene. Good crime scene sketches may provide valuable information and clues that help solve cases.

Some crime scene sketches make their way into the courtroom. During a trial, a witness may use a crime scene sketch to indicate his or her location during the crime. A sketch can also help members of the jury understand the layout of a room or building.

Activity Procedure

1. Distribute the Science Sleuth Activity Package and any special art materials you want your students to use.
2. Tell students to make a sketch of the crime scene. Remind them that they don't have to draw everything as an artist would. They can use squares, circles, and triangles to represent furniture and X's or other letters to represent items.
3. Give students plenty of time, twenty to thirty minutes, to draw the crime scene.

Summary and Discussion

- Ask students:

  "From your research, how do you think a thief could have entered and left the classroom?"

  "How could a person get a python out of the classroom without being detected?"

  "From your drawing, is it likely that Pearl the Python broke open her terrarium and escaped alone? Why or why not?"

Name ______________________________ Date ______________________

Science Sleuth Activity Package: Quick Draw

Background

You've heard the old saying, "A picture is worth a thousand words." That's definitely true in crime scene work. Notes are essential, but they don't always convey the "how" of the story. That's when a sketch comes in handy.

Crime scene sketches don't have to be works of art. Lots of detectives draw stick figures for people and squares or circles to represent furniture, buildings, cars, and so forth. The main purpose of the sketch is to show where important items are located.

You have been called to a crime scene at the local middle school at 7:30 A.M. on Monday. The students haven't arrived yet, but Mr. Bones, the science teacher, has been at school long enough to discover a theft: his beloved classroom pet, Pearl the Python, has been stolen. The Crime Scenario at the end of this package tells you what you see when you arrive.

Activity Directions

1. Read the Crime Scenario carefully.
2. Based on the description, use the blank page attached to your Science Sleuth Activity Package to sketch the crime scene.
3. Remember that this doesn't have to be a work of art. Here are some ideas:

   Start by drawing the outside wall of the classroom.

   Show where the doors are.

   Add the furniture. You can use rectangles or circles or any other kind of symbol to represent the furniture.
4. Your drawing should show the following: the teacher's desk, students' desks, the blackboard, bulletin boards, TV, table, broken glass, hammer, window, classroom door, and closet door. Label each of these items.

Questions for Discussion

- How do you think a thief could have entered and left the classroom?
- How could a person get a python out of the classroom without being detected?
- From your drawing, is it likely that Pearl the Python broke open her terrarium and escaped alone? Why or why not?

Name ________________________________ Date ______________________

Science Sleuth Activity Package: Quick Draw, *Cont'd.*

Crime Scenario

From where you stand at the classroom door, the room appears to be a large square. The door is on one end of the front wall of the classroom, and it leads from the classroom into the hallway. As you take a step into the room, you see a blackboard and a TV mounted on the wall to your immediate left. In front of the board is a teacher's desk and chair. Facing the teacher's desk are thirty student desks arranged in six rows. All desks are empty except for two: the last desk in the second row from the door has a jacket on it, and the first desk in the first row has a backpack in the seat.

From your position, you're facing the only window in the room. It's located on the far wall directly in front of you. Two bulletin boards decorate the rest of this wall to the left of the window. Under the window is a table that holds the remnants of a large, broken terrarium. Glass shards are scattered all over the table. A hammer is lying on the floor under the table. You can also see another door that opens on the wall to your right. It looks like a closet door. A countertop with a sink runs the length of the wall to your left.

Activity 1.4: Get the Picture?

Teacher Briefing

This activity offers two ways for students to make a record of the crime scene. In one, they take photographs; in the other, they make a scale drawing. You may prefer to use one strategy or the other depending on the resources available at your school. Or if you are able to keep the crime scenes set up for a few days, you could do the photography and the scale drawing in separate classes.

Activity Preparation

- Set up two or more crime scenes in your class, depending on how many groups of students will be working on this project. You will want to protect the crime scenes, if possible with the yellow tape real detectives use. With this or some other kind of tape, mark the limits of the crime scenes. Here are some examples of crime scenes:

  Example 1: Draw the chalk line of a body on the floor. Beside the "body," drop a rag stained red. Bring in dirty shoes, and make footprints leading to and from the "body." Leave an open wallet to the side of the "body."
  Example 2: Stand a shoe box on a table with the cover atilt. Have some play money strewn on the table to suggest a robbery. Drop an ID card nearby. Rub some graphite on your finger, and make one fingerprint inside the box lid.
  Example 3: Bring in a stroller with an empty blanket in the seat, and tack a ransom note on the top. Drop some cracker crumbs on the floor next to it, and step on the crumbs to leave a print.

- Make copies of the Science Sleuth Activity Package. Add a blank page to it where students can make their drawing.
- For each student or student group, provide:

  A camera (digital if possible)
  Sticky notes (3 inch by 3 inch)
  Graph paper (4 squares to an inch)
  Compass
  Measuring tape
  Ruler

First, Tell Your Students . . .

Even the best detective in the world cannot remember every detail about a crime scene. That is why it is important to make a record of it. There are a couple of ways to do this, and we are going to practice two: taking photographs and making a scale drawing.

First, detectives walk around the crime scene, making sure that they don't disturb any evidence with their hands or feet. A walk-through helps them get a perspective on the entire crime scene. Then they put flags or labels near the pieces of evidence, taking care not to disturb anything. The next step is to prepare a scale drawing or take photographs, or both.

Activity Procedure

1. As students enter the room, point out the crime scenes and warn them that they must not contaminate the evidence.
2. After you've read the introductory material, assign students to teams and distribute the Science Sleuth Activity Package and the tools you are providing.
3. Tell students to decide among themselves which students will have the following assignments:

    Label and list possible evidence.

    Take photographs of the scene.

    Make a log of the photographs.

    Draw a quick sketch of the crime scene.

    Take measurements and make notes of these for the scale drawing.

    Make the scale drawing.

    Depending on how many students are in each group, a student may have more than one assignment.
4. Tell students to conduct the investigation following the directions on the Science Sleuth Activity Package.

Summary and Discussion

- Ask each student group to tell how many photographs they took of the scene. Did they discover any new evidence when studying the photographs or scale drawings? If so, what is it?
- Based on what they see at the crime scene, what do they think happened? What might their next steps be if they were investigating the crime?
- Why do detectives take a lot of pictures? Why do they make a log of the photographs they take? Answers will vary, but students should explain that pictures help preserve the crime scene. A log provides information about each picture and explains when, and from what angle, each picture was made.
- Why do detectives make scale drawings of crime scenes? Scale drawings show the exact locations and relative sizes of items at a crime scene.
- Which drawing would be larger: one drawn to a scale of one inch equals one foot, or one drawn so that one-quarter inch equals one foot?
- If the crime scene was a two-mile stretch of highway, what kind of scale might you use? (Remember that one mile equals 5,280 feet.) Answers will vary but might include one inch equals one hundred feet.

Name ______________________________ Date ______________________

Science Sleuth Activity Package: Get the Picture?

Background

Detectives know that it's important not to disturb the crime scene by touching evidence or walking nearby. It's also important to make a record of the crime scene, and there are a couple of ways to do this. We are going to practice two: taking photographs and making a scale drawing.

First, detectives place flags or labels near pieces of evidence to help identify them later.

The photographer takes pictures from three perspectives: overview, midrange, and close up. If the crime scene is too big to fit in one shot, overview pictures can be taken in an overlapping sequence that begins in one place and moves clockwise around the scene. In the progressive technique, the photographer begins at the outside of the crime scene and takes pictures moving toward the center.

Detectives must keep a log of all the photographs they take. Later, the log will describe what angle the photograph was taken from and what piece of evidence it shows. To give an idea of size, a ruler can be carefully placed next to the item of evidence.

Without a scale, it might be hard to tell if an object is one inch or one foot long. This brings us to a second way of recording the crime scene: a scale drawing.

The easiest measuring technique is the rectangular method. Detectives make measurements at right angles (90 degrees) to flat surfaces, like walls. They measure objects in the crime scene, distances between them, and distances to the edge of the crime scene. Two measurements must be made of every object. After taking multiple measurements and making quick sketches, detectives return to their offices to make detailed, accurate drawings.

Your Science Sleuth Activity Package has an example of a scale drawing of a crime scene. The scale drawing is broken down into four parts: the title, north arrow, body, and legend. The title, at the bottom right-hand corner, identifies the crime scene. The north arrow indicates which way is north. Usually the arrow points up, and the drawing is positioned to reflect this.

The body of the drawing is the biggest area and is the region where the drawing is made. The legend is used to identify objects, like a sofa, which may be labeled as A and a chair as B, as in the "Scale Drawing of Crime Scene" at the end of the activity package. If there is evidence that the suspect walked through the crime scene, a dotted line is drawn from point of entry to exit.

Activity Directions

1. With your team of detectives, walk around the crime scene, and look at it from different angles.
2. Decide what the key pieces of evidence are. Use sticky notes to label each piece of evidence with a number. Take care not to touch any evidence. (If you are part of the scale drawing team, skip to item 10.)
3. If you are the photographer, take a picture of the entire crime to serve as an overview. If possible, get the overview from several angles.

Name ______________________ Date ______________

Science Sleuth Activity Package: Get the Picture?, *Cont'd.*

4. While you are taking photographs, make sure that you or one of your partners keeps a log describing each photograph.
5. Decide which items need to be photographed at midrange or close up. Place a ruler beside items to give them perspective. Use different angles so you will get all of the features of the evidence.
6. Document everything in your log.
7. If you have taken digital photographs, print them out, arrange them in the order in which they were taken, and check them against the log.
8. Examine the photos carefully with a magnifying glass. Do you see anything that you missed the first time you reviewed these pictures? Does the hand lens reveal any footprints or tracks? A tiny necklace? A scrap of paper? Make notes.
9. Answer these questions:

   How many photographs did you take to get a complete picture of the crime scene?

   ____

   Why do detectives take a lot of pictures at a crime scene?

   ____

   ____

   ____

   ____

   ____

   Why do detectives make a log of the photographs they take?

   ____

   ____

   ____

   ____

   ____

   Did you discover any new evidence when studying the photographs? If so, what is it?

   ____

   ____

   ____

   ____

   ____

If you are part of the photography team, stop here.

Name ____________________ Date ____________________

Science Sleuth Activity Package: Get the Picture?, *Cont'd.*

10. Make a rough sketch of the crime scene on the blank piece of paper at the end of the activity package. Be sure to include each piece of evidence in your rough sketch.
11. Use the compass to find out which direction is north. Indicate north with an arrow on the sketch.
12. In the bottom right-hand corner, give the sketch a title.
13. Reserve an area along one side of the paper where you can draw the legend.
14. Select two spots to serve as your reference points. These could include a piece of evidence or the edge of the crime scene.
15. Working with a partner, measure each piece of evidence from both reference points. Label the distance from each reference point to the evidence.
16. Measure the size of each piece of evidence—both its height and width.
17. Use the graph paper attached to your activity package to make a final scale drawing. Let one inch represent one foot at the crime scene.
18. Neatly transfer all your sketches and drawings to the graph paper.

Questions to Answer

- Why do detectives make scale drawings of crime scenes?

____

____

____

____

- Which drawing would be larger: one drawn to a scale of one inch equals one foot, or one drawn so that one-quarter inch equals one foot? Explain your answer.

____

____

____

____

- If the crime scene was a two-mile stretch of highway, what kind of scale might you use? (Remember: one mile equals 5,280 feet.) Explain your answer.

____

____

____

____

Science Sleuth Activity Package: Get the Picture?, *Cont'd.*

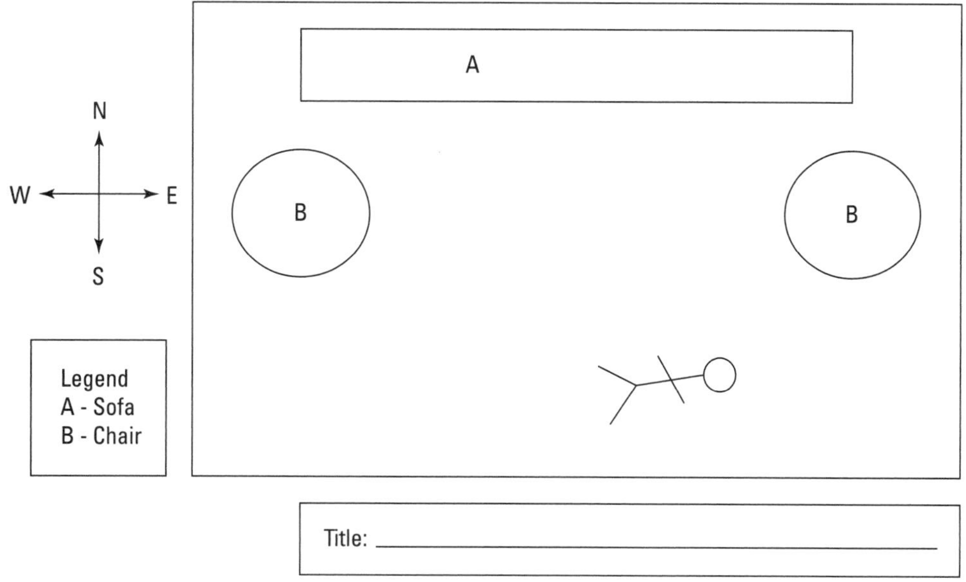

Scale Drawing of Crime Scene

Activity 1.5: Sniffing Out the Solution

Teacher Briefing

In this activity, students conduct an experiment and collect data on odors. In the process, they learn how different kinds of questions require different kinds of scientific investigations. They also learn how evidence supports logical conclusions.

Doing this activity in small groups allows students to draw conclusions for themselves and also collaborate on answers.

Activity Preparation

- For each student group, collect six small containers—film canisters with tops or small margarine cups are ideal.
- Put a blank piece of masking tape on each container, and label them A, B, C, D, E, and F.
- Put a cotton ball inside each container, and close it.
- Select two liquids with distinctive odors, such as coffee and a household cleaner. (Take care when selecting a household cleaner. Some cleaners may irritate the eyes and nose.)
- Select two fruit juices with similar odors (orange juice and lemon juice work well).
- Select two solids with distinctive odors (such as peppermint candy, oregano or rosemary, or soap).
- Shortly before class begins, open all the containers. Put one of the substances in all the A containers, another substance in all the B containers, and so on. Keep track of which substance is in which container:

Container	Substance
A	
B	
C	
D	
E	
F	

- Sort the containers into sets, so that each group will have a full set of containers A to F.
- Make copies of the Science Sleuth Activity Package.

First, Tell Your Students . . .

You've undoubtedly heard of the five senses: seeing, hearing, smelling, touching, and tasting. People are equipped with special organs for each sense. Your eyes are special organs for seeing. Ears make it possible to hear, the nose enables us to smell, the skin is responsible for the sense of touch, and the tongue's taste buds give materials distinctive flavors. When police detectives arrive at a crime scene, their senses are primed and ready for action. Savvy detectives use all of their senses to help analyze clues. Odors may tell an investigator something about who has been at the scene or what has recently happened there.

A person has a pretty good sense of smell, but a dog's ability to detect odors is phenomenal. A dog's nose is forty-four times better at picking up odors than a human's nose. Dogs are super-sniffers because their bodies are especially designed to find odors. That's why the police have come to rely on them so heavily as K-9 partners.

Odors are made up of invisible particles that float in the air. The inside of a dog's nose is loaded with special cells that pick up these odor particles. When weather conditions are right, dogs can detect odors up to one-half mile away. In addition, dogs have plenty of brainpower for processing the odors they detect. A lot more space is dedicated to odor interpretation in a dog's brain than in a human's.

Sniff lineups have proven dogs' abilities to smell out objects. Canines can tell the odor of one person from another, even in a large group. They can also find an individual after smelling a sample of that person's clothing. That's why they are great at finding lost children or tracking prisoners who have escaped. Dogs are such good smellers that they can be trained to hone in on scents of special interest, like drugs or explosives. At an airport, dogs are often used to check boarding passengers and their luggage. Drug-sniffing dogs can also check a line of cars faster than their human counterparts can.

Allthough all of the senses are helpful, this activity concentrates on the sense of smell. You will have an opportunity to find out what the nose knows.

Activity Procedure

1. Distribute the Science Sleuth Activity Packages and smell containers, and assign students to groups.
2. Demonstrate for students the most effective way to smell: pass the container back and forth under your nose, at least two or three inches from your face.
3. Tell students to follow the instructions on the Science Sleuth Activity Packages. They should attempt to identify the odors individually, then compare notes and come up with a group answer also.
4. Give students about thirty minutes to complete the activity.
5. Reveal the answers. If possible, show students the bottle of liquid or the object that created the smell. Let them compare the smell in their container to the smell of the original object if you choose to do so.

6. After everyone has had an opportunity to check their answers against the correct list, gather the class for discussion.

Summary and Discussion

- How many students identified all of the odors correctly? Were the group's collaborative answers better than the individual's?
- Which odors were the hardest to identify?
- Odors can be associated with memories. What odor in your life brings back a memory? For example, do baking cookies make you think of the holidays? Does the smell of tomato sauce and cheese remind you of pizza?

For Extra Credit

Sense of smell can be an important tool for a detective. The captain of your department is worried that some of the detectives may not have a good sense of smell. She has a theory that people who drink a lot of coffee lose their sense of smell. The captain has asked you to develop an experiment to find out whether coffee drinkers have as good a sense of smell as people who don't drink coffee. Suggest an experiment that you could do to test the captain's hypothesis.

Name ______________________________ Date ______________________

Science Sleuth Activity Package: Sniffing Out the Solution

Background

You've been identifying odors your entire life. Think about walking into the house just as a batch of chocolate chip cookies is coming out of the oven. It doesn't take you long to identify the aroma of cookies. Other kinds of odors tell stories too. People often wear colognes or perfumes whose odors may linger in a room as evidence of their visit. A house that smells stale and musty has its own story to tell.

This activity concentrates on the sense of smell, one of the five senses that help people understand their environment. (The other senses are taste, hearing, touch, and vision.) Smell is part of your body's olfactory system. The process of smelling begins when molecules or tiny particles of odorant break away and float into the air. When we inhale, we pull odorants inside the nasal cavity. Humans are sensitive to about ten thousand different odorants. There are plenty of odorant receptors inside the human nose. The roof of each nostril, the *nasal mucosa,* contains about 50 million odorant receptors in a layer called the *olfactory epithelium.* When an odorant particle enters the nose, it dissolves in watery mucus and sticks to little extensions of the cells called *cilia* in the olfactory epithelium. Each of the cilia contains specialized receptors that can bind to the odorants.

Once the odorant is bound in place, the olfactory epithelial cells send messages to the brain along *neurons,* or nerve cells. The messages travel as electrical signals. When the brain receives an electrical signal, it interprets the message. Sometimes the brain can identify a smell or even associate it with something else, like a taste. At other times, the smell is new to the brain.

In this activity, you will have an opportunity to find out what your nose knows!

Activity Directions

1. In your group, take turns smelling each container individually. The best way to smell is to pass the container two or three inches beneath your nose. As you do, close your eyes; it will sharpen your sense of smell.
2. As you finish smelling each odor, write what you think it is in the Data Table for Sniffing Out the Solution at the end of this activity package. If you're not sure, make your best guess. For now, don't share your findings with your partners.
3. Once everyone in your group has had a chance to smell every container, share your answers. If there are different opinions in your group, discuss the differences, and select one smell as the group's choice.
4. Ask your teacher to identify the smells.

Name ______________________________ Date ______________________

Science Sleuth Activity Package: Sniffing Out the Solution, *Cont'd.*

Questions to Answer

1. Did either you or your group correctly identify all of the odors?

2. Are some members of your group better than others at identifying odors?

3. Which smells were the most difficult for members of your group to identify?

4. How well did you do distinguishing the different fruit juices?

Name ______________________ Date ______________

Science Sleuth Activity Package: Sniffing Out the Solution, *Cont'd.*

Data Table for Sniffing Out the Solution

	Container	Substance, Individual Choice	Substance, Group Choice
A			
B			
C			
D			
E			
F			

Activity 1.6: Make a Note of It

Teacher Briefing

In this activity, students collect data through systematic observation. Then they think critically and logically to develop an explanation based on their notes. Although this is written as an activity for small groups, you could also use it as an assessment or evaluation device. If you decide to use this activity to assess student progress, do not hold the group discussion. Instead, collect the Science Sleuth Activity Packages to assess.

Activity Preparation

- Recruit two students or staff members to be Witnesses 1 and 2.
- Make copies of:

  Science Sleuth Activity Package

  Witness Statements 1 and 2 (if you want all students to have a copy of the statements), at the end of the Teacher Briefing

First, Tell Your Students . . .

Detectives record information in their notebooks when they work a crime scene. It might not seem exciting, but taking good notes is one of the most important things a detective can do. Notes help detectives remember clues and stories told by witnesses. Notes must be written neatly so others can read them—no "chicken-scratching" allowed! Long after a notebook is filled and a case is closed, the notebook is filed away so that it can be referred to in the future.

Activity Procedure

1. Distribute the Science Sleuth Activity Package, which includes the "Missing Scientists Crime Scene." Give students a few minutes to study it.
2. Ask students to take notes as the Science Sleuth Activity Package instructs them.
3. Have Alisha read her witness card to the class. Students should take notes as she tells her story.
4. Have Michael read his witness card to the class. Students should take notes as he tells his story.
5. Tell students to follow the directions in their Science Sleuth Activity Package.

Summary and Discussion

Review the students' answers to the questions in their activity package, and discuss differences in them. Here is the key to the questions:

- Do you think that Florence and Isaac came into work today? Explain your answer. *Answer:* Yes. The evidence indicates that they arrived at the office.
- Is there anything missing from the lab? *Answer:* The growth factor is missing.
- Is there any sign of foul play? *Answer:* No.
- What are some possible explanations for the disappearance of Isaac and Florence? *Answer:* Answers will vary.
- What time do Alisha and Michael usually arrive at work? *Answer:* 3:00 P.M.
- What was the last time that Isaac made an entry in the logbook? *Answer:* 10:00 A.M.
- Do you think the missing scientists have been gone for more or less than one hour? Why? *Answer:* More than an hour. Their morning coffee is still on the desk. Neither of them opened their lunch bags.
- Did the owner of the briefcase call the bakery? Did he attend the birthday party? How do you know? *Answer:* The unopened lunch bags indicate that they left before lunch. The call to the bakery was scheduled for 2:00. So the owner of the briefcase probably never called the bakery.
- (a) What time does the mail usually arrive? (b) Had it been picked up by Isaac or Florence? *Answer:* (a) 11:30 A.M. (b) No.
- When do you think the crime occurred? In other words, exactly when do you think Florence and Isaac disappeared? *Answer:* They probably disappeared between 10:00 and noon.

Witness Statement 1, Alisha

Michael and I work the 3:00 P.M. to 11:00 P.M. shift. We replace Isaac and Florence, the 7:00 A.M. to 3:00 P.M. guys. When we got in today, they were nowhere to be found. We don't know if they even showed up for work! They hadn't picked up today's mail in the front office, which usually arrives at 11:30 A.M.

Witness Statement 2, Michael

I was supposed to help Isaac finish our experiment on a new plant growth formula. He told me to get here a little early today so that he could show me how to check on the experiment every hour.

Name ______________________ Date ______________

Science Sleuth Activity Package: Make a Note of It

Background

One of a detective's most important jobs is to take notes. It takes practice to become a good note taker. Detectives learn to compose their notes in short, clear sentences that can be easily understood. Well-written notes avoid vague terms like *close to* or *about.* Instead, detectives try to be specific in their descriptions, using sentences like, "The size 12 black leather men's shoe was found six inches from the front door," instead of, "The big shoe was near the front door."

A crime scene is the place where an investigation begins, so a detective takes lots of notes there. Most of the evidence associated with a crime is located at the scene, so the sooner the detective arrives and starts taking notes, the better. Over time, a crime scene changes: people walk through it, air currents blow evidence away, and fingerprints get smudged. It's easy for some of the evidence to be lost or damaged. Good notes help save information about the condition of the scene at the beginning of the investigation.

The Case

Two scientists are missing, and so is their experiment! It's your job to interview the witnesses and get to the bottom of this dilemma.

Activity Directions

1. Look at the "Missing Scientists Crime Scene" picture at the end of this package; examine it carefully for clues.
2. Make notes here:

   The date and time:

   ____

   ____

   The type of crime or event that has occurred:

   ____

   ____

   The location of the crime scene:

   ____

   ____

   The people present at the crime scene:

   ____

   ____

Name ______________________ Date ______________

Science Sleuth Activity Package: Make a Note of It, *Cont'd.*

3. Listen to Alisha's witness statement and make notes here about her story.

____

____

____

4. Listen to Michael's witness statement and make notes here about his story.

____

____

____

5. If your teacher has assigned you to a group, you may discuss the crime with the other students.
6. Answer the following questions:

   Do you think that Florence and Isaac came into work today? Explain your answer.

   ____

   ____

   ____

   Is there anything missing from the lab?

   ____

   ____

   ____

   Is there any sign of foul play?

   ____

   ____

   ____

   What are some possible explanations for the disappearance of Isaac and Florence?

   ____

   ____

   ____

Name ______________________ Date ______________________

Science Sleuth Activity Package: Make a Note of It, *Cont'd.*

What time do Alisha and Michael usually arrive at work?

____

What was the last time that Isaac made an entry in the logbook?

____

Do you think the missing scientists have been gone for more or less than one hour? Why?

____

____

____

Did the owner of the briefcase call the bakery? Did he attend the birthday party? How do you know?

____

____

____

What time does the mail usually arrive? Had it been picked up by Isaac or Florence?

____

____

____

When do you think the crime occurred? In other words, exactly when do you think Florence and Isaac disappeared?

____

____

____

Science Sleuth Activity Package: Make a Note of It, *Cont'd.*

Missing Scientists Crime Scene

Activity 1.7: Handwriting Never Lies

Teacher Briefing

Students probably think they write their signatures with their hands. It's called "handwriting," after all. In this exercise, they'll learn that the brain also plays a role in how their signatures look. They will also learn one basic tool of handwriting analysis.

Activity Preparation

- Make copies of the Science Sleuth Activity Package.
- Provide each student with:

  Tracing paper
  Ruler

First, Tell Your Students . . .

Sometimes a handwritten document is used as evidence in a crime. A ransom note, for example, may be helpful in identifying a kidnapper. In other cases, detectives may suspect that an important document has been forged. Such a "questioned document" must be analyzed to see if the author is who he or she claims to be. When there is a question of who wrote something, known handwriting samples and questioned documents can be compared.

Handwriting samples are useful to detectives because no two people write exactly alike. A person's one-of-a-kind handwriting comes from the unique qualities of his or her brain and muscles. This individuality is so strong that handwriting can be used for identification.

Activity Procedure

1. Distribute the Science Sleuth Activity Package.
2. Ask students to turn to the section in the Science Sleuth Activity Package labeled "Writing Samples."
3. Tell students to write their name in the usual fashion in space 1.
4. Now ask them to clench their fist and slip the pen or pencil inside so that all four fingers are curved around it. Demonstrate. Explain that this changes the muscles that control their writing. They should write their name again, this time with the clenched fist.
5. Ask students to hold the pen in the crease of their elbow. Demonstrate. Explain again that different muscles are controlling their writing. They should write their name again, this time with the pen in this position.
6. Now ask students to compare the three signatures. They might want to share with other students so that everyone can observe similarities and differences.

7. Point out that while the second two signatures may not be as neat as the first, the general pattern of the signature comes through in all cases.

Now, Tell Your Students . . .

When detectives compare handwriting samples, there are several things they look at: the shape of the letters, the way they slant, and how they connect to each other. The thickness of the line, or line quality, may also be helpful. The way people arrange words on the page and their manner of spelling, grammar, and phrasing can give clues.

Activity Procedure

1. Distribute tracing paper as needed.
2. Ask students to turn to the page in their Science Sleuth Activity Package that is headed "The Case."
3. Ask students to follow the directions on their Science Sleuth Activity Package to examine the note from Ms. McIntosh and see if it matches other samples of her handwriting.

Summary and Discussion

- Ask students: Did Ms. McIntosh write the note Melissa gave her teacher? How can you tell?
- Discuss with students the process they used to compare the signatures. You might ask them to go through the steps of the experiment with you so they understand the scientific method they followed.
- Is it hard or easy to forge someone's signature? *Answer:* Hard; every person's signature is unique.
- What body systems are important in writing? *Answer:* The brain and muscles of the arm and hand.

Name ______________________________ Date ______________________

Science Sleuth Activity Package: Handwriting Never Lies

Background

Sometimes a handwritten document is used as evidence in a crime. A ransom note, for example, may be helpful in identifying a kidnapper. In other cases, detectives may suspect that an important document has been forged. This is called a *questioned document,* and it must be analyzed to see if the author is who he or she claims to be. When there is a question of who wrote something, known handwriting samples and questioned documents can be compared. Handwriting samples are useful to detectives because no two people write exactly alike. A person's one-of-a-kind handwriting comes from the unique qualities of his or her brain and muscles. This individuality is so strong that handwriting can be used for identification.

Handwriting is a complex activity that begins in the brain. Before you start to write, the brain makes a mental picture of how the words and letters will look. Nerves carry that mental picture from the brain, down the arms, and to the hands. The muscles and nerves work together to do the writing, but it never looks exactly like the original mental picture.

Today, we're going to do a little experiment that will offer proof that handwriting is controlled more by the brain than by the muscles. We start with the "Writing Samples" section.

Writing Samples

1. In this space, write your name as you usually do.

2. In this space, hold the pen or pencil in your fist, and write your name again.

3. In this space, hold the pen or pencil in the crease of your elbow, and write your name again.

4. Compare the signatures. Name two ways the signatures are similar. Name two ways they are different.

____

____

Name ______________________ Date ______________________

Science Sleuth Activity Package: Handwriting Never Lies, *Cont'd.*

The Case

Melissa McIntosh returned to science class on Wednesday after being absent on Monday and Tuesday. She presented a written excuse to Ms. Nance, her teacher, saying, "Here is a note from my mom, Betty Sue McIntosh, explaining my absence." A copy, "Note to Teacher," is included at the end of this package.

Ms. Nance is suspicious about the authenticity of this note. The handwriting resembles Melissa's, which makes Ms. Nance wonder if Ms. McIntosh did indeed write the note. Ms. Nance needs some help in handwriting analysis and has called on you!

Activity Directions

1. Perform a "top-of-letter handwriting analysis" on "Note to Teacher." To do this:
   - Place the tracing paper over Betty Sue McIntosh's signature.
   - Make a small dot on the tracing paper at the high point of each letter.
   - Use the ruler to connect the dots with straight lines. Write "Betty Sue" on the tracing paper next to this line.
2. Turn to "Signatures of Melissa and Her Friends" at the end of this package. Do the same thing to the signatures of the suspects: Melissa McIntosh and her best friends, Janine Scott, Reggie Defoor, and Patrice Wong. Make sure you label each line with the first name of the person whose signature it reflects.
3. Compare the zigzag line produced from Betty Sue's signature on the note Melissa brought her teacher to the zigzag lines from the suspects' signatures. Are any of them alike?
4. According to your signature analysis, was the note Melissa gave her teacher written by Melissa's mother, Betty Sue McIntosh? If not, who do you think wrote it?

Science Sleuth Activity Package: Handwriting Never Lies, *Cont'd.*

Please excuse Melissa from school.
She had a bad cold and
I made her stay in bed.
Thanks, Betty Sue McIntosh

Note to Teacher

Science Sleuth Activity Package: Handwriting Never Lies, *Cont'd.*

Melissa McIntosh

Janine Scotte

Reggie Defoor

patrice Wong

Signatures of Melissa and Her Friends

Activity 1.8: Comparative Handwriting Analysis

Teacher Briefing

In this activity, students handle a more sophisticated level of handwriting analysis than in Activity 1.7: they will analyze similarities and differences in handwriting samples and use their findings to draw conclusions. The lesson begins with a discussion of the role handwriting analysis played in the Lindbergh kidnapping case in the 1930s. You may omit this part of the lesson if you choose.

Activity Preparation

- Make several writing samples. Label one page "Sample A." On that page, write:

  Imagination is more important than knowledge.
  Love all, trust a few. Do wrong to none.
  1 6 9 2 $
  A D L I
  k w t

  Either you or your helper should write the following on a third piece of paper: "Please give David Alpert $1,692 from my bank account at Lincoln Bank. I know I should come myself, but I'm working on my keepsake chest, and I need the money for paint and other materials. Thanks in advance, Lola Applegate." Label it "Bank Note."
- Make copies of:

  Writing Samples A and B
  Bank Note
  Science Sleuth Activity Package
  Lindbergh Ransom Note
- Make sure all students have a ruler.

First, Tell Your Students . . .

Detailed analysis of handwriting is important any time the author of a note needs to be identified. Handwriting analysis is used to authenticate the authors of everything from notes, wills, and bills of sale to ransom notes.

Detailed handwriting analysis played an important role in the Lindbergh kidnapping case. Although it happened a long time ago, it is still one of the most notorious kidnapping cases in American history.

In 1934, the child of Charles and Anne Lindbergh was kidnapped. Charles Lindbergh was the first to fly a plane nonstop across the Atlantic Ocean, and he was a hero around the world. An envelope found after the kidnapping contained a single sheet of folded paper. The message on the paper is shown in the "Lindbergh Ransom Note." (Distribute the note to the students.)

Handwriting experts used this ransom letter, with all of its peculiar spelling and loopy letters, to help prosecute the kidnapper. They compared the handwriting in the letter to the handwriting of the primary suspect, Bruno Richard Hauptmann. Hauptmann was found guilty, sentenced to death, and executed. (In fact, to this day, doubts still linger as to whether Hauptmann was guilty.)

Activity Procedure

1. Hand out the Science Sleuth Activity Package, including Writing Samples A and B and the Bank Note.
2. Tell students to follow the directions to see if David was telling the truth.

Summary and Discussion

- Ask students whether the Bank Note was a forgery. You might want to have a show of hands as students may have reached different conclusions.
- Would you agree or disagree with the following statement: "People vary their handwriting slightly each time they write"?
- Ask students to suggest some ways you can tell that a sample of handwriting is forged. Students might suggest using over-the-top analysis, height-of-the-letters analysis, or distance-between-words analysis.

Dear Sir!

Have 50,000 $ redy with 25,000 $ in 20 $ bills 15000 $ in 10 $ bills and 10000 $ in 5 $ bills. After 2–4 days we will inform you were to deliver the mony.

We warn you for making anyding public or for notify the polise the child is in gute care.

Lindbergh Ransom Note

Name ______________________ Date ______________________

Science Sleuth Activity Package: Comparative Handwriting Analysis

Background

Detailed analysis of handwriting is important any time the author of a note needs to be identified. Handwriting analysis is used to authenticate the authors of everything from notes, wills, and bills of sale to ransom notes.

Handwriting analysis is a useful tool detectives use in finding criminals, and it serves as evidence in court. Because it is so important, handwriting experts have developed several tricks of the trade. They sometimes compare handwriting samples using measurements and sharp-eyed inspections. These techniques can reveal characteristics that might be missed in the very basic top-of-letter analysis you used in a previous activity. Today you are going to learn some additional tools of handwriting analysis.

The Case

David Alpert showed up at the Lincoln Bank with a note from his neighbor, Lola Applegate. As you can see, he was asking for a considerable sum of money, so the bank wanted to be sure the note came from Lola (Writing Sample A). They had a writing sample from Lola, and they asked David to write the same words and letters on a piece of paper (Writing Sample B).

Activity Directions

1. Look at the Bank Note provided by your teacher. Then examine Writing Sample A and Writing Sample B.
2. As you begin to examine the Bank Note and the writing samples, keep a record of your findings on the data table.
3. You might begin by looking at the capital letters in samples A and B. For example, measure the height above the line of the capital letter "L." (If the letters are not all the same size, find the height above the line of each example of the letter, then find the average height.) Enter the height (or average height) on the data table in the appropriate column: Sample A or Sample B. The data table is at the end of this package.
4. Measure the height of the letter "L" in the Bank Note. Enter this on the data table.
5. Put a check mark next to the height in the Sample A and Sample B columns that is the closest to the height in the Bank Note.
6. Repeat steps 3 through 5 for the other letters and numbers, and enter your findings on the data table.

Name ______________________________ Date ____________________

Science Sleuth Activity Package: Comparative Handwriting Analysis, *Cont'd.*

7. How much space is there between each word in Writing Sample A and Writing Sample B? (If the distance between words varies, find the average distance.) Compare this to the space between words on the Bank Note. Put a check mark next to the distance in the writing sample that is most similar to the Bank Note.

8. You have compared the Bank Note to the Writing Sample on 10 different points. Based on the information in your data table, which Writing Sample is more like the Bank Note? If your results are not conclusive, compare some other letters.

____

____

9. Based on your findings, would you say that the Bank Note is authentic or a forgery?

____

____

Name ______________________ Date ______________________

Science Sleuth Activity Package: Comparative Handwriting Analysis, *Cont'd.*

Data Table for Comparative Handwriting Analysis

Height of Character	Sample A	Sample B	Bank Note
L			
D			
I			
k			
w			
1			
6			
9			
$			
Space between words			

Activity 1.9: In the Dark—Homework Assignment

Teacher Notes

This interesting activity helps students understand how their eyes work. It's something easy to do in the home, and they might enlist family members to help. This is a good activity for partners, and it may be possible for students to team up and work together at home on this, then bring their codes to school and share them with other students.

Answer Key

5. By waiting fifteen minutes, the rods were able to begin to fully function, helping the eyes adapt to the light.
6. The variable was whether light was present in the room.
7. Answers will vary. One possible hypothesis: you can see better in the dark if your eyes have time to adjust to low light.

Name ______________________________ Date ______________________

Homework Assignment: In the Dark

In this assignment, you observe objects under two different conditions, or *variables.*

The subject of this experiment is vision: How well can you see in the dark? In the first condition, you will leave a room that is well lighted and enter a room that is dark, looking for a hidden object. In the second condition, you will go from a darkened room into another darkened room, looking for the same object.

Can you guess what the variable in this experiment is?

Background

A dark area can be a tough place to investigate. In the dark, a detective might have trouble identifying objects. However, crimes don't always conveniently happen in the daytime, so detectives must learn to do their investigating even when the lighting is poor. There are a few tricks of the trade that help investigators when lighting is low.

Humans depend more on their sense of sight than any other sense. We are able to see because light passes into the eye and strikes a layer of sensitive cells on the back of the eyeball. The front of the eye is covered by the clear, tough cornea. Light travels through the cornea, then through the pupil and lens before it gets to the retina in the back of the eyeball. The amount of light that enters the eye is controlled by the iris, a circular muscle. The retina contains cells that respond to light by generating electrical impulses. These impulses travel along the optic nerve to the brain, where they are interpreted.

There are two types of cells in the retina: rods and cones. These cells were named for their appearance under the microscope. Humans have more rods than cones. Rods are very sensitive to light, so they specialize in forming images when light is dim, and they see only black and white. When an investigator is in a dimly lit room, his or her rods are working overtime. Since rods are not good at distinguishing details, everything looks a little gray and fuzzy in dim light.

Cones require a lot of light to function. These cells can detect the three primary colors: red, green, and blue. All of the other colors are produced when the brain mixes these three basic tones. So during the daytime or in a well-lit room, eyes use the brightest rays available and depend on their cones.

Both rods and cones contain light-sensitive pigments. When light hits the pigments, they change shape and set off a series of chemical changes in the cells that generates an electrical signal.

In this exercise, you'll learn how to carry out a search in low light. You may be surprised to discover what your eyes can—and can't—see at night!

What You'll Need

- Two adjoining rooms, perhaps two classrooms at school or a living room and dining room at home. It should be possible to light both rooms. It's easiest to do this experiment at night, when you can make a room dark by just turning out the lights.
- A partner.

Name ______________________ Date ______________________

Homework Assignment: In the Dark, *Cont'd.*

- An object that can be hidden in plain sight. This should be not too large or small, perhaps the size of a cell phone, a wallet, or a coffee cup.
- A watch or clock with a second hand.

Activity Directions

1. Darken one room, and leave the lights on in the other.
2. While you stay in the lighted room, give your partner an object to place in the darkened room. It should be in plain sight—somewhere that it could be easily seen if you turned on the lights.
3. Check the time, and make a note of it. ______________
4. Have your partner watch the clock while you enter the darkened room and look for the object. When you find it, call out "Time!"
5. Record here how long it took you to find the object. ______________
6. Now darken both rooms, and wait at least fifteen minutes in the same room that was lighted in the first part of the experiment.
7. Ask your partner to place the object in the other room—in the same room but not in the same place as before.
8. Have your partner watch the clock while you enter the second room and search for the object. When you find it, call out "Time!"
9. Record how much time it took to find the object the second time. ______________

Questions to Answer

1. How long did it take you to find the object when you walked from a lighted room into the dark room?

   ____

2. How long did it take you to find the object when you walked from a dark room into another dark room?

   ____

Name ______________________ Date ______________________

Homework Assignment: In the Dark, *Cont'd.*

3. Which was easier to do?

4. Why do you think this was so?

5. Why do you think it was important to wait fifteen minutes before you went to search in the second part of the experiment?

6. Now can you guess what the variable was in this experiment?

7. Can you make a hypothesis based on what you found?

8. What's another experiment you could use to test this hypothesis?

Activity 1.10: Secret Codes—Homework Assignment

Teacher Notes

This assignment is a good activity for partners, and it may be possible for students to team up and work together at home on this. Then they can bring their codes to school and share them with their classmates.

Answer Key

1. The ten code system is quick, easy, and efficient.
2. Answers will vary. Detectives with their own secret code might be able to communicate quickly without giving away info to a suspect.
3. Answers will vary. Hand signals, poses, facial expressions, words, and phrases might make up a code.

Name ______________________________ Date ____________________

Homework Assignment: Secret Codes

Background

A code is another way of communicating, a way that doesn't use conventional languages like English or Spanish. For example, people who are hearing impaired use a set of coded hand signals or sign language. Codes can be used to communicate over distances. Native Americans used smoke signals to send messages from camp to camp.

Modern detectives often use the verbal "ten code" system that has been standardized for messages. For example, "Code 5" means "stakeout," "207" stands for a kidnapping, and "503" represents a stolen vehicle. The code is often shorter than saying the whole thing, and besides, people who aren't police probably won't know what the officers are saying to each other.

One of the best-known codes in the world is Morse code. Samuel Morse (1797–1878) worked for several years to develop a system of dots and dashes that could be used to send messages across hundreds of miles. Used over the telegraph wire, the sound of a short tone stands for a dot and the sound of a long tone represents a dash. Each letter of the alphabet is made up of its own combination of dots and dashes. In Morse code, the message "See you tomorrow" is ••• •• —•—— ——— ••— — ——— —— ——— •—• •—• ——— •—— You can also use Morse Code with a flashlight, turning it on and off quickly for a dot, and leaving it on longer for a dash.

Activity Directions

1. Using the Morse Code in the table at the end of this homework package, write out a short message in this code.
2. Using a flashlight, try sending this message to your partner across a room or yard. See if your partner can figure out what you said.
3. Like the police, you and your partner can make up a special code of your own. Think about five or six simple messages you might want to send.
4. Develop a flashlight code for sending that message. The code can be based on the number of times the light is flashed, the rate at which the light is flashed, or even movements of the light. Here are some ideas:

Word or Message	**Code**
Come here.	Two quick flashes
Wait there.	Three quick flashes
Meet me at headquarters	Move light up and down from ceiling to floor

Name ______________________________ Date ______________________

Homework Assignment: Secret Codes, *Cont'd.*

5. Write your code down on this page. Be prepared to demonstrate your code in class.

Questions to Answer

1. Why do detectives use the ten code system when they talk on their radios?

____

____

____

2. How could you use a secret code to help solve a case?

____

____

____

3. Flashlights are one way to send a code. What are some other ways?

____

____

____

Name ______________________ Date ______________________

Homework Assignment: Secret Codes, *Cont'd.*

Morse Code

A •—	U ••—
B —•••	V •••—
C —•—•	W •——
D —••	X —••—
E •	Y —•——
F ••—•	Z ——••
G ——•	
H ••••	1 •————
I ••	2 ••———
J •———	3 •••——
K —•—	4 ••••—
L •—••	5 •••••
M ——	6 —••••
N —•	7 ——•••
O ———	8 ———••
P •——•	9 ————•
Q ——•—	0 —————
R •—•	Period •—•—•—
S •••	Comma ——••——
T —	Question Mark ••——••

Chapter Two

Inquiring Sleuths Want to Know

What to Ask and How to Remember at the Crime Scene

Investigators, whether they are scientists or detectives, deal with a lot of information. An investigator who is trying to solve a crime may get information from people and the crime scene. Sometimes information comes in quickly, so a good memory is a useful asset. On other occasions, details and data trickle in over a long period of time. No matter when information arrives, it has to be assimilated and applied to the case at hand.

CRIME SCENE DO NOT CROSS

Activity 2.1: Seeing Is Believing

Teacher Briefing

This is a whole-class activity showing students that people's perceptions—including their own—are not always reliable. Over the course of the activity, students will note differences between two witnesses' versions of a single event, and they may find that their own recording of what the witness said was inaccurate. Finally, when they are given a chance to look at the "crime scene," they may find themselves equally unable to describe accurately and completely what they saw. The activity encourages students to pay closer attention as they collect data and draw conclusions.

You can use the questions in item 7 of the Activity Procedure as a way to assess how well students are able to describe the crime after listening to witnesses and observing the scene themselves. In that case, collect the Science Sleuth Activity Packages before holding the summary and discussion.

Activity Preparation

- Make copies:

  Science Sleuth Activity Package
  "What's This?" at the end of the Teacher Briefing
  "Auto Crime Scene" at the end of the Teacher Briefing

First, Tell Your Students . . .

You might think an eyewitness to a crime is all a detective would need to crack a case. But how reliable are eyewitnesses? Detectives have learned that when two or more people witness an event, each sees it a little differently. Everyone has his or her own interpretation of events and objects.

Look at this picture. What do you see? (Distribute "What's This?" and give students a few minutes to study it. Then ask for responses. Many people see an old woman with a scarf over her head. Others see a young lady wearing a feathered cap.)

Today, we're going to see how it feels to be a witness and how accurately we can describe what we see.

Activity Procedure

1. Select two students to be crime witnesses; one of them is Witness 1 and the other Witness 2. Give both of them the "Auto Crime Scene" drawing, and let them have a minute or two to look at it. Then take back the drawing. They are not to show it to anyone else in the classroom.
2. Ask Witness 2 to step outside the classroom while Witness 1 tells the class what happened at the crime scene. Let the other students ask any questions they have, and instruct them to make notes.

3. Then have Witness 1 step outside, and invite Witness 2 to tell what happened in the "Auto Crime Scene" drawing. Again, let students "play detective" and ask questions, making notes on the answers.
4. Ask the "student detectives" to write a few sentences describing what they think the picture of the crime scene will show as a result of listening to Witnesses 1 and 2.
5. Bring Witness 1 back into the room again. Have both witnesses repeat their crime scene descriptions, and invite the class to discuss the differences in the two versions. Here are some discussion questions:

   Did Witness 1 say anything about the crime picture that Witness 2 left out?

   Did Witness 2 give any details that Witness 1 omitted?

   How do Witness 1 and Witness 2 react when they hear their different versions of the crime scene? Does one of them claim to be correct?

   How do your notes differ from what the witnesses actually said?
6. Now distribute the "Auto Crime Scene" to all of your students and give them 30 or 40 seconds to study it. Then have them turn the page face down so they can't see it.
7. Ask them to write down their answers to the following questions:

   Were there any people in the picture? If so, how many were there?

   What were they wearing?

   What were their hairstyles?

   How old were they?

   Where did the crime take place?

   What time of year was it?

   Was someone injured?

   Was property destroyed or stolen? What happened?

   Who committed the crime?

Summary and Discussion

- Have the students turn the "Auto Crime Scene" face up again, and ask them to compare their answers to what they actually see in the picture. Invite discussion about what happened in the picture, and let conflicting opinions about it emerge.
- Ask students to consider how close their description was to the actual picture. Point out all the different versions of "the truth" that emerged in the course of their investigation.

What's This?

Auto Crime Scene

Name ______________________ Date ______________

Science Sleuth Activity Package: Seeing Is Believing

Background

How reliable are eyewitnesses? Detectives know that when two people witness an event, each sees it a little differently. Everyone has a different interpretation of events and objects.

Eyewitnesses can be helpful, but they usually are not 100 percent accurate. Many detectives have interviewed a group of onlookers at a crime scene only to get several different versions of the same event. Even two eyewitnesses who are standing side by side don't often see the same thing! A good detective expects to hear different stories.

What causes these differences in perception? For one thing, some people are more accurate observers than others. Also, what a person sees or hears is affected by his or her life experiences. For example, a girl from the country might not be as sharp at noticing all of the events on a city street as a girl who grew up in that neighborhood. And a city boy might not be as observant about life in the country as one who was raised there.

The Case

For this activity, a crime has occurred near school, and you are the detective interviewing witnesses. Listen to Witness 1 and make notes here about Witness 1's testimony:

____

____

____

____

____

Listen to Witness 2 and make notes here about Witness 2's testimony:

____

____

____

____

____

Based on what you've heard from the two witnesses, write a description of the crime:

____

____

____

____

____

____

Name ______________________________ Date ____________________

Science Sleuth Activity Package: Seeing Is Believing, *Cont'd.*

Study the drawing, "Auto Crime Scene." When your teacher says so, turn the picture face down and answer these questions:

- Were there any people in the picture? If so, how many?

____

- What were they wearing?

____

____

____

- What were their hairstyles?

____

____

- How old were they?

____

____

- Where did the crime take place?

____

____

- What time of year was it?

____

- Was someone injured?

____

- Was property destroyed or stolen? What happened?

____

____

____

- Who committed the crime?

____

____

____

Activity 2.2: Are Eyewitnesses Accurate?

Teacher Briefing

Here's another opportunity for students to collect data and draw conclusions about what they see. They can test the accuracy of their own perceptions and consider the effectiveness of eyewitness testimony when a crime occurs in your own classroom. Be sure to advise your principal and teachers in adjacent classrooms that you are staging a robbery, so they don't misunderstand the commotion.

Activity Preparation

- Alert school administration and teachers in nearby classrooms to this activity and what will be happening.
- Recruit some collaborators—perhaps students or other teachers or school employees—to stage a "crime" for your students.
- Help them create disguises. Make sure they are outlandish so no one will mistake them for real criminals.
- Work out a plan for the crime, keeping it relatively simple. An example would be to have two perpetrators enter the classroom in costume. They might state warnings or wave a "weapon." Make sure that the "weapon" chosen in no way resembles an actual weapon. One will then take something from the classroom. This should not belong to a student to avoid personal distress. To be most effective, the crime should come as a surprise to the students.
- Make copies of the Science Sleuth Activity Package.

First, Tell Your Students . . .

Eyewitnesses to crimes aren't always reliable. Here's a real life story that provides an example.

In the fall of 2002, four banks in Indiana were robbed. Weeks after the fourth robbery, a teller at one of the bank branches spotted Troy Rufra, a financial adviser, while he was grocery shopping on his lunch hour. She called the police and identified Rufra as the man who had robbed the bank. Rufra was arrested and charged with all four robberies, despite his claims of innocence. Further investigation showed that Rufra had an airtight alibi for the date of the fourth robbery. When faced with this evidence, the teller admitted that she really wasn't sure if she recognized Rufra's face because he was often in the bank or because she saw him at the robbery. Charges, which could have resulted in as much as eighty years in prison, were dropped, and Rufra was set free.

Do all eyewitnesses make mistakes? Are some of them just liars? Several factors affect what a person actually perceives. Perceptions of an event don't come only from the images that enter our eyes. They are influenced by lots of factors, such as past experiences, beliefs, and expectations. Stress, lighting, how long a person views an event, and the amount of time between the event and the retelling of it also affect memory. Some studies show that witnesses make mistakes identifying people 50 percent of the time! (This can be the cue for your surprise crime.)

Activity Procedure

1. Your collaborators burst into the classroom wearing colorful disguises—unusual clothes, darkened eyebrows, fake moles, or tattoos. Be creative!
2. They should shout and scream to get everybody's blood pumping! Maybe they say, "This is a stickup! Don't anybody move." They walk quickly through the room, "steal" something (like a teacher's book or purse or perhaps a classroom item) and then leave as suddenly as they entered.
3. Give your students a chance to settle down. Then pass out the Science Sleuth Activity Package, and ask them to take out their pens or pencils. Tell them to write a general description of what just happened.
4. Invite students to read their descriptions aloud. Discuss the differences.
5. Now ask them to answer the questions in their Science Sleuth Activity Package. The list of questions is on a separate page in the activity package; you may want to hand this page out separately so that students don't use these questions as a prompt for their description in step 3.
6. If possible, ask your collaborators to restage the crime, so students can see what actually happened.

Summary and Discussion

- Review the answers to the questions in the Science Sleuth Activity Package.
- Describe the crime that you staged with your partners. Point out any important facts that students left out of their accounts.
- Based on their experience, students can discuss this question: If a person witnesses a bank robbery, why can't the police totally depend on one person's account of what happened?
- Let the students discuss their own experience with being an eyewitness. What made it difficult for them to remember the crime accurately?

Name ______________________ Date ______________________

Science Sleuth Activity Package: Are Eyewitnesses Accurate?

Background

Eyewitness testimony is considered to be a strong form of testimony, and people are convicted and sent to jail based on these kinds of accounts. Yet in the past few years, DNA evidence has shown that many innocent people have been wrongfully convicted by eyewitness testimony.

Do eyewitnesses lie? Some probably do, but most mistakes by eyewitnesses are honest ones. Several factors affect what a person actually sees, or perceives. Perceptions are not simple matters. Perceptions of an event don't come only from the images that enter our eyes. They are influenced by lots of factors, such as past experiences, beliefs, and expectations. Stress, lighting, how long a person views an event, and the amount of time between the event and the retelling of it also affect memory. Some studies show that witnesses make mistakes identifying people 50 percent of the time!

You and your classmates have just been the victims of a robbery. Let's see what kind of witness you make.

Activity Directions

1. Use this space to write down your description of the crime:

____

____

____

____

____

____

____

____

____

____

____

____

____

____

____

____

Name ______________________ Date ______________

Science Sleuth Activity Package: Are Eyewitnesses Accurate?, *Cont'd.*

2. Now answer the following questions:

   How many robbers were there?

   What did they look like?

   Did they say anything?

   What did they do?

   When did they enter the classroom?

   What did they take?

For Extra Credit

Some people think that television stories about police brutality color people's perceptions of police. Let's say that you have been asked to come up with an experiment to find out if viewing a picture of police brutality affects how people think about the police. Describe an experiment that you could carry out that would provide some answers.

Activity 2.3: Train Your Brain

Teacher Briefing

In the previous two activities, students learned that their powers of observation and memory might be less than excellent. In this activity, they learn some techniques for improving their memory. They also learn how to collect evidence accurately and improve their investigative skills.

Activity Preparation

- Make copies of the Science Sleuth Activity Package.
- Decide how you are going to pair students up for the second part of the activity.

First, Tell Your Students . . .

Memory is an important part of detective work. Your memory lets you store information for later use. Memories are processed and stored in your brain.

Neurons, or nerve cells, are located all through the brain, including the regions called the *hippocampus* and *cerebral cortex.* The connections between neurons are called *synapses.* "Memories" are stored when neurons make connections. Stimulation can form new and alter existing synapses, thus allowing us to have memories. The *hippocampus* is the part of the brain that transforms and relays new information into long-term memory. So does the section called the *cerebral cortex,* the biggest part of the brain. Both old and new information is processed and kept in the cerebral cortex.

The memory may be placed in short-term storage for thirty to forty seconds or kept indefinitely in long-term storage. Here is the way the brain works. Sensory organs like the eyes and ears send information to the brain. Unless the brain pays close attention to the information for at least eight seconds, the information will be lost. If the brain holds on to the data for thirty to forty seconds, it becomes part of the short-term memory. Short-term memories are useful, but in detective work, some things must be remembered for a long time. To keep a memory, the brain moves it to long-term storage. Long-term memories are hard-wired into the brain, where they can stay for days, weeks, or even years.

You can change a memory from short term to long term. All you have to do is pay attention to the memory by *pegging* it, that is, associating it with something so you won't forget it. Associative memory techniques help people remember all kinds of things, like long lists of names or foods on a menu. Peg techniques work best if you associate the items you're trying to remember with things that are already familiar to you. The wilder and weirder the association, the easier it is to remember!

Activity Procedure

1. Distribute the Science Sleuth Activity Package.
2. Tell students to follow the directions in their Science Sleuth Activity Package for Method 1.
3. Ask different students to read their lists. You might ask some to describe what links they made between items in their imagined room and items on the "Grocery List."
4. Now ask students to pair up according to the plan you've made. One student will be the coach, and one will be the memory athlete.
5. Tell the coaches to follow the directions in the Science Sleuth Activity Package for Method 2.
6. Let students check their answers. Ask for a show of hands on how many memory athletes got everything right and how many coaches did.

Summary and Discussion

- Ask students whether they did better in the first or second exercise. Point out that in one case, they could look at the list, while in the other case, half of them only heard the list read. Also point out that in the second case, half of the students weren't using the pegging memory device. Solicit differences in accuracy, and discuss possible reasons for them.
- Some people remember important facts by learning them as rhymes such as, "Thirty days hath September, April, June, and November . . ." By learning a rhyme, are you storing information in your short-term memory or your long-term memory? *Answer:* Long-term memory.
- Brainstorm some examples of short-term memory and long-term memory.
- Pegging or associating an item with something else helps you remember the item. How could you use the same technique to remember a person's name?
- At a busy crime scene, why do detectives need to move information from short-term memory into long-term memory?

Name ____________________ Date ____________________

Science Sleuth Activity Package: Train Your Brain

Background

Since memory is an important part of detective work, it's a good idea to keep yours sharp. Memories are created by, and stored in, your brain. If you want to improve your memory, you have to do a little brain training.

Brain training is similar to muscle training. To improve your muscle strength, you work out with weights. To sharpen your memory, you work out your brain. There are a few tricks of the trade that can help your brain remember important information.

A memory can be placed in long-term storage or short-term storage. Some short-term memories last just for a minute or two before they disappear (just long enough for you to jot down an important clue!). Short-term memories can be moved to long-term storage. They are hard-wired into the brain, where they can stay for days, weeks, or even years.

You can change a memory from short term to long term. All you have to do is associate, or *peg,* it with something so you won't forget it. Peg techniques work best if you associate the items you're trying to remember with things that are already familiar to you. The wilder and weirder the association is, the easier it is to remember!

Making Memories

There are two methods for changing a memory from short-term to long-term storage. In one case, you work alone to peg important information in your brain. In the other, you work with a coach to help you remember material.

Method 1

1. Imagine a place you know really well, like your bedroom or the classroom. Close your eyes and "see" the room inside your head. Imagine all of the things that are there: the bed, the desk, the pictures on the wall, the closet, and the door to the hallway, for example. If you're using the classroom, visualize the teacher's desk, the chalkboard, a bulletin board, and other decorations.
2. Look at the "Grocery List" at the end of this package. In your imagination, place the first item on the list—pickles—somewhere in the room you have imagined. For example, you could imagine putting the pickles near a picture. Repeat in your mind where you've put the item by thinking, "Pickles near picture, pickles near picture."
3. Do the same thing with every item on the list. Each time you add a new item, repeat the entire list in your head.

Name ______________________________ Date ______________________

Science Sleuth Activity Package: Train Your Brain, *Cont'd.*

4. Sit back and relax for a second.
5. Without looking at the grocery list, write down the items here:

____

____

____

____

____

Method 2

1. Following your teacher's directions, pair up with another student. Decide between you which one will be the coach and which will be the memory athlete.
2. The coach should read the items on the "Detective Equipment List" (at the end of this package) one at a time, giving the memory athlete a few moments to "place" each item in his or her imagined room.
3. When the list is completed, put it aside. Both coaches and athletes write the list here in exact order:

____

____

____

____

____

____

____

____

____

____

4. Pick up the list again, and check your answers. Which one of you came closer to getting everything right?

Science Sleuth Activity Package: Train Your Brain, *Cont'd.*

pickles
eggs
Green beans
musterd
cat food

Grocery List

fingerprint brush
fingerprint powder
camera
notebook
measuring tape
latex gloves
empty envelopes
tweezers
magnifying glass

Detective Equipment List

Activity 2.4: Motive, Motive, Motive

Teacher Briefing

Students use evidence and higher-order thinking skills to consider possible strategies for solving a problem. This activity works well with small groups in which students can brainstorm ideas.

Activity Preparation

- Make copies of the Science Sleuth Activity Package.

First, Tell Your Students . . .

The *motive* of a crime is the reason for carrying out the criminal act. Motives may be as simple as anger, jealousy, or a need for money. Knowing the motive behind a crime can help detectives find the criminal.

Activity Procedure

1. Distribute the Science Sleuth Activity Packages, and divide the class into detective teams of two or three students each.
2. Depending on the age and maturity of your students, you may want to hand out the material on each crime separately and give the team a limited amount of time to brainstorm motives in that crime before moving on to the next one.
3. Now ask students to return to each crime and consider what steps they might take to investigate it. What evidence would they collect? Who would they interview?

Summary and Discussion

As a class, discuss each crime. Who was everybody's favorite suspect? What was the motive? What strategy did the different teams develop for investigating the crime?

Name ______________________ Date ______________________

Science Sleuth Activity Package: Motive, Motive, Motive

Background

Detectives know that if they can learn the "why" behind a crime, they can often crack the case. The "why," or reason for doing something, is the *motive.* Discovering why a crime was committed can sometimes lead a detective to the criminal.

In this activity, you and your student partners will be given some information on three crimes and a list of possible suspects in each case. For each case, you will brainstorm motives; then you will consider an investigative strategy for solving that case.

Name ______________________ Date ______________________

Science Sleuth Activity Package: Motive, Motive, Motive, *Cont'd.*

Case 1: Frog Baby

The Indiana detectives who handled the slippery theft of Ball State University's Frog Baby Fountain had a tough problem on their hands: multiple suspects. Frog Baby is a bronze statue of a little girl dangling a frog from each hand. It has been a landmark at Ball University since the early 1900s. Students treat the sculpture like a good-luck charm, and many visit the statue of Frog Baby before exams to rub her nose.

Now, someone has stolen Frog Baby. Two big questions need quick answers: Who did it? Why do such a thing?

The Suspects

Darrell, school prankster

Lou, owner of A Touch of Class art gallery

Francisca, a member of a debate team at a rival school

Professor Taylor, teacher who is retiring after forty years at Ball University

Louisa, a former student who flunked out and was once investigated for sending threatening e-mails to the school's president

Activity Directions

1. Brainstorm possible motives for each suspect, and write them in the data table. Be creative!
2. Review the list and circle the motive that you think is most likely for each suspect.
3. Now consider who is the most likely suspect.

Data Table for Case 1: Frog Baby

Suspect	Possible Motive(s)
Darrell	
Lou	
Francisca	
Professor Taylor	
Louisa	

Name ______________________________ Date ____________________

Science Sleuth Activity Package: Motive, Motive, Motive, *Cont'd.*

Case 2: Carjacking Jackpot

As Mr. Larson sat at a stoplight, he was bumped from behind by a pickup truck. Larson got out to inspect the damage to his 1960 Rolls Royce and to talk to the driver of the truck. When he did, a young man jumped out of the passenger side of the truck, pushed Larson to the ground, and jumped into the Rolls. Both vehicles sped off before Larson could even get on his feet.

The Suspects

Tom Allen, the driver of the truck

Spike Malone, a young man whose fingerprints are found on the steering wheel when the Rolls Royce is recovered

Cedric Mountrose, a rival collector of vintage cars

Paul Bauer, the owner of the house where the Rolls Royce was recovered

Activity Directions

1. Brainstorm possible motives for each suspect, and write them in the data table. Be creative!
2. Review the list and circle the motive that you think is most likely for each suspect.
3. Now consider who is the most likely suspect.

Data Table for Case 2: Carjacking Jackpot

Suspect	Possible Motive(s)
Tom Allen	
Spike Malone	
Cedric Mountrose	
Paul Bauer	

Name ______________________ Date ______________

Science Sleuth Activity Package: Motive, Motive, Motive, *Cont'd.*

Case 3: Burned-Down Clubhouse

The Reggie Jackson Little League clubhouse was burned to the ground, leaving four hundred Little League players without a headquarters. At the scene, investigators found evidence that the fire had been set on purpose.

The building housed all of the league's equipment, as well as a safe where a small amount of money that was collected from the sales of tickets and soft drinks was stored.

The Suspects

Phil Brutus, a player who was recently suspended from a Little League team

Mary Worth, a mother who is responsible for the ticket and soft drink sales

George Bigfella, the owner of a sporting goods store

Letitia Rose, owner of the building, which is heavily insured

Activity Directions

1. Brainstorm possible motives for each suspect, and write them in the data table. Be creative!
2. Review the list and circle the motive that you think is most likely for each suspect.
3. Now consider who is the most likely suspect.

Data Table for Case 3: Burned-Down Clubhouse

Suspect	Possible Motive(s)
Phil Brutus	
Mary Worth	
George Bigfella	
Letitia Rose	

Name ______________________ Date ______________________

Science Sleuth Activity Package: Motive, Motive, Motive, *Cont'd.*

An Investigative Strategy

For each crime, select a possible suspect, and decide how you would investigate that person's role:

Case 1: Frog Baby

Suspect: ______________________

Investigative Strategy: ______________________

____

____

____

____

Case 2: Carjacking Jackpot

Suspect: ______________________

Investigative Strategy: ______________________

____

____

____

____

Case 3: Burned-Down Clubhouse

Suspect: ______________________

Investigative Strategy: ______________________

____

____

____

____

Activity 2.5: Just the Facts, Ma'am

Teacher Briefing

In this activity, students collect and evaluate evidence and then draw logical conclusions based on what they've learned. Before you start the activity, you might want to discuss note-taking strategies with the students. How will they organize their notes? How will they remember later who said what?

The Science Sleuth Activity Package provides some structure for note taking.

As an assessment vehicle or for extra credit, either in class or as a homework assignment, you might ask students to write a crime report based on what they've learned.

Activity Preparation

- Make copies of the Science Sleuth Activity Package and the Witness Statements at the end of the Teacher Briefing.
- Decide which students will read the witness statements.
- Depending on how realistic you'd like to be, you might want to give the witnesses props to suggest who they are and maybe name tags too.

First, Tell Your Students . . .

When detectives interview witnesses, they jot down all the facts they learn in a notebook. Later, back at the police station, they put the noteworthy details of an incident into an official report.

A detective notebook usually is pocket-sized so it can be carried anywhere, and it has lined pages. Detective notes are short and to the point—that's why they're called *notes!* They include "just the facts," such as who, what, where, when, and how.

Notes must be neat enough for a detective to be able to read and understand them weeks, months, or even years later—no chicken-scratching allowed! When they are filled up, notebooks are added to the case file so they can be referred to later, if needed.

When taking notes from witnesses, detectives have to decide what information is useful and what is not. Witnesses may tell detectives all kinds of things, much of which is irrelevant to the case.

If the stories of two people confirm—or as police say, *corroborate*—one another, it makes their versions more believable. In the same way, some of the witnesses' testimonies cannot be confirmed, and that makes them a little more suspicious.

You have been called to help investigate an accident. All you know is that there's been a wreck, but no one seems to agree on who, or what, caused it. Grab your note pad, and get ready to take down the facts.

Activity Procedure

1. Distribute the Science Sleuth Activity Packages.
2. Give students a few minutes to look at the "Car Wreck Crime Scene" in their package and make notes.
3. Introduce the witnesses. Provide enough introduction of each witness to help students connect them with the figures in the crime scene drawing.
4. Tell the students to make notes on what each witness says.
5. Give students some time to consider the information they've gathered.

Summary and Discussion

- At the end of the activity, hold a class discussion. Ask students to draw some conclusions about the accident based on what they've seen and heard:

  Was all of the information you gathered from the witnesses useful to solving this case? Explain your answer.
  According to each witness, where was Mary at the time of the wreck?
  Do Jeremy's and Rudy's stories agree? Which do you find more believable? Why?
  Does Felicia's version support the account given by either of the drivers? If so, which one?
  From the information you gathered, what do you think actually happened?
- Let students discuss their answers to the questions above. What did they learn about detectives' work? What did they learn about witnesses? Are they happy with the notes they took? What would they do differently the next time they investigate a crime?

Witness 1: Mary Chin

Mary is a ten-year-old girl with a basketball who is sniffling and wiping her eyes as she tells her story:

> *I was practicing shooting hoops in my driveway. Next week we're having basketball tryouts, and Coach Johnson will pick the team. So what happened is, I missed the goal, and the ball hit the top of Mom's car and bounced down the driveway. I wanted to catch it before it got to the street. This is my brother's basketball, and I knew he'd be mad if it got flattened in the road. So I chased it down the driveway, and just as I got my fingers on it, I heard a loud crash and horns blowing. Those noises scared me so much I dashed to the other side of the street where it was safe. At least I saved my brother's ball—so I'm not in trouble with him.*

Witness 2: Rudy Miller

Rudy is the driver of the older car, who is wiping his forehead with a handkerchief or tissue as he tells his story:

> *I've had my car for ten years, and I've never had a wreck. Why, I've never even gotten a scratch on this ole beauty. That girl almost scared me to death. In fact, I may need to go to the hospital—my heart's still racing! I was just driving along, under the speed limit, when she stepped out into the road right in front of me. I hit the brakes so hard that my car skidded—you can see the skid marks. That black sports car was tailgating me, so he crashed right into my rear bumper. You'd think people wouldn't follow so close! At least the girl's safe.*

Witness 3: Jeremy Marshall

Jeremy is the driver of the newer car. Here's his story:

> *This is my mother's new convertible—she's only had it a week. I begged her to let me drive it. I wanted to roll the top down and look cool for my friends. Now I won't be impressing anybody because I'll be grounded for the rest of my life! I want you to know that I wasn't speeding. I couldn't have speeded if I had wanted to—the guy in that old car in front of me was just puttering along like he had all day. I was careful to stay a safe distance away from him. Did you see all those stickers on his rear bumper? Anyway, since there's no passing on this windy street, we were both just crawling along. All of a sudden, I heard tires squeal. Next thing I know, that old car's bumper was in my grill. He just stopped in the middle of the road without giving me any signal. I feel sick; every time I look at Mom's car, my stomach flips over. I've got to call her, and I dread it, but maybe she won't be too mad since this wasn't my fault. That guy should have his license revoked!"*

Witness 4: Felicia Gunnell

Felicia was walking her dog down the street. Here's her story:

> *I take Skippy out for a walk three times a day. We just moved to this street after living in the country, you know, and we like to be outside. We get out even when it's raining and snowing! Of course, we like living in a neighborhood now, but it's a change. Well, we were right over there, on the sidewalk near Mary's house, when I saw Mary running toward the street. She was looking down, just running really fast. I could see cars coming down the street, and I just knew she was going to get hit. But the driver of that old car was going real slow. The driver of the convertible was gunning his engine like he might pass or something, but he never did. The driver of the old car was watching Mary too and slammed on his brakes. I don't think Mary ever knew that she was in the way because when the car stopped, she jumped straight up in the air and scooted to the other side like something was biting at her heels!*

Name ______________________ Date ______________________

Science Sleuth Activity Package: Just the Facts, Ma'am

Background

When detectives interview witnesses, they jot down all the facts they learn in a notebook. Later, back at the police station, they put the noteworthy details of an incident into an official report. Detective notes are short and to the point—that's why they're called notes! They include "just the facts," such as who, what, where, when, and how.

Now it's your turn to see what noteworthy facts you learn from witnesses at the scene of an investigation. Remember, no two people tell stories that are exactly alike. But if the stories of two people confirm—or as police say, *corroborate*—one another, it makes their versions more believable. In the same way, some of the witnesses' testimonies cannot be confirmed, and that makes them a little more suspicious.

The Case

You have been called to help investigate an accident. All you know is that there's been a wreck, but no one seems to agree on who, or what, caused it. Get ready to take down the facts.

Activity Directions

1. Look at the "Car Wreck Crime Scene" drawing at the end of this package. Based on what you see, think about the following:

   Who is involved?

   What happened?

2. Now you'll hear what the witnesses have to say. Be aware that it's not unusual for witnesses to tell you more than you need to know—they may throw in information that has nothing to do with the incident under investigation. It's your job to listen to their stories. As you do, ignore the unimportant details, and write down the facts that you think are important to this case.

   Mary Chin says:

   ____

   ____

   ____

Name ____________________ Date ____________________

Science Sleuth Activity Package: Just the Facts, Ma'am, *Cont'd.*

Rudy Miller says:

____

____

____

Jeremy Marshall says:

____

____

____

Felicia Gunnell says:

____

____

____

Questions to Answer

Now that you've heard four different versions of the incident from the witnesses, you probably have a lot of notes. You may have picked up on some differences in the witnesses' stories. Your next job is to find out what parts of the notes are facts and what parts aren't. Answering these questions in your notebook may help you decide if one or more of the witnesses is bending the truth:

1. Was all of the information you gathered from the witnesses useful to solving this case? Explain your answer.

____

____

____

____

Name ______________________ Date ______________________

Science Sleuth Activity Package: Just the Facts, Ma'am, *Cont'd.*

2. According to each witness, where was Mary at the time of the wreck?

   Rudy says:

   ____

   ____

   ____

   Jeremy says:

   ____

   ____

   ____

   Felicia says:

   ____

   ____

   ____

   Mary says:

   ____

   ____

   ____

3. Do Jeremy's and Rudy's stories agree? Which do you find more believable? Why?

   ____

   ____

4. Does Felicia's version support the account given by either of the drivers? If so, which one?

   ____

   ____

5. From the information you gathered, what do you think actually happened?

   ____

   ____

   ____

Car Wreck Crime Scene

Activity 2.6: Which Came First?

Teacher Briefing

In this exercise, students learn how to organize information and arrange evidence in a logical sequence. You can decide whether you want the students to work individually, in pairs, or in small groups.

Activity Preparation

- Make copies of the Science Sleuth Activity Package.
- Make sure students have scissors.

First, Tell Your Students . . .

Detectives gather information from different sources. Then they have to go through their notes and try to arrange this information in a way that helps them understand how the crime unfolded. What happened first? Next? Last? Sometimes figuring out the order of events in a crime can help solve the case.

In this activity, you will try to arrange information in the correct sequence.

Activity Procedure

1. Hand out the Science Sleuth Activity Package, including the "Index Cards" at the end of the package. Ask students to cut out the index cards so that they can rearrange the cards—and the evidence—in any order they choose.
2. Tell the students to read the notes from the crime scene on the cards, and then arrange the cards in a logical sequence so that they present information in a way that makes sense.
3. Give students some time to arrange the cards. Then divide the class into small groups, and have them compare their work. Encourage students to discuss similarities and differences in the findings of each group.

Summary and Discussion

- Have the whole class put together a list of evidence. Ask:

  From the evidence presented, was Ms. Arrington aware of the meeting of the Science Club executive officers?

  Based on the information you have so far, who do you think is the most likely suspect in the koi theft?

  Is it possible that someone other than the individuals mentioned on the cards stole the koi?
- Discuss with your students the process of sequencing events in this crime. How did they decide which card should go first? Are there any cases where more than one order would make sense? Why? Did organizing the cards help them solve the crime?

Name ________________________ Date ________________

Science Sleuth Activity Package: Which Came First?

The Case

Ms. Arrington, the principal of your school, calls at 8:00 P.M. to report that the school's prized koi has been stolen. She wants you to help solve this case, and quickly. You know the koi she's talking about—a beautiful fish that Ms. Arrington placed in an aquarium in the lobby the year the school opened. Thousands of students have passed that exotic-looking fish every day for the last twelve years. You cannot believe that it is gone!

The first investigator at the scene did a good job of collecting information. He wrote each important fact from the crime scene on an index card. But then he dropped the cards, and now they are no longer in sequential order. It's your job to arrange the files in a logical sequence.

Activity Directions

1. Cut out the "Index Cards" at the end of this package.
2. Read the information on each index card.
3. Arrange the cards in a logical sequence so that they present information in a way that you can interpret.
4. Copy the information from the cards here in the order you've chosen:

____

____

____

____

____

____

____

____

____

____

____

____

____

____

____

Name ______________________________ Date ______________________

Science Sleuth Activity Package: Which Came First?, *Cont'd.*

5. Answer these questions:

   From the evidence presented, was Ms. Arrington aware of the meeting of the Science Club executive officers?

   ____

   ____

   ____

   ____

   ____

   ____

   ____

   Based on the information you have so far, who do you think is the most likely suspect in the koi theft?

   ____

   ____

   ____

   Is it possible that someone other than the individuals mentioned on the cards stole the koi? Explain your answer.

   ____

   ____

   ____

   ____

   ____

   ____

   ____

   ____

   ____

   ____

   ____

6. As your teacher directs, discuss your crime scenario with another student or group of students.

Science Sleuth Activity Package: Which Came First?, *Cont'd.*

The Drama teacher, Mr. Kent, walked through the lobby at 5:45pm. He didn't see anyone in the lobby. The koi was swimming in the aquarium at that time.

The executive board of the Science Club had a meeting at school from 5:00pm to 6:00pm.

At 6:05pm Ms. Arrington went into the lobby to be sure that everything was locked. That's when she discovered the Koi missing. She also saw drops of water on the floor leading from the aquarium to the front door.

The sign-in/sign-out sheet for the club meeting showed that Bob left at 5:41pm, Kim at 5:49pm, Lou at 5:52pm, Ty at 5:55pm, and Rena at 5:59pm.

Ty's parents picked him up about 6:00PM in front of the school.

The front door of the school was unlocked until 5:15pm. All of the other exterior doors were locked at 3:30 after students went home for the day.

Bob and Kim walked home.

Bob, Lou, Rena, Kim, and Ty are members of the Executive board of the Science Club.

Rena rode home with Lou. His brother picked them up a few minutes after 6:00pm.

Ms. Arrington was in her office from 3:30pm to 6:05pm. Before leaving the school, Kim stopped by the office to tell Ms. Arrington goodbye.

Activity 2.7: The Missing Laptop

Teacher Briefing

Here's another exercise that lets students develop their skills in logical thinking and interpreting evidence. Whereas Activity 2.6 was based on verbal reports, this activity uses a picture as evidence.

Activity Preparation

- Make copies of the Science Sleuth Activity Package.

First, Tell Your Students . . .

Sometimes detectives can figure out the order in which events occurred from the physical evidence at the crime scene. The case you are investigating today is a good example.

Activity Procedure

1. Hand out the Science Sleuth Activity Package.
2. Point out that the tracks in the "Missing Laptop Crime Scene" in their package are labeled A, B, and C to identify different kinds of footprints.
3. Tell your students to study the drawing, and see what they can learn from it.
4. Give them some time to work by themselves or with other students.

Summary and Discussion

Discuss the following questions with your students:

- Which set of tracks belongs to Sam: A, B, or C? How do you know?
- Were tracks B made by an adult or child? Explain your answer.
- Which set of tracks was made first? Which set was made last? How do you know?
- Which set of tracks probably came from the person who took Sam's laptop? Why do you think so?

Name ______________________ Date ______________________

Science Sleuth Activity Package: The Missing Laptop

The Crime

After lunch, Sam decided he needed to find a relaxing place to study. He packed up his papers, laptop computer, and a big towel and headed down to the beach. Sam searched the beach and deliberately picked a quiet place where he could work without interruption. The sand was smooth in all directions, and there was no one else in sight.

The warm sun made Sam a little sleepy, and he decided to take a nap before getting to work. Setting his laptop aside, Sam lay back, pulled his hat over his face, and promptly dropped off to sleep. When he woke up, he was horrified to see that his laptop was gone.

Sam immediately started calling for help. Luckily, a tourist was walking along the edge of the ocean taking pictures. She heard Sam's cries and came to see what she could do to help. Noticing a lot of tracks in the sand around Sam's towel, the tourist decided to snap some photos of them in case they might be useful later.

The photographs made by this quick-thinking tourist turned out to be some of the best evidence in this case. This photo is shown in the "Missing Laptop Crime Scene" drawing, which is at the end of this package.

To help you in your work, the tracks are labeled A, B, and C. Study the drawing, and see what you can learn from it.

Activity Directions

1. Closely examine the footprints in the "Missing Laptop Crime Scene" drawing.

Questions for Discussion

1. Which set of tracks belongs to Sam: A, B, or C? How do you know?
2. Were tracks B made by an adult or child? Explain your answer.
3. Which set of tracks was made first? Which set was made last? How do you know?
4. Which set of tracks probably came from the person who took Sam's laptop? Why do you think so?

Science Sleuth Activity Package: The Missing Laptop, *Cont'd.*

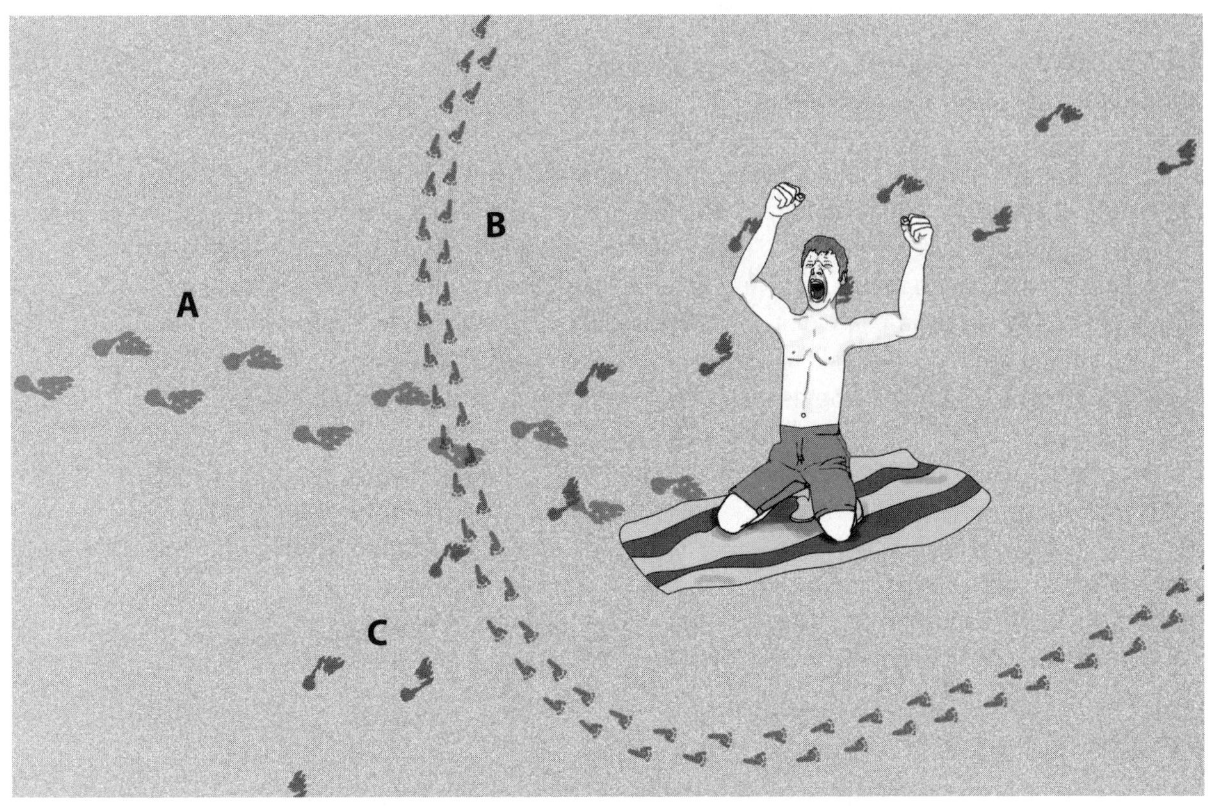

Missing Laptop Crime Scene

Activity 2.8: A Picture-Perfect Mystery

Teacher Briefing

Here's another crime scene for students to analyze. In this case, they're asked to interpret the evidence to answer questions about when the crime occurred and what happened.

Activity Preparation

- Make copies of Science Sleuth Activity Package.

First, Tell Your Students . . .

Detectives like to get to a crime scene as quickly as possible. The crime scene can reveal much about when the crime occurred, and detectives know that if some materials are left exposed to the air, they undergo chemical reactions like spoiling and rotting. Most of these chemical reactions take place at a predictable rate. So detectives can use these reactions to help them determine how long the materials have been in place.

In other situations, detectives may look to see whether certain chemicals have changed from one state or phase of matter to another. Change of phase is not a chemical change; it is a physical change, and it occurs at a predictable rate. For example, there may be ice cubes in a glass of water at a crime scene. Since not all of the solid ice has changed to liquid water, detectives know that the crime occurred very recently.

Detectives are usually called to check out the scene of a crime as soon as it is discovered. In some cases, a person comes across a scene just minutes after the crime takes place. Other times, the scene isn't discovered for days or weeks. Either way, the detective must decide when the crime happened.

Detectives learn a lot about the time of a crime when they analyze the crime scene and look for reasons to explain the evidence they find. They can use their knowledge of how long it naturally takes things to change—ice to melt or dust to accumulate—and calculate how long a scene has been intact. For example, if there are ice cubes in a glass of water sitting at the crime scene, the detective might be quite sure that the crime just happened. A layer of dust is a pretty good clue that things have been sitting out for a while and may indicate that the crime happened days earlier.

Activity Procedure

1. Hand out copies of the Science Sleuth Activity Package.
2. Tell students to look at the "Kitchen Crime Scene" at the end of their package. This is how the crime scene looked when it was discovered by two detectives on July 11.
3. Ask them to analyze the picture closely, looking for evidence.
4. Give students some time to work individually or in groups of two or three.

Summary and Discussion

Have the students gather as a class and ask:

- Based on the evidence in the picture, how long do you think it has been since someone was in the house? Defend your answer.
- Does it seem to you that the people who live here left of their own free will? Why or why not?
- How many people were here last? Explain your logic.
- Give the approximate ages of the people who were here.
- Explain how you came to these conclusions.

Name ______________________ Date ______________________

Science Sleuth Activity Package: A Picture-Perfect Mystery

Background

Detectives are usually called to check out the scene of a crime as soon as it is discovered. In some cases, a person comes across a scene just minutes after the crime takes place. Other times, the scene isn't discovered for days or weeks. Either way, the detective must decide when the crime occurred.

Detectives learn a lot about the time of a crime when they analyze the crime scene and give a reason for the evidence they find there. They can use their knowledge of how long it naturally takes things to change—ice to melt or dust to accumulate, for example—and calculate how long a scene has been intact. For example, if there are ice cubes in a glass of water sitting at the crime scene, the detective might be quite sure that the crime just happened. A layer of dust is a pretty good clue that things have been sitting out for a while and may indicate that the crime happened days earlier.

Activity Directions

1. Look at the "Kitchen Crime Scene" drawing, at the end of this package. This is how the crime scene looked when two detectives arrived on July 11.
2. Analyze the drawing closely. Look for evidence that might indicate something about the last time there was a person at this scene.

Questions for Discussion

1. Based on the evidence in the picture, how long do you think it has been since someone was in the house?
2. Does it seem to you that the people who live here left of their own free will? Why or why not?
3. How many people were here last? Explain your logic.
4. Give the approximate ages of the people who were here.
5. Explain how you came to these conclusions.

Kitchen Crime Scene

Activity 2.9: A License to Remember—Homework Assignment

Teacher Notes

This activity provides students with some additional strategies for improving their memory.

Name ________________________________ Date ________________________

Homework Assignment: A License to Remember

This assignment will help you to improve your memory with some techniques that detectives use.

Background

Detectives are good at checking out crime scenes, but that's not their only skill. They are also great at *remembering* what they see. Since it's nearly impossible to remember absolutely everything, detectives carry a notebook to jot down critical information. Still, there are times when detectives have to remember precise details until they get an opportunity to write them down. This means putting their short-term memory to good use.

Short-term memory is the part of the brain that can hold onto items for a minute or two. Usually short-term memory can store seven or eight pieces of information at a time. That means you can use it to remember a phone number or a license plate, among other things. Believe it or not, you can "exercise" your memory to keep it in tip-top shape and even improve it! Developing good memorization strategies can help a detective in an investigation.

Detectives look at the license plate on a car because the numbers and letters on it can be used to identify that vehicle. Each car is assigned its own unique license plate number. So if detectives see a car speeding away from a crime scene, they will first look at and memorize the license plate, then check out the rest of the car. License plates are kept in files that link the number of the plate to the owner of the car. With a license plate number, detectives can find out the name and address of the car owner.

Memorization Strategies

Good short-term memory skills are vital to detectives. If a suspicious car is speeding away, they might need to remember the numbers on its license plate. What if they have only a few seconds to look at the plate? There are several memory-enhancing techniques. In this experiment, you will try two methods of improving your memory. Test yourself to see which of the two gives you the better results.

Repetition Method

1. Without looking closely at the two license plates on the drawing at the end of this package, cover the second plate with a piece of paper.
2. Now look at the first license plate. In your mind, repeat the numbers and letters on it a few times.
3. Remove the paper from the other plate and use it to cover the first plate.
4. Try to recall the numbers and letters on the license plate and write them down here.________________________________
5. Check your answer. Did you get it right? If not, try again.

Name ______________________ Date ______________

Homework Assignment: A License to Remember, *Cont'd.*

Chunk-and-Associate Method

One way to remember numbers is to group them together in chunks. You may find it easier to remember several small groups of numbers than a long list of individual ones. For example, look at the number 12253012. You could repeat that number to yourself several times, or you could divide it into smaller chunks: 12 25 30 12. When the number is separated into parts, you no longer have to remember eight individual numbers; you can remember four large ones.

This technique works especially well if you can separate a long number in chunks that are already familiar to you. In the numbers 12 25 30 12, the first two numbers form 12/25, the date of Christmas. What about 30 12? Do those numbers mean anything to you? Can you connect them to your life at all? (For example, 30 might be your street number, and 12 might be your age.)

Let's try out your new strategy on the second license plate in the drawing:

1. Without really looking at the second license plate, cover the illustration of the first one.
2. Now closely examine the second license plate. Divide the individual numbers on this plate into chunks, or larger groups.
3. Repeat the groups of numbers to yourself three times.
4. Without looking at the license plate, write down the license number here.

   ____

5. Check your answer. Did you get it right? If not, repeat it a few more times and try again.

Questions to Answer

1. Which memory-enhancing technique was better for you: the repetition method or the chunk-and-associate method? What kind of evidence did you use to draw this conclusion?

   ____

   ____

   ____

2. A license plate is one set of numbers that can be remembered by chunking. What are some other numbers that people remember by breaking them into small chunks?

   ____

   ____

   ____

Name ______________________ Date ______________________

Homework Assignment: A License to Remember, *Cont'd.*

3. Many social security numbers are nine digits. When a person is issued a social security number, it is written as a three-digit number, followed by a two-digit number, followed by a four-digit number. For example, the social security number 123456789 is written as 123 45 6789. Why do you think social security numbers are written like this?

____

____

____

____

____

4. Why does a detective need to have a good memory?

____

____

____

____

____

Homework Assignment: A License to Remember, *Cont'd.*

Two License Plates

Activity 2.10: What Are Your Questions?—Homework Assignment

Teacher Notes

In this activity, students formulate their own questions for witnesses.

Name ______________________________ Date ______________________

Homework Assignment: What Are Your Questions?

In this homework assignment, you are going to study a crime and develop appropriate questions to ask witnesses.

Background

To collar a robber, detectives may need to ask some smart questions. The answers to the questions help detectives sift through the evidence before the robber's trail goes cold.

The kinds of questions a detective asks influences the answers he or she will receive. Some questions are *direct:* "Where were you at 9:00 P.M. on January 21?"

Open questions let the person who is questioned expand on the answer. One type of open question begins, "How do you feel about . . . ?"

A *probing question* is designed to get more information about something. "Tell me more about . . ." is one way to start a probing question.

Closed questions usually require a yes or no answer, for example, "Did you see a man run by?"

Leading questions attempt to persuade someone to think a certain way. "Did you notice any scars on the suspect's face?" or "Don't you think the perpetrator was a young person?" leads the person who is being asked to give a certain answer.

One type of question that is rarely used in detective work is the *rhetorical question,* one that doesn't really have an answer. "Why do people commit crimes?" might be something detectives wonder, but they would rarely ask a witness this.

No matter what kinds of questions detectives ask, they are more likely to get an answer if they ask it in a relaxed, friendly way. Witnesses feel safer, and more comfortable, with a person who is not antagonistic.

The Crime

The Athlete's Closet, a local business, has been burglarized. This business carries expensive athletic apparel, and every bit of merchandise is missing except for one stack of baseball sliding pants. It is 9:00 P.M. when you get a call reporting the crime.

Activity Directions

1. Look at the "List of Witnesses" and "Notes from the Crime Scene" at the end of this package.
2. You have time to ask each witness three quick questions, so you want to ask questions that will supply you with as much information as possible.
3. Use the following data table to write all the questions you can think of for each witness. Give yourself a time limit—say, fifteen minutes. Detectives at crime scenes can't sit around thinking about questions. They have to start interviewing. You can use extra paper if you need it.

Name ______________________ Date ______________________

Homework Assignment: What Are Your Questions?, *Cont'd.*

Person to Be Questioned	Questions
Shandra Owens	
Rob Gray	
Trevor McAdams	
Beatrice Simpson	
Natasha Wright	

4. Now review the questions you have written for each witness and decide which three are most likely to provide you with good, solid clues to solving this crime.
5. Rank the questions as to their relative importance. Write 1 by the most important clue, a 2 by the second most important clue, and so on.

Questions to Answer

1. What is the most important question you want to ask about this crime?

____

____

____

2. How many original questions did you come up with?

____

3. Classify each question as direct, open, probing, closed, leading, or rhetorical.

____

____

____

____

____

Homework Assignment: What Are Your Questions?, *Cont'd.*

Shandra Owens – store owner

Rob GRAY – last employee to leave work today

Trevor McAdams / Beatrice Simpson – custodians who cleaned store

Natasha Wright – last customer in store

List of Witnesses

Homework Assignment: What Are Your Questions?, *Cont'd.*

Back window is damaged, NOT pried open.

Front door is open & unlocked.

Store safe is open & empty.

There are several strands of long black hair stuck in front door frame.

Piece of chewing gum stuck to building outside front door.

Whitechalk dust spilled on store floor.

There are two sets of footprints in white chalk dust.

Soft drink can is sitting on countertop. Can has lipstick prints.

One glove is lying on floor near window.

Chapter Three

Opening Up a Can of Worms

Using Earth Science in Crime Scene Investigations

At crime scenes, investigators collect physical evidence in hopes of tying a suspect to a crime scene. Physical evidence is any material at the scene that provides information about that crime. Impressions such as shoe prints, tool marks, tire marks, and fingerprints can be valuable clues. A good investigator knows how to spot physical evidence at the scene, preserve it, and transport it to the lab. By working with physical evidence, students can learn some of the basic principles of physical science, good observation skills, and logical thinking.

Activity 3.1: Finger the Felon

Teacher Briefing

Working in small groups, students learn how to take fingerprints and how to classify them according to characteristics such as loops, arches, and whorls. Although it's lots of fun, this activity is potentially messy. You may want to arrange special tables covered with paper where students do the actual fingerprinting. Or you could provide paper for students to cover their desks.

Activity Preparation

- Make five to ten fingerprint cards for each students. You may simply copy the "Model Fingerprint Card" at the end of the Teacher Briefing onto a hard-surfaced paper. Better still, you might create large index cards in this format.
- For each student group, you need:
  Black ink pad
  Fingerprint cards
  Magnifying glass
- Make copies of the Science Sleuth Activity Package.
- Make sure you have plenty of soap and water, as well as paper towels, so that students can clean up before they leave your classroom.

First, Tell Your Students . . .

One of the most useful forms of evidence at a crime scene is a fingerprint. No two people have exactly the same fingerprints, not even identical twins, and our fingerprints never change over the course of our lifetime. Fingerprints helped law enforcement solve a tough case in Miami. Derrick James, a.k.a. Spider Man, was an accomplished burglar who could climb up the side of a thirty-story building without ropes and hooks. In a series of robberies between 1994 and 1998, James robbed more than 130 homes of their fine jewels, cash, and credit cards.

His technique for getting in homes was simple. James pulled up to waterfront homes in a small boat. He hooked his boat ladder onto their balconies and pulled himself up. From there, he could scale to any height with the incredible strength of his arms and legs. James was so sure-footed and confident of his ability to climb that he often wore loose-fitting sandals for scaling the sides of buildings.

His downfall came after crime scene investigators found fingerprints at one of the "Spider Man" burglaries. Prints taken from the scene matched a database of fingerprints and sealed the fate of Spider Man.

State and federal law enforcement agencies keep fingerprints of people who have been arrested, along with others that they gather for various reasons.

For this activity, the Forensic Services Division of your state bureau of investigation has hired you to gather some of these fingerprints. The prints you collect will be filed in the computerized fingerprint classification system so they can be quickly retrieved when a comparison to a suspect needs to be made. Before filing each print, you must inspect and classify it.

Activity Procedure

1. Distribute the Science Sleuth Activity Packages and Fingerprint Cards, and divide students into small groups of two or three.
2. The Science Sleuth Activity Package includes directions on making fingerprints, but you may want to demonstrate the process first with one or more students.
3. For the demonstration:
   a. Fill out the name and date on the top row of the card.
   b. Roll (from left to right) the index finger of the student's right hand lightly on the black ink pad.
   c. Roll (from left to right) the inked finger lightly onto the appropriate space on the fingerprint chart.
   d. Repeat the procedure until you have prints of all ten fingers.
   e. Have the student clean up.
4. Have students follow the instructions in the Science Sleuth Activity Package.

Summary and Discussion

Discuss the following questions with your students:

- Are the fingerprints on each finger exactly alike? Explain your answer. *Answer:* No. Each finger has a unique print.
- Do all of a person's fingerprints have any similarities? If so, what are they? *Answer:* Answers will vary. All of a person's prints show whorls, loops, and arches, but they are not exactly alike.
- Why do you think that detectives and police take fingerprints from all ten fingers? *Answer:* At the crime scene, they may find a print of only one or two fingers, so it's important to have a complete set.
- Based on what you have learned about fingerprints, do you think that the patterns of prints on all of your toes are just alike? Explain your reasoning. *Answer:* Like fingerprints, each toe print is likely to be different.

For Extra Credit

A biometric trait is any unique physical characteristic like a fingerprint or voiceprint. Make a list of human traits (other than fingerprints and voiceprints) that you believe may be biometric. Using the library or the Internet, do some research to discover other biometric traits.

Fingerprint Card **Name**________________________ **Date**_______________

Right Thumb	Right Index	Right Middle	Right Ring	Right Little
Left Thumb	Left Index	Left Middle	Left Ring	Left Little

Predominant Pattern of Fingerprints

Model Fingerprint Card

Name ______________________ Date ______________________

Science Sleuth Activity Package: Finger the Felon

Background

Take a close look at your thumb. See all of those tiny ridges on the skin? Those are *friction ridges,* and they help you hold onto things. A fingerprint is an impression, or print, of those ridges. Fingerprints can be a big help to a detective because no two individuals have prints that are exactly the same.

For this activity, the Forensic Services Division of your state bureau of investigation has hired you to gather fingerprints. The prints you collect will be filed in the computerized fingerprint classification system so they can be quickly retrieved when a comparison to a suspect needs to be made. Before filing each print, you must inspect and classify it.

Activity Directions

1. Collect the Science Sleuth Activity Package and some Fingerprint Cards from your teacher, and join your detective team.
2. Prepare a Fingerprint Card for your own prints. To do so:
   a. Fill out your name and date on the top row of the card.
   b. Roll the index finger of your right hand lightly on the black ink pad.
   c. Roll the inked finger lightly onto the appropriate space on the fingerprint chart. If you do not get a clear print on the card, try again.
   d. Repeat the procedure until you have prints of all ten fingers.
   e. Wash your hands with soap and water.
3. Examine one of your fingerprints with a magnifying glass. Compare this print to prints on the "Basic Fingerprint Patterns" sheet at the end of this package.
4. Identify the primary pattern on your fingerprint as looped, arched, whorled, or mixed. Use the capital letters L (looped), A (arched), W (whorled), or M (mixed) to make a note of this pattern next to the fingerprint on your fingerprint card.
5. Do the same with the other fingerprints.
6. What is the main pattern of fingerprints on your card? Write that name in the blank at the bottom of the fingerprint card. If your prints are a mixture of patterns, write "mixed" in the blank.
7. Compare notes with your teammates. Did anyone find making fingerprints particularly hard or easy? Share tips.
8. In whatever time you have left, take the fingerprints of other members of your detective team and classify them by type. Keep these prints in a safe place so you can use them for the next lesson.

Name ______________________________ Date ______________________

Science Sleuth Activity Package: Finger the Felon, *Cont'd.*

Questions for Discussion

1. Are the fingerprints on each finger exactly alike? Explain your answer.
2. Do all of one person's fingerprints have any similarities? If so, what are they?
3. Why do you think that detectives and police take fingerprints from all ten fingers?
4. Based on what you have learned about fingerprints, do you think that the patterns of prints on all of your toes are just alike? Explain your reasoning.

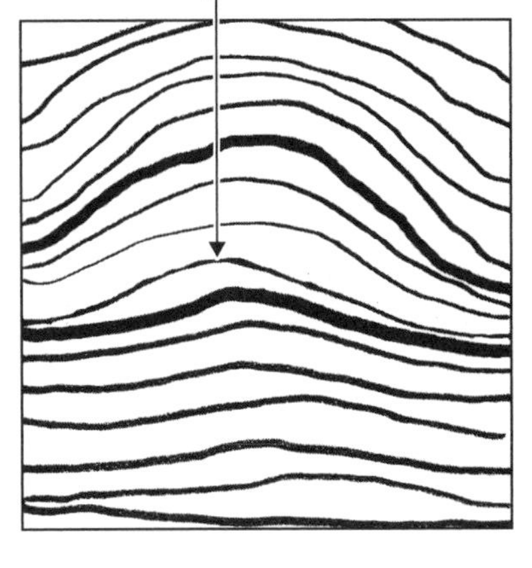

Basic Fingerprint Patterns

Activity 3.2: Sealed with a Kiss

Teacher Briefing

In this experiment, students learn how to examine evidence and draw conclusions based on comparison. In small groups, they are asked to design a simple experiment that will let them draw a conclusion about the perpetrator of a crime. If you feel your students aren't ready to do this, you can walk them through the steps.

Activity Preparation

- Ask five girls and one boy to help you by making lip prints, using the same lipstick, on blank index cards. Five of your helpers will need to make one lip print for each student group. The sixth helper—the perpetrator—will make two sets of lip prints.
- Label one set of the perpetrator's lip prints "Found at Crime Scene," and put them aside.
- Label the other six sets of prints Suspect A, Suspect B, and so on. Or choose more colorful names.
- Make sets for student groups so that each group will have a complete set of suspect prints.
- For each group of students, you will need:

  Lip prints on blank index cards
  Magnifying glass
  Ruler
  Tape
  Two or three lipsticks (optional)
  Blank index cards
- Make copies of the Science Sleuth Activity Package and "Common Lip Patterns" at the end of the Teacher Briefing.

First, Tell Your Students . . .

Like fingerprints, prints from other body parts may be used as evidence. Lip prints from a crime scene can be compared to a suspect's lip prints to see if there is a match. In court, lip prints are considered strong evidence. For this reason, prints may be collected at crime scenes. Some lip prints can be collected on transparent tape. Others are visualized by dusting and then photographed.

There are five basic patterns seen in lip prints: short vertical grooves, long vertical grooves, rectangular grooves (some of which form crisscross patterns), grooves that form diamond patterns, and branching grooves (see the handout for these patterns). An individual may show more than one pattern.

Activity Procedure

1. Distribute the Science Sleuth Activity Packages, and assign your students to detective teams of two or three.
2. Ask student groups to work together to design an experiment that will help them discover who the Kissing Vandal is.
3. As groups turn in their experiments, make sure they are on the right track. Then give them a set of "Suspect Prints," the lip print "found at the crime scene," and the "Common Lip Patterns" handout.
4. Give them thirty to forty minutes to conduct their experiment.

Optional Activity

1. Give each group of students a lipstick and six blank index cards.
2. In each group, one member applies the lipstick and makes a set of lip prints on each index card.
3. Have the students compare the prints made by the same person and discuss how they look alike and how they are different.

Summary and Discussion

- Who is the Kissing Vandal? How did you reach your conclusion?
- What tools did you use to compare the lip prints? Are there any other tools that might have been helpful?
- Does a lipstick lip print mean that the only possible suspects in the crimes of the kissing vandal are females? *Answer:* No.
- Tell the students that one of their suspects was a man. Ask if they can tell which one. Reveal the answer.
- For the optional activity, point out that lip prints do not have clear patterns of ridges like those used in fingerprinting. Ask students if they think a lip print could be conclusive evidence that a person is guilty of a crime, and then discuss their answers. *Answer:* No, because lip prints are not unique. They can narrow down the list of suspects, but they're not solid evidence.

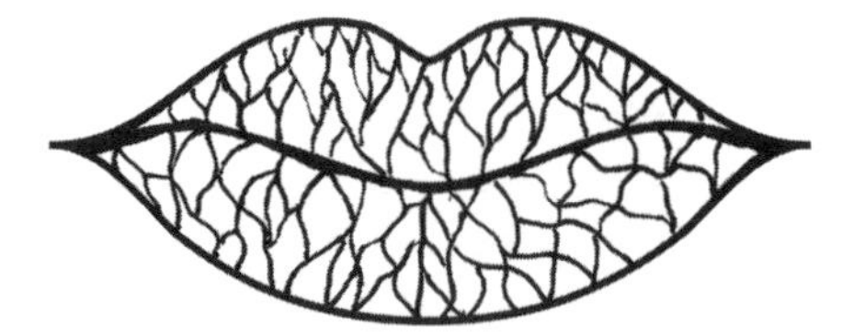

Branching grooves

Rectangular grooves

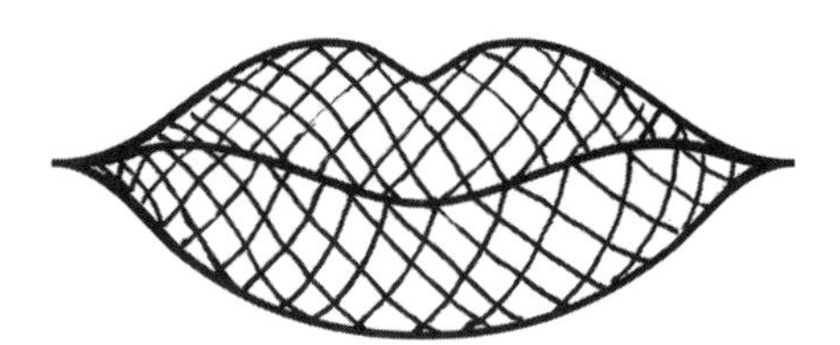

Diamond grooves

Short vertical
(up and down) grooves

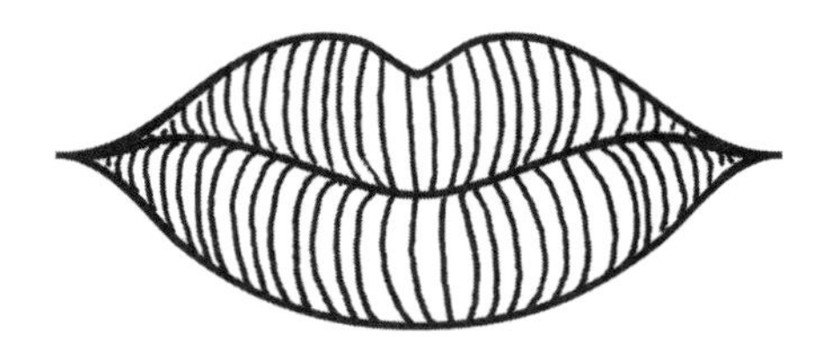

Long vertical
(up and down) grooves

Common Lip Patterns

Name ______________________ Date ______________________

Science Sleuth Activity Package: Sealed with a Kiss

Background

Today you are going to use lip prints to solve a crime. It is your job to design and carry out an experiment that can help you identify the criminal.

The Crime

Someone has been spray-painting cars in the school parking lot. To date, three cars have been damaged, and the cost of cleanup is high. Detectives suspect that the same person committed each crime and that the culprit is a female because she always leaves the same signature: a kiss planted on the side mirror in bright, red lipstick.

Lots of students and teachers walk among the parked cars on the way to other parts of the campus, but the school officer has a plan to narrow down the number of suspects. Each day he jots down the names of people he sees in the parking lot. He figures that the culprit's name must be on his list on the days that the Kissing Vandal strikes.

Yesterday the Kissing Vandal struck again and the resource officer has six suspects. Each of the six suspects has been asked to make a lip print using a bright red lipstick. The resource officer also has a lip print he took from the side mirror.

Activity Directions

1. Working with your group, design an experiment to identify the Kissing Vandal. Spend a few minutes deciding what you want to do. Then in the first row of the data table at the end of this package, describe the experiment you plan to conduct.
2. You know what evidence is available. What will you need to conduct your experiment? In the second row of the data table, make a list.
3. Show your plan to your teacher. If your teacher approves of your plan, ask for the materials you need to carry out your experiment.
4. As you conduct your experiment, keep good records. Enter your data in data tables that you construct.
5. Look over the data you have collected, and see if they lead you to any conclusions. Once you have drawn a conclusion, write it in the last row of the data table.

Name ______________________________ Date ______________________

Science Sleuth Activity Package: Sealed with a Kiss, *Cont'd.*

Data Table for Sealed with a Kiss

Describe the experiment you would like to conduct

List the materials you need to carry out the experiment

State the conclusions that you drew from your experiment

Activity 3.3: The Invisible Prints

Teacher Briefing

Lifting invisible, or latent, fingerprints takes a bit more skill than taking fingerprints with an ink pad. Also, in this activity, students not only identify prominent characteristics of fingerprints, but also compare them to identified fingerprints to draw conclusions. Note that this activity presupposes that you have already done Activity 3.1 with your class.

So that students can compare the prints they "lift" to prints taken in a more conventional way, we suggest keeping the same student groups you used in Activity 3.1. Ask all students to bring their own collection of prints from that activity to class with them.

Activity Preparation

- Make sure you have for each student:

  A drinking glass that is free of existing prints (Your cafeteria may be able to provide a tray fresh from the dishwasher.)
  Latex gloves
  A small soft-bristle paint brush
- Make sure you have for each group:

  A set of ink fingerprints for everyone in the group
  Baby powder or cocoa (about a half-cup)
  Clear tape
  Several index cards—white if you use cocoa and dark if you use baby powder
  Magnifying glass
- You may want to set up the work stations with the supplies before beginning.

First, Tell Your Students . . .

Fingerprints are made up of several compounds produced by the body. Pores in the skin of fingers secrete sweat, amino acids, and oils.

Fingerprints may be visible. Visible prints do not need any special treatment to be viewed. They may be preserved by photographing. The impressions of fingerprints made in soft material are described as plastic fingerprints. They can usually be photographed with assistance from special lighting. Latent prints are more difficult. First, they must be located and then visualized. Some of the materials used to visualize latent prints include powders and chemicals.

Activity Procedure

1. Distribute the Science Sleuth Activity Package.
2. Students make their prints on the drinking glass. Tell them to pick the glass up toward the bottom, as they normally would, and to set it down on the counter carefully.
3. Tell students to put on their latex gloves. *Caution:* First ask whether any students are allergic to latex.
4. Now students need to turn their backs to the table and close their eyes while you—wearing latex gloves—switch the glasses around so everyone gets someone else's glass.
5. Tell the students to handle the glass only with gloves on and to follow the instructions in the Science Sleuth Activity Package.

Summary and Discussion

- Discuss the process of lifting prints. What was hard about it? Why did they wear gloves?
- Did the fingerprints lifted from the glass look like the fingerprints taken with ink?
- Were they able to match the prints on the glass with someone in their group?
- How do detectives use fingerprints to help solve crimes?

Name ______________________________ Date ______________________

Science Sleuth Activity Package: The Invisible Prints

Background

Fingerprints are important pieces of evidence in solving crimes. They are also vital to prosecutors, who use them in the courtroom to tie a suspect to a crime. Because each fingerprint is unique, the courts accept them as evidence of personal identification.

Criminals often leave their prints at a crime scene. Of course, the prints are not always obvious; most crime scene prints do not even show up unless they are treated. Investigators have a special name for prints that cannot be seen unless they are treated: *latent prints.*

There are several ways to process latent prints. They can be dusted with powder or treated with special chemicals.

In this experiment, you will use a tried and true method for finding latent prints: fingerprint dusting.

Activity Directions

1. To make your prints on the drinking glass, pick the glass up toward the bottom, as you would if you were going to take a sip, and then set it down on the counter carefully.
2. Put on your latex gloves.
3. Turn your back or close your eyes while your teacher rearranges the glasses.
4. You now have a glass with a set of unknown fingerprints on it. First, you will find and lift the prints. Then you will try to match them to ink prints of your detective team.
5. Dip your brush into the fingerprint powder. Your teacher may have provided black powder and white cards or white powder and dark cards. Either way, the lifted prints should show up clearly.
6. Apply the powder to the surface of the drinking glass in a light, twirling motion. Avoid getting a lot of powder on the drinking glass. Excess powder will ruin the fingerprint.
7. Gently brush any extra powder away from the print.

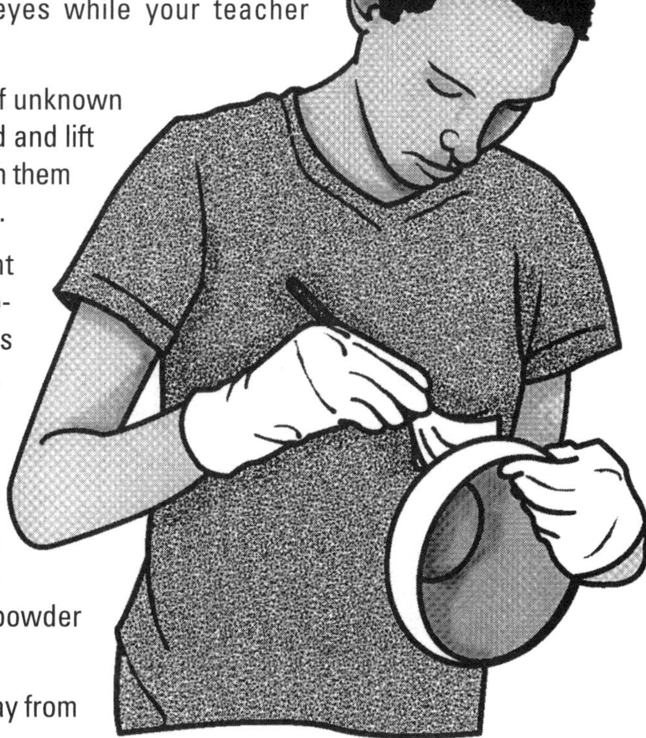

Dusting for Fingerprints

Name ______________________ Date ______________________

Science Sleuth Activity Package: The Invisible Prints, *Cont'd.*

8. To lift a print, remove a short section of transparent tape from the tape dispenser. Press the sticky side of the tape onto the powdered print.
9. Carefully pull off, or "lift," the print from the surface of the drinking glass. Press the sticky side of the tape (and the print) onto an index card.
10. Lift another fingerprint from the glass, and tape this second fingerprint to another index card.
11. To identify prints, examine them with a magnifying glass. Classify them as looped, arched, whorled, or mixed. Write the type of print on the card. For help on classifying fingerprints, see "Basic Fingerprint Patterns" (in Activity 3.1).
12. Now compare the latent prints to the ink prints you took of your teammates during another class. Write the name of the person whose prints match the latents you lifted.

Questions for Discussion

- What was hard about lifting prints?
- Why did you wear gloves?
- Was it easy to match the fingerprints you lifted from the glass to the fingerprints taken with ink?
- How do detectives use fingerprints to help solve crimes?

Activity 3.4: If the Shoe Fits

Teacher Briefing

Students will enjoy preparing a cast of shoe impressions and matching it to possible perpetrator shoes to identify a criminal. Because a lot of materials are required, divide students into groups to conduct the experiment. Although they will work in groups of two or three, it will take the whole class to solve the crime.

This activity can be completed with plaster of Paris or dental stone. Plaster of Paris is less expensive, but dental stone hardens faster. Plaster of Paris casts need to set for at least thirty minutes before handling; dental stone is ready to handle in ten minutes. However, both materials should be left to harden overnight before they are examined closely.

Because the casts that students make have to harden overnight, this experiment covers two class periods: one for making a cast and the second for comparing the cast to the crime scene cast.

Activity Preparation

- Collect shoes that are similar in size and style—for example, all running shoes or all loafers. Check the lost and found at school for shoes, bring shoes from home, or ask each student group to bring one shoe to school. You need one shoe for each student group.
- You will need to make a cast of one of the shoes in your collection, following the directions in the Science Sleuth Activity Package. This is good practice, so that you can help students who have trouble with the process. In addition, you are making an impression of the guilty person's shoe, which students will compare to the impressions they make to identify the burglar.
- Using the masking tape, label the shoes (Suspect A, B, C, D, and so on).
- Set up work areas for each student group with one suspect's shoe and the following materials:

  A pan or tray large enough to hold a shoe; cat litter boxes work well
  Five to six cups of sand
  Hair spray
  Two to three pounds of plaster of Paris
  One-gallon freezer bag with a zipper
  About three cups of water
  Medium-size soft-bristle paint brush
  Spoon
  Ruler
  Magnifying glass
- Make copies of the Science Sleuth Activity Package.

First, Tell Your Students . . .

At virtually all crime scenes, the perpetrator has walked in and out of the area. That means there's a possibility that footprints were left behind and that the shoes of suspects are key pieces of evidence. Shoe evidence may be in the form of a two-dimensional track or a three-dimensional impression. A shoe impression can reveal the kind and size of shoe worn by the perpetrator, among other things. This kind of evidence narrows the list of possible suspects.

Mike Trimpe, a Cincinnati crime fighter, is a superhero when it comes to shoe impressions. Trimpe specializes in difficult and unusual cases. He solved one case with a slice of bread. At the scene of a burglary, detectives found a piece of bread that had been stepped on. Police sent Trimpe the bread, along with the shoe of a suspect who was in their custody. Trimpe examined the shoe and the print on the bread and found them to be an exact match. In addition, he spotted a speck of dirt pressed into the bread that matched the dirt on the suspect's shoe. The shoe evidence proved to be enough to convict the burglar.

Of course, using shoe prints is not always easy. A shoe impression made in soil or snow will not last forever; rain, wind, or even changing temperatures can alter it. When detectives find a shoe impression, they preserve it in a cast. Two great materials for making casts are plaster of Paris and dental stone. Both are powders that can be mixed with water to form solids.

In this experiment, your class is being asked to help solve a crime at a nearby preschool.

Activity Procedure

1. Pass out the Science Sleuth Activity Packages, and assign the students to detective groups of two or three.
2. Several tasks will need to be done. Depending on the age and maturity of your students, you may need to help them with the assignments:
   - Fill the box halfway with sand, and make a clean impression of the shoe.
   - Examine the shoe impression, and spray it lightly with hair spray to keep soil particles from shifting.
   - Measure the length and width of the impression, and record the information.
   - Lift the hardened cast out of the sand, and use a soft brush to remove soil clinging to the cast.
3. The casts have to be left overnight to harden completely. The remainder of the experiment can be completed during the next class period.
4. Allow students to examine the cast that you made—the one that was taken in the play area at the preschool. Let them compare it to the cast that they have made and reach a conclusion about whether their suspect is or is not the burglar.

Summary and Discussion

- Ask if any of the groups believe that they have the burglar's shoe. Have them explain what similarities led to their conclusion. In the event that two or more groups think they have the right shoe, let each one make a cast. Then have a representative from each group examine the casts and reach a conclusion.
- Why do detectives make casts of shoe impressions? Can a shoe cast prove beyond a shadow of a doubt that the owner of the shoe committed the crime? Explain your reasoning. *Answer:* Detectives make casts to preserve the shoe impression, which might be damaged over time. A shoe cast is rarely conclusive evidence all by itself.
- When you added water to the plaster of Paris powder, you started a chemical reaction. Some chemical reactions produce heat and are described as *exothermic*. Others use heat and are called *endothermic* reactions. Is the reaction between water and plaster of Paris exothermic or endothermic? How do you know? *Answer:* The reaction was exothermic because it produced heat.

Name ______________________ Date ______________________

Science Sleuth Activity Package: If the Shoe Fits

The Case

When preschool teacher Lizzie Primo arrived at school one morning, she was astonished to find that a planter from the school's play yard had been stolen. Fortunately, the play yard was covered a few inches deep in sand, so the thief left plenty of shoe prints.

The police found no sign of a break-in, but they made a cast of one of the prints left by the thief. Lizzie knows that she locked the door and the gate to the preschool last night. The prints are from adult size shoes, and only four grownups have keys to the preschool. Lizzie has asked the four adults—Suspects A, B, C, and D—to give her one of their shoes.

Now she wants you to make casts of the suspects' shoes to see if any of them match the burglar's shoe prints.

Activity Directions

1. Join your detective team, and review the Science Sleuth Activity Package and the materials your teacher has provided.
2. Divide up the chores to get the job done. Here are some possible roles:

   Fill the box halfway with sand, and make a clean impression of the shoe by pressing the shoe firmly into the sand without letting it wiggle back and forth.

   Examine the shoe impression, and spray it lightly with hair spray to keep soil particles from shifting.

   Measure the length and width of the impression and record the information.

   Lift the hardened cast out of the sand, and use a soft brush to remove soil clinging to the cast.
3. Half-fill the tray with sand. Then take the shoe your group is testing and make a clean impression by pressing the shoe firmly into the sand without letting it wiggle back and forth.
4. Lightly spray the impression with hair spray to keep soil particles from shifting.
5. Let everyone in the group measure the length of the impression and the width across the toes. Record those measures here:

   Length of impression: ____________________.

   Width of impression: ____________________.

Name ______________________________ Date ____________________

Science Sleuth Activity Package: If the Shoe Fits, *Cont'd.*

6. Make a sketch of the impression in this space. Note any unusual marks in the impression that might have been made by a cut or tear in the sole of the shoe.

7. Half-fill the freezer bag with plaster of Paris, and add enough water to dampen the powder. Close the bag. Take turns kneading the contents until it is about the consistency of pancake batter. If it gets too thin, you can add a little more plaster of Paris. If it is too thick, add a little water. Make sure everyone gets a chance to feel the bag, and describe here how it feels:

   ____

   ____

   ____

   ____

8. Now it's time to pour the plaster of Paris into the impression. Instead of pouring it directly onto the sand, which might be displaced, put a tablespoon in the impression and slowly pour the plaster of Paris onto the spoon, letting it overflow to fill the impression. You might need two people to do this: one to hold the spoon and another to do the pouring. It's also possible to take turns so everyone gets a chance. Fill the impression completely, letting the material overflow a little. Remove the spoon.
9. Leave the cast in place overnight. The experiment will continue in the next class period.
10. *Next class period:* Now that the cast has hardened, gently lift it out of the sand. Use a soft brush to remove any sand clinging to it.
11. Examine the cast to see if it is a good likeness of the impression. Use a magnifying glass to inspect marks on the impression.
12. Compare your cast to the cast that was made in the preschool play yard.

Name ______________________ Date ______________________

Science Sleuth Activity Package: If the Shoe Fits, *Cont'd.*

Questions to Answer

1. Does the cast your team made match the cast from the crime scene?

2. What points are similar?

3. Are there any differences?

4. Do you think that the shoe cast could prove beyond a shadow of a doubt that the owner of the shoe stole the planter? Why or why not?

5. When you added water to the plaster of Paris powder, you started a chemical reaction. Some chemical reactions produce heat and are described as *exothermic.* Others use heat and are called *endothermic* reactions. Is the reaction between water and plaster of Paris exothermic or endothermic? How do you know?

Activity 3.5: Earn Your Good Marks

Teacher Briefing

This activity will probably take two class sessions to complete: one in which students examine and characterize tool marks and a second in which they compare the marks they've created with the tool marks created in the imaginary crime. They will work in groups.

Activity Preparation

- Collect a variety of tools: three or four screwdrivers with different head types and in different sizes, a crowbar, a pair of pliers, and a file perhaps.
- Label the tools (A, B, C, and so on), and assemble them at the front of your classroom.
- Hammer a nail into a wood block for each student group; then use one of the screwdrivers to try to remove the nail.
- At each group work station, provide:

  An empty egg carton
  Some modeling clay—enough to make a piece the size of a small egg for each tool.
  A wood block with a nail embedded in it and tool marks
  Labels and tape
- Make copies of the Science Sleuth Activity Package.

First, Tell Your Students . . .

Crooks usually force their way into the places they burglarize and use many different kinds of tools to break in. Tools leave clues called tool marks, which are created when two materials interact with each other. When the hard tool is used to pry open a soft material, it leaves an impression on the soft material.

The characteristics of a tool mark depend on the kind of tool used, the hardness of the surface the tool is used on, and the force applied to the tool. Tool marks can tie a person to a crime scene if the marks are unique to the tool.

Tool marks can be grouped into four basic categories: impressed (or static) marks, striated (or dynamic) marks, crush marks, and multistroke marks. When a hard object like a screwdriver is pressed into a softer object, like a window sill, an impression mark is made in the soft material. Striated or dynamic marks are created when two objects move past one another because the hard object scratches the softer one. For example, when a key is scraped along the hood of a car, the finish of the car is damaged. Wire cutters compress material between two points, forming a ridge in the material. If crush marks are created, one might assume that a tool like wire cutters was used. Multistroke marks result when tools like files and saws move back and forth over a surface.

Activity Procedure

1. Read "The Crime" in the Science Sleuth Activity Package to the class.
2. Distribute the Science Sleuth Activity Packages to students, and assign them to detective teams.
3. Ask each student team to choose a representative. That person can select two or three of the suspect tools—depending on how many tools you have and how many student groups there are—to take back to his or her group. **Warn students that tools can be dangerous if they are used incorrectly, and caution them to be careful.**
4. Tell students to follow the directions in the activity package to make impressions of all the suspect tools.
5. As each group finishes with one set of tools, a delegate will return them to your desk and select others.
6. Depending on the amount of class time you have, the rest of the activity may be postponed until a second class.
7. Distribute the blocks of wood with the nails and tool marks. Tell students that the blocks were taken from Mr. Salvador's barn door.
8. Tell the students to follow the directions in the activity package to see if they can identify the tool that was used to pry open the barn door.
9. Give students time to reach a conclusion.

Summary and Discussion

When students have finished making the impressions, discuss these questions:

- No two tools are exactly alike. Describe some of the differences in the tool marks made by different screwdrivers.
- How could a crime scene investigator or detective use a set of reference tool marks to help solve a crime? *Answer:* Marks from unknown tools could be compared to a data base of known tools.
- Describe the marks made by a tool that compresses material, such as a pair of pliers. *Answer:* Pliers and other compressing tools push materials together.
- Describe the marks made by a saw. *Answer:* Saws show repeated back-and-forth movement.

After students have compared their casts and tried to identify the tool used in the burglary, discuss these questions:

- Which technique was better for identifying the tool that made the tool mark: examining the mark directly or examining the impression of the mark? Is your answer the same for all tools?

- With a show of hands for each tool, have individual students show which tool they think was used in the burglary.
- With a show of hands for each tool, have team representatives indicate which tool they think was used in the burglary.
- Are the results different? Which one is correct?
- How can you tell if a door has been pried open with a tool? *Answer:* There will be tool marks.
- How could a tool mark be used to help solve a crime? *Answer:* Tool marks might link particular tools to a crime scene.

Name ______________________________ Date ______________________

Science Sleuth Activity Package: Earn Your Good Marks

Background

At a crime scene, detectives look for tool mark evidence. If any is found, they photograph it and then make a cast. A cast can reveal details about the unique characteristics of a tool. Each tool has individual traits that result from its wear and tear. It is extremely unlikely that any two tools will have the exact same marks.

Tools suspected of making tool marks at the crime scene must be carefully collected and stored to avoid damaging their unique characteristics. The suspected tools can be compared to casts made at the crime scene.

In this experiment, you will create samples of tool marks in balls of clay. Then you will use these samples to draw conclusions about the tool used in an imaginary burglary.

The Crime

Ever since Mr. Salvador was a boy, he has loved tractors. For the past ten years, he has been collecting antique tractors and restoring them to their original glory. So far, he has found and worked on nine of these antique machines, and they are all real beauties. On weekends, Mr. Salvador loads his tractors onto a double-decker trailer and takes them to competitions. He has won a dozen blue ribbons so far.

While he is at work during the week, Mr. Salvador keeps his tractors in the barn in his backyard. Recently the lock on the barn door broke, so he secured the door with a long nail. When he got home from work today, Mr. Salvador noticed the barn door swinging open. In a panic, he raced across the backyard and into the barn, only to find two of his prized tractors missing.

Mr. Salvador has four neighbors, and he thinks one of them was responsible for the theft. The police have gathered tools from each of the suspects. In this activity, you will identify the tool marks on Mr. Salvador's barn door by comparing them to impressions made of the tools taken from suspects.

Activity Procedure

1. Pick a delegate from your group to select a couple of tools for you to begin your work.
2. While waiting, take a piece of modeling clay about the size of a small egg, and roll it into a ball. Make several balls of clay this way.
3. Examine each tool to see if you can find any unique identifying marks—scratches, nicks, or breaks. If so, note these marks on the data table provided at the end of this package. Make sure to check the label on the tool, and record your notes in the space next to that tool.
4. Make an impression of the tool in a ball of clay by pressing the tip into the clay and then removing it.
5. Place the piece of clay in one of the depressions of the empty egg carton. Identify the piece of clay by writing the label of the tool—for example, "Tool A"—next to it.

Name ______________________ Date ______________________

Science Sleuth Activity Package: Earn Your Good Marks, *Cont'd.*

6. Repeat steps 3 through 5 for each of the suspect tools until you have tested all of them.
7. No two tools are exactly alike. Describe some of the differences in the marks made by different tools.

   ____

   ____

   ____

   ____

8. Obtain the piece of wood with the pried nail from your teacher.
9. Compare the marks on the wood to the impressions of the tool marks. You may also ask your teacher to see the original tool.
10. Examine the tool marks in the block of wood. When you find a clearly recognizable tool mark, describe it here. Then write the name of the tool that you think made the mark.

    ____

    ____

    ____

    ____

11. Take a small piece of modeling clay and knead it in your hand until soft. Press the softened clay onto one of the tool marks on the piece of wood. Carefully remove the clay and examine the impression. Describe the impression here.

    ____

    ____

    ____

    ____

12. Compare the impression from the piece of wood to the impressions of suspect tools in your egg carton. Write the name of the tool that you think made the mark.

    ____

    ____

13. Did you pick the same tool both times? Ask your team members what tool they think made the marks. Are their answers different? Discuss the differences, and come to a conclusion on behalf of the group.

Name ______________________________ Date ______________________

Science Sleuth Activity Package: Earn Your Good Marks, *Cont'd.*

Data Table for Earn Your Good Marks

Tool	**Description of Tool**	**Description of Identifying Marks on Tool**	**Description of Tool Impression**
Tool A			
Tool B			
Tool C			
Tool D			
Tool E			

Activity 3.6: The Case of Blood Splatter

Teacher Briefing

In this activity, students are asked to design an experiment that will allow them to create a hypothesis about the relationship between the size and shape of a blood splatter and the distance that the blood fell. The design of the experiment is as important as conducting the experiment and collecting results.

Of course, we are talking about fake blood here, and you will want to make this clear to your students.

Activity Preparation

- Make fake blood. Here are two recipes:

  Recipe 1
  1/2 cup water
  1 tablespoon cocoa powder
  3–4 tablespoons corn syrup
  1/2 to 1 teaspoon red food coloring

  Mix the cocoa powder with water until smooth. Add other ingredients and stir. If bubbles or foam form in the fake blood, spoon it off.

  Recipe 2
  2/3 cup Oriental "cherry" dipping sauce
  1/3 cup water
  1/2 teaspoon red food coloring
  2–3 drops green food coloring

  Thoroughly mix the cherry dipping sauce with water. Add the food coloring, then let the mixture sit a few minutes before using.

- For each student group, you will need:

  Fake blood (about one-fourth cup per student group)
  Medicine dropper
  Drinking straw
  Yardstick or meter stick
  Small bowl or jar
  White paper
  Cardboard
  Drop cloth
  Graph paper
- Make copies of the Science Sleuth Activity Package.

First, Tell Your Students . . .

When liquids splatter against a solid object, they create a pattern that depends on several factors. One of them is the height from which the liquid falls. Detectives can use data they collect and work backward to figure out how far blood fell to create a particular splatter pattern.

Activity Procedure

1. Divide students into small groups, and ask them to work together to develop a procedure for testing the relationship between the size of blood splatter and the distance the blood drop falls.
2. As teams develop their plan, review their experimental designs and provide feedback or guidance as needed.
3. Let teams select the materials they need and draw conclusions.

Summary and Discussion

- Ask students what they learned about the relationship between the diameter of a blood drop and the height from which the blood falls. *Answer:* The diameter of a blood drop decreases as the height from which the blood falls increases.
- Have students describe the appearance of the outside edge of a blood drop that fell a short distance and one that fell a longer distance. *Answer:* The outside edge of a drop that falls a short distance will be fairly round and smooth. As the distance grows, the outside edge will become less smooth.
- Ask students whether the surface that the blood strikes might affect the pattern of blood drops. What kind of experiment could test this? *Answer:* Some surface materials are absorbent and will soak up blood; others are not.
- How do you think a detective might use blood drop evidence when trying to solve a crime? *Answer:* A detective might be able to tell how far a drop of blood fell before striking the floor. This could give clues as to what happened during the crime.

Name ______________________________ Date ______________________

Science Sleuth Activity Package: The Case of Blood Splatter

Background

The forensic science class at your school has asked you and your partners to develop a report that will show the relationship between the size of the splatter and the distance the blood fell. They know that the students in this class are the most experienced investigators in your school. They're counting on your report to help rookies learn something about blood splatter evidence.

First, you'll be meeting with your investigative team to figure out an experiment you can do to show the relationship between a blood splatter pattern and the distance blood falls. Then you will show the plan to your teacher and select the materials you need for your experiment from the supplies at the front of the classroom. Finally, you will conduct your experiment and organize your findings in a graph and several drawings.

Activity Directions

1. Work with your partners to brainstorm some ways you could collect the data you need. When you have a good idea for an experiment, write it in the row titled "Procedure for Your Experiment" in the data table at the end of this package. Be sure to list all of the steps of your proposed procedure.
2. Now look at the list of materials presented here:

   Simulated blood

   Medicine dropper

   Drinking straw

   Yardstick or meter stick

   Small bowl or jar

   White paper

   Cardboard

   Drop cloth

   Graph paper

   Which ones will you need to conduct your experiment? Writer the list in the second row of the data table.
3. Show the plan to your teacher, and gather the materials you need to conduct your experiment.

Name ____________________ Date ____________________

Science Sleuth Activity Package: The Case of Blood Splatter, *Cont'd.*

4. In your science notebook, design a data table to collect your results.
5. Use the results of your experiment to create a report to share with your colleagues.
6. Conduct you experiment, and collect the data.

Questions for Discussion

1. Based on your experimental results, what is the relationship between the diameter of a blood drop and the height from which the blood falls?
2. Describe the outside edge of a blood drop that fell from a short distance and one that fell farther.
3. How might the surface that blood strikes affect the pattern of blood drops?
4. How do you think a detective might use blood drop evidence when trying to solve a crime?

Name ______________________ Date ______________________

Science Sleuth Activity Package: The Case of Blood Splatter, *Cont'd.*

Data Table for The Case of Blood Splatter

Procedure for your experiment	
Materials needed	

Activity 3.7: Shattered Glass

Teacher Briefing

In this activity, students learn something about fracture patterns in glass. Then they review some evidence from a case and draw conclusions. Because the only materials needed here are colored highlighters, this activity can be done with individual students, or you can assign student groups.

Activity Preparation

- For each student or student group, provide highlighters in three different colors—preferably yellow, blue, and green.
- Make copies of the Science Sleuth Activity Package and distribute them before beginning this discussion, so students can look at the "How Glass Shatters" drawing.

First, Tell Your Students . . .

If you throw a rock or anything hard at a piece of glass, chances are good it will break. There are some scientific rules about what really happens when glass breaks.

First, glass will break on the opposite side of where it was struck. For example, if you're standing outside and throw a rock at a window, most of the broken glass will fall inside the building. Some smaller amount of glass, the *backscatter,* may be projected backward in the direction from which the blow came. People who break into homes by shattering windows may have some backscatter blown back on their clothes, an important clue for detectives.

When glass breaks, it forms two kinds of fracture lines. You can see how this works if you'll look at the drawing, "How Glass Shatters," at the end of your Science Sleuth Activity Package. *Radial fractures* start at the point of impact and run straight out in all directions. In a radial fracture, the glass breaks on the side opposite the applied force. *Concentric fractures* form between the radial fractures on the same side of the glass where the impact took place. When new fracture lines form, they stop when they hit older fracture lines.

Activity Procedure

Instruct your students to follow the directions in the package.

Summary and Discussion

- Remind students that fracture lines will stop if they meet existing fracture lines. Which set of fractures occurred first: A, B, or C? Ask students how they know. *Answer:* C. None of its fracture lines are interrupted. The second strike occurred at A and the last strike at B.
- In a fracture where very little loose glass was produced, ask students whether they would expect that glass to be on the side of the strike or opposite the strike. Have them explain their reasoning.
- Based on the information available about the fractures in Terrance's windshield, do they think all three strikes were caused by pieces of gravel falling off a truck?
- Manny, Gina, and Lynn offered different information about what happened to Terrance's windshield. Who do students believe? Why?

Name ______________________________ Date ______________________

Science Sleuth Activity Package: Shattered Glass

The Crime

Three months ago, Terrance bought a car and paid for it with money he had earned at his part-time job. He's very proud of this car and keeps it squeaky clean and in excellent running order.

Yesterday Terrance took his car to his insurance company because the windshield is badly cracked in three places. He says that three pieces of gravel fell off a large truck in front of him. Where each piece of gravel hit, the glass broke in all directions. Terrance asked the insurance company to pay for a new windshield.

The insurance agent wants to be sure that rocks really did all of the damage Terrance reported. In interviews with people who have recently seen Terrance and his car, the agent learns some interesting, but confusing, information. Manny says that Terrance came to school one day with just two, not three, sets of fracture lines in the windshield. Gina reports that Terrance was very angry one day, and she saw him punch his car a few times. Lynn says she saw Terrance hit the inside of his windshield with his fist.

When you examine the car and the windshield, you find a few shards of glass on the windshield at point B. You can't find any glass inside the car, but the car's interior appears to have been cleaned recently. Now, take a close look at the fracture lines in the drawing of Terrance's windshield (see the drawing at the end of this activity package) and see what information you can give the insurance agent.

Activity Directions

1. Using "How Glass Shatters" (at the end of this package) for background information, review "Terrance's Windshield" (also at the end of this package) and complete this data table.

Data Table for Shattered Glass

Fracture	Location of Glass Fragments	Side of the Glass Where Radial Fractures Are Found	Side of the Glass Where Concentric Fractures Are Found

Name ______________________________ Date ____________________

Science Sleuth Activity Package: Shattered Glass, *Cont'd.*

2. Determine which strike point (A, B, or C) was created first. You can identify this point because none of the radial lines radiating from it touch any other cracks or fractures.
3. Highlight this first strike area in yellow.
4. Determine which strike point (A, B, or C) was created second. You can identify this strike point because its radial lines hit only those produced by one other strike point.
5. Highlight this strike area in green.
6. Determine which strike point (A, B, or C) was created last. You can identify it because its radial lines strike the lines created by the other two strikes. Highlight this area in blue.

Questions to Answer

1. Remember that fracture lines will stop if they meet existing fracture lines. Which set of fractures occurred first, A, B, or C? How do you know?

____

____

2. In a fracture where very little loose glass was produced, would you expect that glass to be on the side of the strike, or opposite the strike? Explain your reasoning.

____

____

____

3. Based on the information that you have about the fractures in Terrance's windshield, do you think all three strikes were caused by pieces of gravel falling off a truck?

____

____

4. Three people have come forward with information for you, but you don't know who to believe. Manny says Terrance came to school one day with just two sets of fracture lines in the windshield. Gina says Terrance was very angry one day and hit the car a few times. Lynn says that she saw Terrance sitting inside his truck and hitting the windshield with his fist. But according to Terrance, he was a passenger when three pieces of gravel hit the windshield. Which one of these people would you believe? Why?

____

____

____

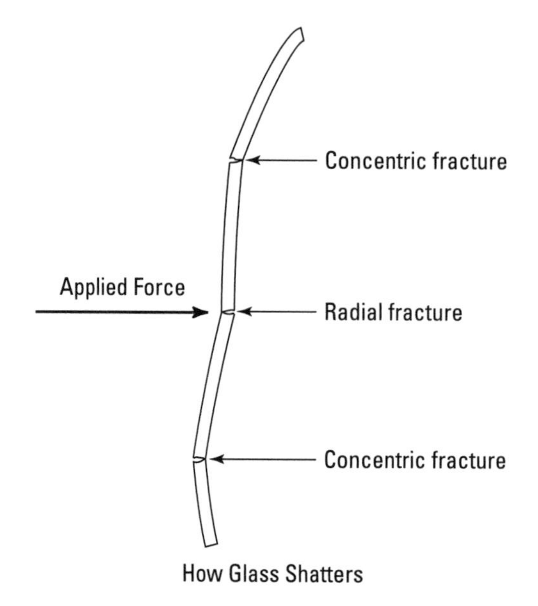

How Glass Shatters

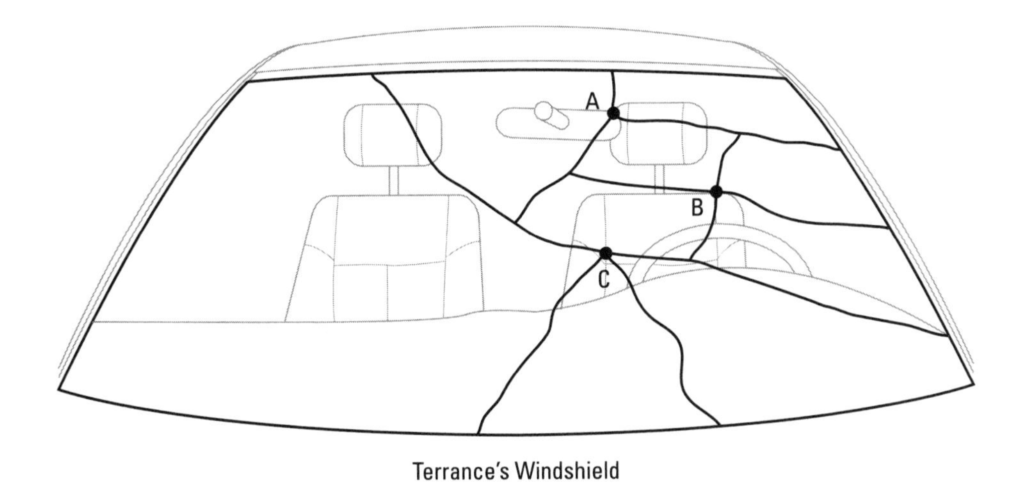

Terrance's Windshield

Activity 3.8: Dirty Evidence

Teacher Briefing

In this activity, students analyze soil from a crime scene and compare it to known samples of soil. Students examine the texture of the samples under a microscope.

Activity Preparation

- Collect soil samples from six locations, and put them in bags. The samples should not be obviously different from each other, only slightly different. In other words, don't pick samples like pure white sand, red clay, and dark black humus. Instead, select six areas where the soil seems similar. You will need enough soil in five of the samples to fill a small paper cup for each group. For the sixth sample, you will need enough to fill the paper cups and to provide a "crime scene" sample in an envelope.
- Label the bags of soil A through F.
- Choose one sample as the crime scene sample, and put some in an envelope for each of the student groups. Label it "From Bob Trundell's Yard." Note which sample you used here: Sample _______ is from Bob Trundell's yard.
- For the other soil samples, label cups A through F for each student group, and fill the cups with the appropriate samples. To save yourself some of this work, label the bags in which you have collected the soil A through F. Students will then label and fill their own paper cups.
- Set up a work station for each student group with:

  Six paper cups with labels marked or unmarked
  Microscope
  Ruler (marked in millimeters)
  Drinking glass (about eight ounces in size) or jar
  Spoon
  Stopwatch
  Water
- Make copies of Science Sleuth Activity Package.

First, Tell Your Students . . .

Detectives have been getting the dirt on perpetrators for a long time. As early as 1908, detectives used soil to help solve a murder. After the death of Margaeth Filbert in Bavaria, Germany, detectives were suspicious of a local fellow who had a reputation for stealing. When detectives visited the suspect at his home, he claimed that he had never seen Miss Filbert.

The detectives noticed that he had a lot of mud on his shoes, and the victim's body had been discovered in a muddy area. Police questioned the suspect's wife about her husband's shoes, and she explained that she had cleaned his shoes the night before. The suspect said that he'd gotten his shoes muddy when walking through his fields. The field where the suspect claimed to have been walking contained light-colored soil derived from milky quartz, and it was also home to a flock of geese.

Georg Popp, a local chemist and geologist, was called in for help. Popp examined the muddy shoes closely and discovered that the region in front of the heel showed three distinct layers of mud. Popp reasoned that the innermost layer was probably the oldest. The innermost layer contained a lot of goose droppings, like the soil in the suspect's fields. The second layer was made up of red sandstone, which was common in the place where Margaeth Filbert's body was found. The third layer contained coal dust. Bloody clothes, which the police suspected belonged to the killer, were found in a part of town where coal dust was common. Mr. Popp's examination suggested that the suspect was a liar and that he murdered Miss Filbert.

The same approach is used today in forensic geology. Forensic scientists compare soil found on the shoes or clothes of a suspect to soil from a crime scene. There are thousands of kinds of soil, and the samples from one location are different from samples in another spot. Some of the ways soils vary are by color, types of minerals, content, and texture.

Activity Procedure

1. Hand out Science Sleuth Activity Packages, and assign students to groups.
2. Give each group an envelope containing soil "From Bob Trundell's yard."
3. If you have provided the other soil samples at the work stations, skip to step 4. Otherwise, tell students to label their paper cups A through F and to collect a soil sample from each bag of soil labeled on your desk.
4. Instruct your students to follow directions in their Science Sleuth Activity Packages.

Summary and Discussion

- Ask students if they found evidence of Frank McDonald's guilt or innocence in the theft of Bob Trundell's coins. Discuss their findings and how they reached their conclusions.
- In Arizona, theft of large cacti is a serious problem. This larceny takes place when people dig up the cacti that are growing on protected federal land. The thieves take the cacti into nearby towns and sell them to unsuspecting home owners, who plant them in their yards. How could you use soil evidence to help determine whether a cactus has been stolen from federal property? *Answer:* Soil on the roots of the cacti could be compared to soil on protected land. If it matches, the cacti were stolen.
- In Alabama, vandals have been throwing clods of dirt at a cargo train as it travels through town. When the clods hit the train, they break up and spread dirt everywhere. The railroad crew never discovers the problem until the train comes to a stop and begins to unload. How could you use soil evidence to find out where to start looking for these dirt-tossing vandals? *Answer:* Soil is unique. The clods of dirt could be matched to certain types of soil in Alabama.
- How can a detective use soil evidence to help solve a crime? *Answer:* Soil evidence shows whether a person was in an area.

Name ______________________ Date ______________________

Science Sleuth Activity Package: Dirty Evidence

Background

Detectives have been getting the dirt on perpetrators for a long time. Forensic scientists compare soil found on the shoes or clothes of a suspect to soil from a crime scene. There are thousands of kinds of soil, and the samples from one location are different from samples in another spot. Some of the ways soils vary are by color, types of minerals, content, and texture. Today you and your detective partners are going to use some of these variations to analyze evidence.

The Crime

Your neighbor, Bob Trundell, buried some old coins in his backyard when he went away for the weekend. When he came home, it looked as if someone had been digging in the yard, and the coins were gone. Trundell thinks his gardener, Frank McDonald, stole them.

Police find a lot of dirt on McDonald's clothes, but he says that the dirt comes from other clients. He says he hasn't been in Trundell's yard for more than a week, and his wife says she washed all of his dirty clothes last Friday.

Police have sent you some samples and asked you to do the science.

Activity Directions

1. Examine six samples of soil taken from Frank McDonald's clothes.
2. Using the data table at the end of this package, describe the color of each soil sample.
3. Sprinkle a few grains of each soil sample on a white sheet of paper. Examine the grains with a microscope, and describe the appearance of the grains in the data table.
4. The rate at which soil settles out of water is related to that soil's physical traits. Perform a rate-of-sedimentation test on the soil samples. To do so, half-fill the drinking glass with water. Put one teaspoon of soil sample A in the glass of water. Stir briskly to mix. Start the stopwatch. When all of the soil has settled to the bottom of the glass, stop the stopwatch. Record the time sedimentation took for all of the samples on the data table.
5. Take the soil sample from the envelope marked "From Bob Trundell's yard." Repeat steps 2 through 4 on this soil sample. Record your findings on the data table.
6. Based on the data you collected, was Frank McDonald in Bob Trundell's yard since last Friday? Does this prove he took the old coins?

Science Sleuth Activity Package: Dirty Evidence, *Cont'd.*

Data Table for Dirty Evidence

Soil Sample	Color	Appearance Under Microscope	Sedimentation Time
A			
B			
C			
D			
E			
F			
Soil from Bob Trundell's yard			

Activity 3.9: Fingerprint Frequency—Homework Assignment

Teacher Notes

Once students have learned the basic skills of taking fingerprints, this activity gives them a chance to take an experiment from start to finish: developing a hypothesis about fingerprint frequency, constructing an experiment to test it, doing the experiment, and reporting results. Thus, you could use this activity as a special project to be done over the course of two or three weeks.

Answer Key

3. In a classroom of thirty students, Delores found the results that are summarized here:

Delores's Experiment

Primary fingerprint pattern	Males	Females
Loops	69%	31%
Whorls	19	51
Arches	10	2
Mixed	4	16

a. What is the most common fingerprint pattern found in females in this group of students? What is the most common fingerprint pattern found in males? *Answer:* Females: whorls; males: loops.

b. Would it be correct to assume that since only 4 percent of the males in Delores's class have mixed fingerprints, only 4 percent of all males have mixed fingerprints? *Answer:* No. Frequencies could be different in each classroom.

c. How could a detective use the information in the table in an investigation? *Answer:* If the fingerprints at a crime scene are loops, he or she knows that there is a 69 percent chance that the perp will be male.

4. How do detectives and investigators use the scientific method? *Answer:* The scientific method is a technique for solving problems that can be applied to the science lab or the investigation of a crime. After making observations and suggesting hypotheses, detectives carry out tests to see if their hypotheses are sound.

Name ______________________________ Date ______________________

Homework Assignment: Fingerprint Frequency

Recently you learned how to take and analyze fingerprints in your class. Here's a chance to use your experience to develop a hypothesis and an experimental procedure, then do the experiment and draw conclusions.

Background

Fingerprints are fascinating pieces of evidence. You know that they can be used to place a person at a crime scene. What else do you know about them? Would you find the most loops in a sample of boys' fingerprints or girls' fingerprints? How about swirls and arches? Are the fingerprints of older people different from the fingerprints of younger people?

Detectives use the same approach to problem solving that scientists do, a technique called the *scientific method.* The scientific method has five basic steps:

1. Statement of the problem
2. Statement of a hypothesis (an idea about the answer to the problem)
3. An experiment to test the hypothesis
4. Analysis of the results of the experiment
5. Conclusions from the experimental analysis

These five steps do not have to be done in this order, but most people using the scientific method find this order helpful.

In this activity, you will put your detective skills to work to solve a problem. First, you will state a hypothesis about the frequency of fingerprint patterns. You will develop a procedure to find out whether your hypothesis is true. From this procedure, you will collect evidence and draw conclusions.

What You'll Need

- Index cards
- Ink pad
- Soap and water
- Magnifying glass
- Ruler
- Transparent tape

Activity Directions

1. Develop a hypothesis about fingerprint frequency that you can test. For example, your hypothesis might be that loops can be found more often in girls' fingerprints than in those of boys', or that arches are common in boys and rare in girls. Once you decide on a hypothesis to test, write it in the Data Table for Fingerprint Frequency.
2. Decide what you would need to do to find out whether your hypothesis is true. In other words, what kind of experiment will you do to prove or disprove your hypothesis? In the second row of the data table, describe the experiment you plan to do.

Name ______________________ Date ______________

Homework Assignment: Fingerprint Frequency, *Cont'd.*

3. Before you proceed, show your hypothesis and your experimental plan to your teacher, and follow any advice you get.
4. During your experiment, keep good records. Collect and enter data in data tables that you construct.
5. Once you have drawn a conclusion, write it in the last row of the data table.

Questions to Answer

1. Did you find your hypothesis to be true or false?

   ____

2. If you found it to be false, what could you do next?

   ____

   ____

3. In a classroom of thirty students, Delores found the results that are summarized here:

Primary fingerprint pattern	Males	Females
Loops	69%	31%
Whorls	19	51
Arches	10	2
Mixed	4	16

   What is the most common fingerprint pattern found in females in this group of students? What is the most common fingerprint pattern found in males?

   ____

   Would it be correct to assume that since only 4 percent of the males in Delores's class have mixed fingerprints, only 4 percent of all males have mixed fingerprints?

   ____

   ____

   How could a detective use the information in Delores's table in an investigation?

   ____

   ____

4. How do detectives and investigators use the scientific method?

   ____

   ____

Name ______________________ Date ______________________

Homework Assignment: Fingerprint Frequency, *Cont'd.*

Data Table for Fingerprint Frequency

Hypothesis

Describe the experiment you plan to conduct

State the conclusions that you drew from your experiment

Activity 3.10: Tracking Down the Intruder—Homework Assignment

Teacher Notes

This activity has two pieces. The first is a straightforward experiment with the parameters all spelled out for the students. In the second, students are asked to develop their own experiment and data tables. What they did in the first part should provide a model for the second.

This activity presupposes some knowledge of graphing. You may need to supplement with other pieces of your curriculum.

Answer Key for Footprints

1. Look over the data table and the graph. According to your results, is there a link between the height of a person and the length of stride? If so, what is it? *Answer:* As height increases, length of stride increases.
2. A detective found two sets of tracks at a crime scene. The stride length of one set of tracks measured 27 inches. The stride length of the other set of tracks measured 19 inches. What do these tracks tell you about the people who made them? *Answer:* One person is much taller than the other.
3. Your boss has asked you to solve a problem for him. He wants to know if a detective can tell whether a person is walking or running by examining impressions of that person's tracks. Describe an experiment that will help you solve this problem. *Answer:* One is having students walk through a sandy area, then examining the prints. The prints could be compared to those of a person running through the sandy area.
4. Write an outline of an experiment that would enable you to estimate the weight of a person from impressions of his or her tracks. *Answer:* Answers will vary.

Answer Key for Bicycle Tracks

1. Does the weight of a suspect affect the bicycle tire impressions that suspect makes? If so, how? *Answer:* The heavier the suspect, the deeper the tire impressions are.
2. Does the height of a suspect affect the bicycle tire impressions that suspect makes? If so, how? *Answer:* Height alone does not affect the tire impressions.
3. Do you think the bicycle track evidence will be enough to convict one of the three suspects? Why or why not? *Answer:* Answers will vary. One possible answer is that the suspect could have been riding around the clubhouse without being the thief.
4. Which vehicle would you expect to make the deeper tire impressions: a compact car or a large car? Why? *Answer:* Probably a large car, which would be heavier unless the compact car was loaded with cement.
5. What other kind of information might a detective get from bicycle tire tracks? *Answer:* Answers will vary. One possible answer is that a detective can determine the direction of movement and path followed from tire impressions.

Name ______________________________ Date ______________________

Homework Assignment: Tracking Down the Intruder

Background

Some people are tall, and others are short. Some people are lean, and others are chubby. In this set of activities, you learn something about what you can tell about a person's size by the tracks he or she leaves behind.

What You'll Need

- Access to an outdoor area of sand or soft soil
- Rake
- Bicycle
- Flashlight
- Yardstick or tape measure
- Measuring cup
- Bathroom scale

Footprints

Foot impressions at a crime scene may show how many people were in the area and in which direction those people were traveling. They can reveal details about the people who made them, such as their height, weight, or speed of their travel.

Activity Directions

1. Ask three or four people to join you in this activity. Line up all the members of your group by height. Call the tallest person in the group Suspect A, the next tallest Suspect B, the next tallest Suspect C, and so forth.
2. Measure the height of each suspect, and record those heights in the data table.
3. Use the rake to smooth an area of sand or soft soil.
4. Ask Suspect A to walk across the smoothed sand.
5. Measure the length of Suspect A's stride—the distance from the toe of one track to the heel of the track in front of it. Record that length in the data table.
6. Repeat steps 3 through 5 with each of the other suspects.
7. Create a graph to display the data you have collected. Place "Height of Suspect" on the *x*-axis and "Length of Stride" on the *y*-axis.

Name ______________________________ Date ____________________

Homework Assignment: Tracking Down the Intruder, *Cont'd.*

Data Table for Footprints

	Height	**Length of Stride**
Suspect A		
Suspect B		
Suspect C		
Suspect D		

Create Your Graph Here

Name ______________________ Date ______________________

Homework Assignment: Tracking Down the Intruder, *Cont'd.*

Questions to Answer

1. Look over the data table and the graph. According to your results, is there a link between the height of a person and the length of stride? If so, what is it?

___

___

___

2. A detective found two sets of tracks at a crime scene. The stride length of one set of tracks measured 27 inches. The stride length of the other set of tracks measured 19 inches. What do these tracks tell you about the people who made them?

___

___

___

3. Your boss has asked you to solve a problem for him. He wants to know if a detective can tell whether a person is walking or running by examining impressions of that person's tracks. Describe an experiment that will help you solve this problem.

___

___

___

4. Write an outline of an experiment that would enable you to estimate the weight of a person from impressions of his or her tracks.

___

___

___

___

___

___

___

___

___

___

___

Name ______________________ Date ______________________

Homework Assignment: Tracking Down the Intruder, *Cont'd.*

Bicycle Tire Tracks

Tire tracks can provide a lot of information at a crime scene. Impressions of tires from the crime scene may indicate that a suspect was there and provide helpful evidence. Here's your case:

When the Ready Riders arrived at their track today for afternoon practice, they were shocked to find that their clubhouse has been burgled. The Ready Riders store a lot of important things in the clubhouse, such as their helmets, flags, and other gear. They also store the money they use to buy refreshments after each practice. The intruder at their clubhouse took two bike helmets and all of the refreshment money.

Luckily, three suspects have been taken into custody, and there are some impressions of bicycle tires in the soil around the clubhouse. The police are now trying to decide which one is the most likely perpetrator. The three suspects and some of their vital information are summed up here:

Suspect	Height	Weight in Pounds
Pete	6 feet 1 inch	120
Guy	5 feet 6 inches	150
Buddy	5 feet 9 inches	200

The police chief wants your help. She needs to know if there is a relationship between the way a bike impression looks and the weight or height of a cyclist. With the information you provide, the crime may be solvable!

Activity Directions

1. Decide on an experiment you could carry out that would tell the chief whether bicycle tire tracks provide information about a rider's weight or height. Describe the experiment you plan to do in the first row of the data table for bicycle tire tracks.
2. Make a list of materials that you need in the second row of the chart.
3. Show your plan to your teacher. If your teacher approves of your plan, gather the materials and carry out your experiment.
4. As you carry out your experiment, keep good records. Collect and enter data in data tables that you construct.
5. Once you have drawn a conclusion, write it in the last row of the data table for bicycle tire tracks.

Name ____________________ Date ____________________

Homework Assignment: Tracking Down the Intruder, *Cont'd.*

Data Table for Bicycle Tire Tracks

Describe the experiment you plan to conduct

List the materials you need to carry out the experiment

State the conclusions that you drew from your experiment

Name ______________________ Date ______________

Homework Assignment: Tracking Down the Intruder, *Cont'd.*

Questions to Answer

1. Does the weight of a suspect affect the bicycle tire impressions that suspect makes? If so, how?

2. Does the height of a suspect affect the bicycle tire impressions that suspect makes? If so, how?

3. Do you think the bicycle track evidence will be enough to convict one of the three suspects? Why or why not?

4. Which vehicle would you expect to make the deeper tire impressions: a compact car or a large car? Why?

5. What other kind of information might a detective get from bicycle tire tracks?

Chapter Four

When the Beaker Bubbles Over

Using Physical Science in Forensic Science

The field of forensic science includes many disciplines. Two of the most important are chemistry, the science of matter, and physics, which includes the study of motion and forces. In this chapter, students learn about the physical and chemical properties of matter as they relate to solving crimes. In doing so, they conduct chemical analyses, carry out examinations and comparisons, perform investigations, and gather and process data. Fibers, latent fingerprints, food, and paper are some of the materials that they chemically investigate. Students also learn how an understanding of forces and matter can help them reconstruct the events at a crime scene.

Activity 4.1: Paper Detective

Teacher Briefing

Students create and characterize a collection of papers of different kinds. Then they identify the characteristics of an unknown paper sample. While you may do this activity in small groups, each individual can conduct the tests if you have enough supplies.

Activity Preparation

- You will need to collect samples of several different kinds of paper—for example, newspaper, notebook paper, copier paper, stationery, construction paper, and glossy paper from a magazine. The samples can be just a couple of inches square.
- You may want to save time by presorting packets of the different paper samples that students will test.
- Take some pieces of one kind of paper, and write on it: "There is a bomb in the school." You will need to make several copies of this note, all on the original paper.
- For each student or group, provide:

  Microscope or magnifying glass
  Ultraviolet light
  Black construction paper or poster board
  Ballpoint pens
  Copy of the note
  Samples of several types of paper
- Make copies of the Science Sleuth Activity Package.

First, Tell Your Students . . .

Because criminals often use paper in the course of their crime—writing notes, for example—learning something about the different properties of paper is useful for detectives. It may give them clues about where the suspect lives or works, and it may even link the suspect to the crime.

Activity Procedure

1. If you are conducting this experiment in small groups, assign students to groups.
2. Distribute the Science Sleuth Activity Package and the paper samples.
3. Tell students to follow the directions in their activity packages.
4. As they finish their data tables, students should bring them to you for review. Then you will provide a copy of the suspicious note for them to study.

Summary and Discussion

Discuss the following questions with your students:

- Which type of paper that you examined has the largest fibers in it?
- Which samples of paper are coated with sizing?
- Why do investigators need a set of reference papers?
- What kind of paper was used to write the ransom note?
- How could you use this knowledge to help Mr. Hanson discover who was writing the notes?

Name ______________________ Date ______________________

Science Sleuth Activity Package: Paper Detective

The Case

"There is a bomb in the school." Principal Hanson couldn't believe his eyes—another bomb threat! Returning to his office, he found the note taped to his door. This was the third bomb threat in a week! Like the first two, this turned out to be a false alarm, but everyone had to leave the school while police searched for it. People were scared, and classes were disrupted.

Who is writing these notes? Mr. Hanson wonders. He calls you to his office and asks if there is anything you can do to help him find the author. You tell Mr. Hanson, "Let's start with what we have: this piece of paper. It might provide us with a lead."

A suspicious paper must be compared to known paper samples to determine its source, and to do that, you need a set of reference papers. In this experiment, you will create a set of reference papers that can be used for comparison purposes. Then you will use those papers to help you learn more about the note to Mr. Hanson.

Activity Directions

1. Examine the paper samples provided by your teacher. In the left-hand column of the data table at the end of the package, record what kind of paper each piece is, for example, "newspaper."
2. Tear off a small piece of one of the papers so the fibers are exposed.
3. Place the torn paper against a black background and examine the torn edge with a magnifying glass or use a microscope to study it. In the second column of the data table, describe the fibers along the torn edge. In the third column of the data table, sketch the appearance of the paper under magnification.
4. Test the sample to see if it reflects ultraviolet (UV) light. To do so, darken the room as much as possible. Turn on the UV light and hold it over the paper sample. *(Caution: Do not look directly at the UV light.)* If the paper emits a bright white glow, it is reflecting fluorescent light. Write *yes* in the fourth column of the data table. If the paper looks the same as it does under normal light, write *no* in the fourth column of the data table.
5. Some types of paper are coated with *sizing,* a material made of gelatin or starch, which prevents the paper from acting as a blotting pad and absorbing too much ink. To determine if the sample is coated with sizing, rest the tip of a ballpoint pen on it for about thirty seconds. If a large spot of ink forms, the paper lacks sizing. If a large spot of ink does not form, the paper is coated with sizing. In the last column of the data table, record your findings.
6. Repeat steps 1 through 6 for each of your paper samples, recording your findings on the data table.
7. When your table is completed, show it to your teacher. Test the bomb threat note paper your teacher gives you in the same way you tested the other papers.
8. Compare the characteristics of paper used in the bomb threat note with the samples you examined earlier. Based on this comparison, what kind of paper is this note written on?

   ____

Name ______________________ Date ______________

Science Sleuth Activity Package: Paper Detective, *Cont'd.*

Data Table for Paper Detective

Kind of Paper	Description of Fibers Under Magnification	Sketch of Fibers Under Magnification	Fluoresces Under UV Light (Yes or No)	Coated with Sizing (Yes or No)

Activity 4.2: Cookie Confusion

Teacher Briefing

In this activity, students learn how to detect the presence of fat in food. Because it involves one of their favorite foods, the students also learn a bit of useful information about nutrition. In the process, they collect and analyze data and then draw conclusions. No cookie is 100 percent fat free, but some will have substantially less fat—and thus make much smaller grease spots on the brown paper used in this experiment.

Activity Preparation

- Collect several different kinds of cookies; besides selecting different varieties—chocolate chip, peanut butter, oatmeal raisin—one of the cookies must be low fat or fat free. It would be good if it's not identifiable by appearance. For example, use two kinds of chocolate chip cookies: one fat free and one regular.
- Sort the cookies into the appropriate bags labeled Sample A, Sample B, Sample C, and so on. Keep the original packaging, but do not show it to students until the experiment is completed. Complete the table here so you will know which cookies are in which bag:

	Type of Cookie
Sample A	
Sample B	
Sample C	
Sample D	
Sample E	
Sample F	
Sample G	

- To save time, you may further sort the cookies so that each student group will have a small bag—say, a waxed paper sandwich bag—with a cookie from each sample. These bags should be labeled Sample A, Sample B, and so on.

- For each student group, provide:

  Brown paper bags
  Waxed paper sandwich bags
  Labels
  Scissors
- Make copies of the Science Sleuth Activity Package.

First, Tell Your Students . . .

The Food and Drug Administration (FDA) is a federal agency that regulates the ingredients in foods, medicines, cosmetics, and other consumer items. FDA scientists try to make sure that these products are safe and that they contain the ingredients their labels say they contain.

Since fat-free foods have been introduced to the market, consumers have bought them in large quantities. Too much fat in the diet is linked to several serious diseases.

Activity Procedure

1. Distribute the Science Sleuth Activity Packages, and divide students into research teams. If you have sorted the samples into bags for each group, skip to step 4.
2. Bring out the bags of samples. Invite students from each group to come forward and collect a small sample from each bag, using waxed paper sandwich bags.
3. Provide different colored labels with each large bag of samples, and remind students to attach one of these colored labels to their sandwich bag and label it with a pen: Sample A, Sample B, and so forth.
4. Tell students to follow the directions in their Science Sleuth Activity Package.

Summary and Discussion

- Ask students how they determined whether a cookie contains fats. Based on the results of their experiments, which cookie has the most fat? Is there a low-fat or fat-free cookie in the samples? Could they tell that cookie by taste?
- Reveal the original packages for all of the samples. Discuss ingredients if you wish.

Name ______________________ Date ______________________

Science Sleuth Activity Package: Cookie Confusion

The Situation

The Civic Club decided to have a cookie sale to raise money for a student trip to Washington, D.C. Your principal, Mr. Huffman, agreed to let the club members sell homemade cookies during the afternoon break. However, he attached one important stipulation: at least some of the cookies must be fat free. Mr. Huffman is all about healthy eating and does not want the school to promote anything that might not be nutritious.

The aroma of home-baked cookies draws you toward the school lobby. You see a long line of students waiting to buy cookies. Wow, do those smell good! But the club members haven't opened for business. It turns out that the cookies got mixed up, and now no one can remember which cookies are low fat or fat free. It's important to know so that they can put an accurate label on the low-fat/fat-free cookies.

You and your classmates come to the rescue.

Activity Procedure

1. With members of your student team, collect samples of each type of cookie. Be careful to use the labels your teacher provides to identify where each cookie came from: Sample A, Sample B, Sample C, and so on.
2. At your work station, describe each cookie in the data table provided at the end of this package.
3. For each cookie sample, cut a small square of brown paper, about 5 inches by 5 inches.
4. Label the squares of paper: Sample A, Sample B, and so on.
5. Making sure that you take a cookie and a square of paper marked with the same sample name, test each cookie for the presence of fats. To do so, rub the cookie into the brown paper.
6. Observe what happens. If the paper does not change, the cookie does not contain fat. If the paper becomes translucent, then fat is present. *Translucent* means that some light can pass through the paper but you cannot see through it.
7. Record your findings in the data table.
8. Repeat the procedure with the other cookies and pieces of brown paper. Extend the data table if you need space to record your findings.
9. Which do you think makes more translucent smudges on the brown paper: food that is high in fat or low in fat? Explain your reasoning.

   ____

   ____

   ____

10. Based on your answer, arrange the cookies you tested in order from the one that has the most fat to the one that has the least fat.

Name ______________________ Date ______________________

Science Sleuth Activity Package: Cookie Confusion, *Cont'd.*

Data Table for Cookie Confusion

Cookie	Kind of Cookie	Appearance of Paper	Fats Present (Yes or No)
Sample A			
Sample B			
Sample C			
Sample D			
Sample E			
Sample F			
Sample G			

Activity 4.3: Stick It to 'Em

Teacher Briefing

In this activity, students get to be engineers, designing and building a device that detectives could use to make latent prints visible at a crime scene.

When you are working on this project, keep in mind that superglue contains cyanoacrylates, which can cause extreme eye and nose irritation. Try not to breathe any superglue fumes, and make sure you do your work in a well-ventilated area. **Teachers will need to judge the maturity of their students in deciding whether to proceed with this activity.**

Activity Preparation

- Discuss the use of superglue with the principal as needed.
- Provide:

  Superglue
  Several types of small containers (such as empty coffee cans with lids, 8-inch by 8-inch cardboard boxes, small food containers with lids, empty cereal boxes, or empty milk cartons)
  Cotton balls
  String
  Transparent tape
  Paper clip
  Scissors
  Stapler
  Weather stripping (about 12-inch-long strips)
  Clay or modeling dough (about the size of a golf ball)
  Aluminum foil
  Stopwatch
  Ruler
  Small objects—perhaps poker chips—bearing latent fingerprints
- Make copies of the Science Sleuth Activity Package.

First, Tell Your Students . . .

You have learned that fingerprints are important pieces of evidence that can help link a suspect to a crime scene. Most fingerprints are latents, the type that can't be seen with the naked eye. Sometimes you can find latents by dusting them with fingerprint powder, but this doesn't work well with fragile prints. Also, if conditions are extremely dry or hot, fingerprints may dry up. Therefore, investigators sometimes use chemicals that react with the compounds in fingerprints and make the prints visible. Several chemical techniques can be used to enhance fingerprints. Each test is based on different chemical reactions.

In one type of test, the item that contains latent prints is put in a closed container with iodine crystals. Iodine crystals vaporize quickly. The vaporized iodine binds with unsaturated fatty acids in the invisible fingerprints to make them visible. (Note that this is related to what you learned in Activity, 4.2 "Cookie Confusion.") Another useful chemical that can reveal invisible prints is ninhydrin. It reacts with free amino and carboxyl groups in proteins. Silver nitrate can also be used because it reacts with chloride ions in the print.

Superglue fuming is a quick and easy way to find latent prints. It is done by placing the item containing a fingerprint in a small chamber. Liquid superglue is also put in the chamber, and then the top is sealed in place. Sometimes the chamber is warmed to speed vaporization of the glue. On a very warm day, warming may not be necessary. Sometimes it may be necessary to add moisture to the chamber because the fingerprints will disappear if they become dry. Moisture can be added to the chamber by placing a wet cotton ball or a small bowl of water on the floor of the chamber.

Your job is to experiment with several designs of superglue fuming chambers and come up with one that is small enough to take with you on a case. For extra credit, you can write an owner's manual so that a person who is not familiar with the technique of superglue fuming can use your chamber.

Activity Procedure

1. Alert students: "When you are working on this project, keep in mind that superglue contains chemicals that can cause extreme eye and nose irritation. Try not to breathe any glue fumes, and make sure you do your work in a well-ventilated area."
2. Review the criteria for a fuming chamber with the class:

   The chamber should fit in your crime scene kit.

   The chamber should keep fingerprints moist enough to develop properly.

   The chamber should be able to warm the prints and the superglue if temperatures are cool.

   The chamber should develop prints in less than twenty minutes.

   The chamber should require no more than twenty drops of superglue to develop a set of prints.
3. Distribute the Science Sleuth Activity Packages, and divide students into research teams of two or three.
4. Give students time to develop a plan for the chamber. If you have concerns about safety issues, you can conclude the activity here, comparing various group approaches with the class.
5. If you decide to go forward, review student plans, and let them select materials for construction.
6. As students complete their superglue fuming chambers, provide a small item with latent prints so that they can test it.

Summary and Discussion

1. Why might a detective need a portable superglue fuming chamber? *Answer:* Fragile fingerprints might need to be fixed at the crime scene.
2. Why should you fume fingerprints in a well-ventilated area? *Answer:* Superglue produces fumes that can cause headaches.
3. Why should a superglue fuming chamber include a method to keep fingerprints moist? *Answer:* Fingerprints contain moisture. Once they dry up, they disappear.

For Extra Credit

After you have tested the superglue fuming chamber, write an owner's manual that explains how to use it (in other words, write a procedure like the ones in this book). Be sure to be clear and logical, and write step-by-step instructions.

Name ______________________________ Date ______________________

Science Sleuth Activity Package: Stick It to 'Em

Background

Cyanoacrylate, or superglue, is an inexpensive chemical that can be used to help reveal latent fingerprints. It works well with prints on nonporous materials—anything that a drop of water will roll off, like glass, plastic, metal, rubber, or the cover of a magazine. Superglue contains a polymer that bonds to moisture and organic compounds in the print. A print visualized with superglue can remain intact for years.

Superglue fuming is done by placing the item containing a fingerprint in a small chamber. Liquid superglue is also put in the chamber, and then the top is sealed in place. Sometimes a catalyst is needed to warm the chamber enough to vaporize the glue. On a very warm day, warming may not be necessary. In other cases, it may be necessary to add moisture to the chamber because the fingerprints will disappear if they become dry. Moisture can be added to the chamber by placing a wet cotton ball or a small bowl of water on the floor of the chamber.

Your job is to experiment with several designs of superglue fuming chambers and come up with one that is small enough so that you could take it with you on a case. For extra credit, you can write an owner's manual so that a person who is not familiar with the technique of superglue fuming can use your chamber.

When you are working on this project, keep in mind that superglue is a chemical that can cause extreme eye and nose irritation. Try not to breathe any superglue fumes, and make sure you do your work in a well-ventilated area.

Activity Directions

1. Review the criteria for a portable superglue fuming chamber:

   The chamber should fit in your crime scene kit.

   The chamber should keep fingerprints moist enough to develop properly.

   The chamber should be able to warm the prints and the superglue if temperatures are cool.

   The chamber should develop prints in less than twenty minutes.

   The chamber should require no more than twenty drops of superglue to develop a set of prints.

2. Meet with your research team, and discuss a design for a superglue chamber.
3. Assess your design according to the following criteria. Write *yes* or *no* in the last column of the data table at the end of this package.
4. Sketch the design below the data table, label the parts, and show it to your teacher.

Name ______________________ Date ______________________

Science Sleuth Activity Package: Stick It to 'Em, *Cont'd.*

5. If your teacher provides materials, select the materials you need to build the chamber.
6. After your portable superglue fuming chamber is complete, test it on a material containing latent prints, as provided by your teacher.

Questions for Discussion

1. Why might a detective need a portable superglue fuming chamber?
2. Why should you fume fingerprints in a well-ventilated area?
3. Why should a superglue fuming chamber include a method to keep fingerprints moist?

Name ______________________ Date ______________________

Science Sleuth Activity Package: Stick It to 'Em, *Cont'd.*

Data Table for Stick It to 'Em

Criteria: This Superglue Fuming Chamber:	Yes or No
Fits in a crime scene kit	
Provides a method to keep fingerprints moist	
Provides a method to warm superglue	
Develops prints in less than twenty minutes	
Uses fewer than twenty drops of superglue	
Develops fingerprints on a sample provided by the teacher	

Activity 4.4: Burning Evidence

Teacher Briefing

Students observe and study the physical properties of different fibers. While this activity depends on eyes-only observation of fibers as they burn, you could add an observation under microscope.

Here are some notes on what students should observe as they burn various kinds of fibers:

Fiber	Flame (Color, Action, Smoke)	Ash (Shape, Color, Hardness)	Odor
Wool and silk	Orange, sputters, no smoke	Irregular, black, crumbles easily	Burning hair
Cotton and linen	Yellow or amber	Feathery, gray, crumbles easily	Burning paper
Rayon	Orange or no color	Little or no ash	Burning paper
Nylon	Blue base with orange tip, sputters, white smoke	Rounded like small beads	Celery or wax
Polyester	Orange, sputters, black smoke	Shiny and rounded like small beads	Sweet fruit
Acetate	No color, sizzles, no smoke	Black and shaped like small beads	Vinegar
Acrylic	White-orange, sputters, black smoke	Irregular, black with a hard crust	Acidic

Activity Preparation

- Gather samples of five different types of blue or black fibers (such as cotton, linen, wool, rayon, polyester, acetate, or acrylic). For four types, you will need a piece of each fiber for each group. For the fifth type, you will need two pieces for each group.

- Keep each fiber type in a separate bag. Label them Sample A, B, C, and so on, and keep a record of their content in this table:

	Fiber Content
Sample A	
Sample B	
Sample C	
Sample D	
Sample E	
Fiber from jacket sleeve	

- Choose one type of fiber as the "crime scene" fiber. Place one piece of it into an envelope for each student group, and label it: "From Sleeve of Jacket Left in Library."
- For each team, provide:

  Candle (or laboratory flame unit)
  Safety goggles
  Matches
  Nonflammable surface (such as a trivet, aluminum pie plate, or brick)
  Long tongs or tweezers
  Sample fibers and fiber from jacket sleeve
- Make copies of the Science Sleuth Activity Package.

First, Tell your students . . .

Fibers do not all look alike. They can be identified by several properties: color, texture, shape, size, and strength. All fibers can be classified into two big groups: natural and synthetic. Natural fibers come from animals or plants. Cotton and linen are natural plant fibers; wool and silk are from animals (wool is sheep's hair, and silk is made by caterpillars). Synthetic fibers are made using chemical reactions. Synthetic fibers tend to be very uniform in size and shape, and individual fibers show few variations.

Depending on their makeup, fibers react differently when burned. By observing a fiber as it burns, an investigator can determine its composition. This kind of information is essential in finding out where the fiber came from.

Fibers make up clothes, rugs, and some furniture. The physical contact involved in many crimes means that fibers are deposited at the crime scene or carried away from it. Edmund Locard (1877–1966), the father of forensic science, said that every contact leaves a trace. If a person enters a room, something of that person will be left in the room, and something of that room will be transferred to the person. In many investigations, the type of material that is transferred is fiber. Fibers can be instrumental in crime fighting.

Activity Procedure

1. Distribute the Science Sleuth Activity Packages, and divide students into research teams of two or three.
2. Have each team take a sample from each of the fiber bags. Make sure they label their samples according to the bag from which they came: Sample A, B, C, D, and E.
3. Distribute envelopes marked, "From Sleeve of Jacket Left in Library."
4. Tell students to follow the directions in their Science Sleuth Activity Package, **being extremely careful with the flame and burning procedure.**

Summary and Questions

- Ask students if they were able to match the crime scene fiber with one of the samples taken from teenagers in the school. Discuss their findings.
- Identify the fibers used for Samples A, B, C, D, and E. Have students discuss the properties of each fiber. Are there any practical applications of what they've learned? For example, if polyester burns especially fast, is it good to use for clothes?
- A man was murdered after a long struggle with his attacker. The victim was wearing a black wool jacket and blue jeans. Within an hour, a murder suspect was taken into custody by detectives. There were several black fibers on his shirt. If you conducted a flame test on one of these fibers, what information could the test give you? *Answer:* The wool from his shirt would burn with an orange, sputtering flame, producing an irregular ash and the smell of burning hair.
- You enter a lab where forensic tests are being conducted and smell a sharp odor of vinegar. From your experimental results, what is most likely the source of this odor? *Answer:* Acetate.
- You have been asked to test an unknown fiber to see if you can identify it. When it burns, the fiber produces a sweet odor, similar to the smell of very ripe fruit. In the flame, the fiber sputters and causes the flame to turn orange. The ash forms small, hard beads. What is this fiber? *Answer:* Polyester.
- How can detectives use fiber evidence to help solve a case? *Answer:* Fibers can be used to link a suspect to a crime scene.

Name ______________________________ Date ______________________

Science Sleuth Activity Package: Burning Evidence

The Case

The school librarian went back to school one evening, and when she put her key in the lock, she heard a commotion. Inside, a number of books had been taken from the shelves and scattered on a table. It looked as if the intruder had been surprised by her return and fled through an open window. He left behind a jacket. Close inspection of the jacket revealed black fibers inside one sleeve.

The school guard found five teenagers in the school or on the playground. Nobody admitted that he was missing a jacket. However, all of them were wearing black sweaters. The school librarian is hoping you can tie one of the suspects to the incident in the library by matching fibers from his sweater to the fibers from the jacket.

To learn more about fibers, you will carry out some flame tests and compare the characteristics of different fibers as they burn. **Be very careful when working around open flames.**

Activity Directions

1. One or more members of your research team should obtain samples of each fiber from bags marked Sample A, Sample B, Sample C, Sample D, and Sample E. Make sure you put each fiber in a separate envelope and label it with its sample identity.
2. Obtain the crime scene sample from your teacher.
3. Put on your safety goggles.
4. Light the candle or other source of flame, and set it on a nonflammable surface.
5. Using a pair of long-handled tongs or tweezers, pick up the fiber in the Sample A envelope.
6. Move the fiber into the flame. Note whether the flame changes color, sputters, or smokes when the fiber begins to burn. Record your observations in the second column of the data table at the end of this package.
7. Remove the burned fiber from the flame, and examine the ash. Note the shape, color, and hardness of the ash. Describe these ash characteristics in the third column of the data table.
8. If the burning fiber produced an odor, describe it in the fourth column of the data table.
9. Repeat steps 4 through 8 with the other samples of fibers and with the sample taken from the crime scene.
10. From your experiment, can you tell which sample fiber—A, B, C, D, or E—is connected to the jacket left in the library?

    ____

Name ______________________________ Date ______________________

Science Sleuth Activity Package: Burning Evidence, *Cont'd.*

11. Your teacher will identify the kind of fiber used in each sample. Add these identifications to the last column of the data table.
12. What do you know now about the properties of each kind of fiber?

____

____

____

____

____

____

____

____

____

____

Name ______________________ Date ______________________

Science Sleuth Activity Package: Burning Evidence, *Cont'd.*

Data Table for Burning Evidence

Sample	Flame (Color, Action, Smoke)	Ash (Shape, Color, Hardness)	Odor	Kind of Fiber
A				
B				
C				
D				
E				
Sample from crime scene				

Activity 4.5: Gabby's Gone

Teacher Briefing

In this activity, students learn the technique of chromatography and use it to separate the components of ink. They analyze evidence in the form of chromatograms. This can be done in research teams, but if you have a relatively small class or enough materials, you might consider doing this as a partner activity.

Activity Preparation

- Collect three brands of felt-tip pens with water-soluble ink—enough so that each student pair or group will have a set of three.
- Label the different brands of pen Suspect A, Suspect B, and Suspect C.
- Using one of the suspect's pens, write the following note: "If you ever want to see your parakeet alive again, leave $1,000 in a backpack in the alley tonight at midnight."
- Do a chromatography test on the pen you used to write the note, following the directions in the Science Sleuth Activity Package.
- Label the chromatography "birdnapper's note," and use a color copier to make enough copies for each student group.
- For each student group, provide:

  A set of Suspect A, B, and C's pens
  Copy of chromatography from the birdnapper's pen
  Coffee filter
  Pencil
  Wide-mouth quart jar and water
- Make copies of the Science Sleuth Activity Package.

First, Tell Your Students . . .

Many of the materials we use everyday are mixtures. Examples of mixtures are ocean water, soil, soda, and soup. Ink is also a mixture. The components of ink can be separated by chromatography, a technique for separating the parts of a mixture.

Activity Procedure

1. Distribute the Science Sleuth Activity Packages, a copy of the chromatography of the birdnapper's note, and materials.
2. Assign students to teams or partners.
3. Tell students to follow the directions in the activity package.

Summary and Discussion

- Each piece of paper with its bands of colors is called a chromatogram. Do any of the chromatograms look alike? If so, which ones? *Answer:* The answer depends on your choices.
- How does chromatography separate the components of a mixture? *Answer:* As water travels through the paper, it dissolves the components of ink and carries them along with it. Lightweight components travel farther than heavy ones.
- What do these chromatograms tell you about the pen that wrote the ransom note? *Answer:* One of the chromatograms of ink samples matches the chromatogram of ink from the note. The matching ink may have been used to write the note.
- How can chromatography be used to help solve a crime? *Answer:* Chromatography can be used to link a suspect's ink pen to a note written at a crime scene.
- If ink from one of the pens belonging to Mark's roommates matches the ink on the ransom note, does that prove that the roommate "birdnapped" Gabby? Why or why not? *Answer:* Just because the roommate's pen was used to write the note doesn't mean that roommate took Gabby. Somebody else could have used the pen. Nevertheless, Mark has a good clue.

Name ______________________________ Date ______________________

Science Sleuth Activity Package: Gabby's Gone

The Case

Yesterday when your good friend Mark got home, he was greeted by a silent house and this awful note: "If you ever want to see your parakeet alive again, leave $1,000 in a backpack in the alley tonight at midnight." His talkative parakeet, Gabby, was missing!

Mark shares his house with three roommates—Tom, Dick, and Harry—and none of them likes Gabby. Before his roommates came home, Mark took a pen from each one's desk. Mark gave police the note and the three pens. The police ran a chromatography test on the ink in the note, but before they could test the pens, more pressing work arrived.

Knowing your detective skills, Mark turns to you for help. He retrieves the three pens and the note's chromatogram from the police. If you can get the job done, he may be able to find Gabby before it's too late.

You do a little research and find out that crime labs use a technique called chromatography. It is a way of separating the components of a mixture by using *capillary action.* Different manufacturers use different compounds in their inks. Two black inks made by two different manufacturers will contain different compounds.

You assemble your materials and get ready to work.

Activity Directions

1. Cut three strips from the coffee filter, each strip about 6 inches long by 3/4 inch wide.
2. Label the three strips A, B, and C at one end, and draw a line with a pencil about a half inch from the other end:

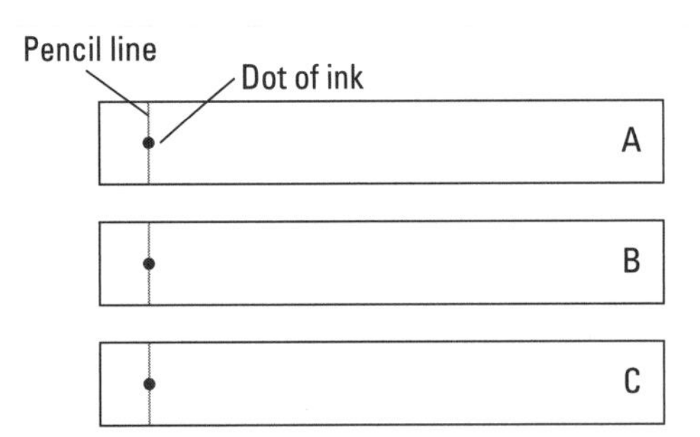

3. Label the three pens A, B, and C.
4. Put a dot of ink from pen A just above the pencil line on Strip A. Repeat Step 4 for pen B and pen C.
5. Fill half the quart jar with water.

Name ______________________________ Date ______________________

Science Sleuth Activity Package: Gabby's Gone, *Cont'd.*

6. Tape the label end of all three pieces of paper to a pencil, as shown in the chromatography setup here. Lay the pencil across the mouth of the jar so that the ink end of each strip just barely touches the water. (If you have too much water in the jar, pour some out. If you need more water, add some.)

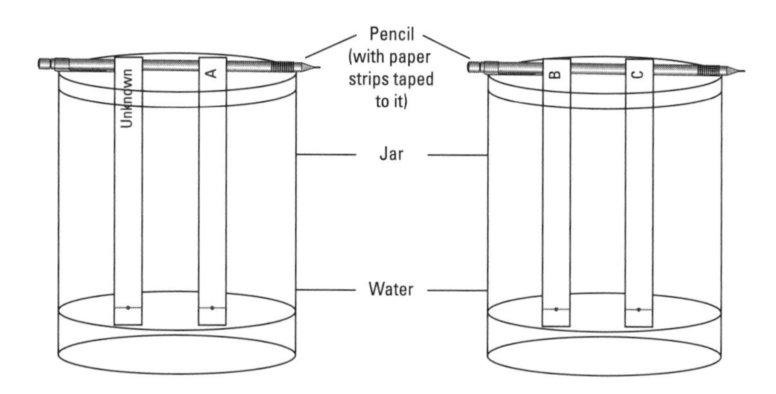

7. The filter paper absorbs water, and it travels up the paper by capillary action. As the water passes the ink spot, it will dissolve the spot and carry the ink along with it. Some of the dyes in the ink will be carried farther than others.
8. After twenty minutes, examine the papers to see if there are any bands of color above the dot. If so, remove the papers, and set them aside to dry. If bands of color have not formed yet, wait another twenty minutes before removing the papers from the water.
9. Compare the chromatography from the birdnapper's note with your work. Suspect A is Tom, Suspect B is Dick, and Suspect C is Harry. Can you tell which one took Gabby?

____

____

Activity 4.6: Cutting Agents

Teacher Briefing

In this activity, students develop a procedure to characterize three unknown white powders. After conducting their experiments, they use logic to identify the powders.

The three white powders are all edible, and the sugar could be easily identified by taste. As a result, we start out the exercise with the powders labeled Cutting Agents A, B, and C. The students will perform some initial experiments to identify the powders. **Make it clear to your students that none of the substances contains drugs.**

Activity Preparation

- Obtain a package or box of baking soda, powdered sugar, and cornstarch.
- Take the materials out of their original packaging and put them in bags labeled Cutting Agent A, Cutting Agent B, and Cutting Agent C. Record here which substance went in which bag:

	Substance
Cutting Agent A	
Cutting Agent B	
Cutting Agent C	

  Alternatively, you could make a package of each substance for each student group in your class.
- For each student group, provide:

  Vinegar
  Iodine
  3 medicine droppers
  3 paper cups
  3 metal spoons
  Matches and candle or other heat source
- Make copies of the Science Sleuth Activity Package. See the "Characteristics of White Powders" sample.

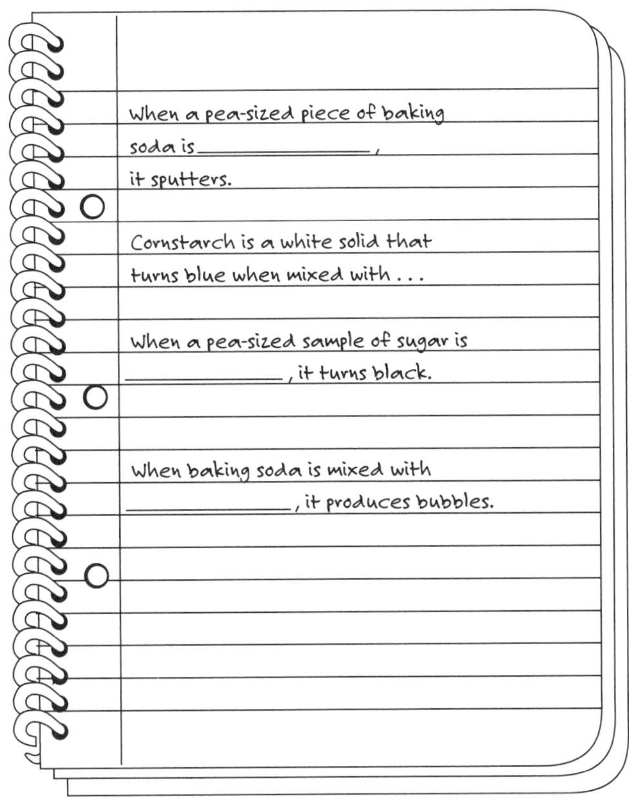

Characteristics of White Powders

First, Tell Your Students . . .

Drug identification is a routine procedure for investigators. Detectives may need to know the name of a drug in an overdose case or the chemical composition of unknown substances in a suspect's possession. Many chemical reactions can be used to identify drugs, and these are usually conducted in a lab.

One quick way to test a drug is simply to identify its cutting agent. Cutting agents are white powders that dealers add to their "goods" to extend them. Drug dealers usually add the same agent to all of a certain type of drugs. Recently, in the town where you live, drug dealers have been adding baking soda to cocaine, cornstarch to heroin, and powdered sugar to methamphetamine.

Activity Procedure

1. Distribute the Science Sleuth Activity Packages, and divide students into detective teams of two or three.
2. Tell students to look at their materials and tools, and develop a procedure for identifying the three cutting agents.
3. When they have a procedure, they will show it to you for approval and retrieve samples of the three cutting agents.
4. Give students thirty to forty minutes to conduct their experiments.

Summary and Discussion

- Ask students to identify Cutting Agent A, B, and C, and check them against the list you made during your activity preparation.
- Ask students how they went about developing their procedure. Did they need to revise it as they worked? In what way?
- The police pulled over a speeding car. The driver looked unusually nervous, so they asked for permission to search the car. In the trunk, the police found a small bag of white powder. You tested the powder and found that it dissolves in water, does not react to iodine or vinegar, and produces a black solid when heated. What is this powder? *Answer:* Sugar.
- How can chemical tests like the ones you developed be used to help solve crimes? *Answer:* Chemical tests help investigators identify materials and link those materials to crime scenes or suspects.

Name ______________________________ Date ______________________

Science Sleuth Activity Package: Cutting Agents

Background

In today's class, you're going to develop a procedure for identifying the substance in unknown white powders. You will begin by working out an experiment that shows the characteristics of three unidentified white powders in four situations:

- When mixed with vinegar
- When heated in a flame
- When mixed with water
- When mixed with iodine

Activity Directions

1. Work with your group to develop a procedure for testing the white powders. When you are ready, show it to your teacher and collect samples of Cutting Agents A, B, and C.
2. Carry out your procedure, and take notes about what happens using the data table provided at the end of this package.
3. Ask your teacher for the clues that can help you identify which cutting agent is powdered sugar, which is baking soda, and which is cornstarch.

Name ______________________ Date ______________________

Science Sleuth Activity Package: Cutting Agents, *Cont'd.*

Data Table for Cutting Agents

	Cutting Agent A	Cutting Agent B	Cutting Agent C
Effect of vinegar			
Effect of heat			
Effect of water			
Effect of iodine			
Identity of substance			

Activity 4.7: Floating Down the River

Teacher Briefing

By determining how long it takes an object to move from one location to another, students calculate speed. If you have a river or stream near your school, this would make a wonderful field trip with a scientific objective. However, you can accomplish the teaching goal in your classroom, using a student to carry the block of wood along an imaginary stream between the start and finish lines. The advantage of doing this in class is that you can run the exercise using students moving at different speeds.

Activity Preparation

- To do this as a field trip, you will need blocks of wood that are large enough to be visible as they float down the stream. When you arrive at the stream, you will designate a starting and finishing line.
- In your classroom, use lines of chairs or a rope barrier to designate the starting and finishing lines.
- You will need:

  Blocks of wood large enough to be easily visible
  Measuring tape
  Calculator
  Stopwatch
- Make copies of the Science Sleuth Activity Package.

First, Tell Your Students . . .

How long does it take you to get to school each day? How long would it take you to travel fifty miles in a car traveling fifty miles per hour? To answer these questions, you must understand the concept of speed. Speed is the distance an object travels in a given amount of time. If you know the rate at which an object is moving and the distance the object travels, you can calculate that object's speed.

Activity Procedure

1. Distribute the Science Sleuth Activity Packages.
2. Have students measure the distance between the starting and finishing lines. Have more than one student take the measurement and compare results so that you're sure to have an accurate number.
3. Ask everyone to record the number in their Science Sleuth Activity Package.
4. Have a student get ready at the finish line with a stopwatch.

5. When that student says, "Go," drop the block of wood into the stream at the starting line, or have a student carry the wood from the start to finish line at a speed short of running.
6. Have the student with the stopwatch read off the time it took for the block of wood to move from start to finish, and make sure students record this number in their Science Sleuth Activity Package.
7. If you choose, you can ask other students to carry the block from start to finish, recording each time separately.
8. Tell students to follow the directions in their Science Sleuth Activity Package to calculate the speed of the block of wood.
9. Then have students estimate whether the package carrying the gold coin could have been the one dropped in the river by the litterbug.

Summary and Discussion

- According to your experimental results and calculations, could the wooden box have traveled seven miles down the creek in eight and a half hours?
- Do you think that the man throwing material off the bridge seven miles up the river could be guilty of this crime? Explain your reasoning. *Answer:* If the answer to question 1 is yes, then the man could be guilty of the crime. The box would have had time to float the distance of seven miles by the time the neighborhood boys found it.
- After a heavy rain, the stream is swollen with more water than usual rushing along at a faster-than-normal pace. Would you expect a storm to increase or decrease the speed at which materials travel down the river? *Answer:* Increase.

Name ______________________ Date ______________________

Science Sleuth Activity Package: Floating Down the River

The Case

On Saturday morning, two kids in your neighborhood made an amazing discovery while wading in the creek at the end of the street. They picked up a small wooden box and opened it to find a gold coin. It looks important—and valuable—so they brought it to you. You asked them a few questions and learned that they found the box about 8:30 A.M.

Just this morning, you were reading an article in the paper about an arrest on Friday night. About midnight, a man was picked up and taken to the police station for littering. He was throwing material into the creek from a bridge about seven miles upstream from where the kids found the box. He claimed that he was cleaning out his car. Could this be the same man who threw the box into the creek? Could the gold coin be stolen property that he was trying to get rid of? Before you call the police station to report that their suspect may have committed a bigger crime than littering, you decide to find out more. For one thing, you need to know if that box could have gotten to your house so quickly. Could it make the trip from seven miles upstream in eight and one-half hours?

Today we are going to study speed. If you think about the words we use to talk about speed, you'll have a hint about how to do this calculation. When we talk about car speed, for example, we refer to miles per hour. So speed is the distance something travels divided by the time it takes to do so.

Activity Directions

1. With your student team, measure the distance between the starting and finishing points. Measure more than once to be sure you are correct.
2. Record the distance here:

   ____

3. With a stopwatch, measure how long it takes a block of wood—or a student carrying one—to move from the starting to finishing points. Record the time here (if you do this in your classroom, more than one student may carry the block; record all the times here):

   Time A ______________________________________

   Time B ______________________________________

   Time C ______________________________________

   Time D ______________________________________

Name ______________________________ Date ______________________

Science Sleuth Activity Package: Floating Down the River, *Cont'd.*

4. Determine the speed or rate at which the block travels from the start to finish points using this formula:

   Speed = Distance traveled/Time required to travel that distance, or $S = D/T$

   Use this space to make the calculation.

5. Now that you know the speed of the stream in feet per second, you can calculate whether the block of wood could have floated from the bridge to where the kids found it in eight and a half hours or less. To find out, you first must convert eight and a half hours to seconds. Here's a formula:

   Time in seconds = 8.5 (time in hours) × 60 minutes × 60 seconds

   Record this calculation here.

   You must also convert the total distance (7 miles) to feet. Since there are 5,280 feet in one mile, use the formula:

   $$\text{Distance in feet} = 7 \text{ miles} \times \frac{5280 \text{ feet}}{1 \text{ mile}}$$

   Record this calculation here.

Name ______________________________ Date ______________________

Science Sleuth Activity Package: Floating Down the River, *Cont'd.*

6. Next, substitute the numbers in the formula:

   Distance = Speed of the stream/time in seconds

   Record this calculation here.

7. According to your experimental results and calculations, could the wooden box have traveled seven miles down the creek in eight and a half hours?

   ____

8. Do you think that the man throwing material off the bridge seven miles up the river could be guilty of this crime? Explain your reasoning.

   ____

   ____

   ____

   ____

   ____

9. After a heavy rain, the stream is swollen with more water than usual rushing along at a faster-than-normal pace. Would you expect a storm to increase or decrease the speed at which materials travel down the river?

   ____

Activity 4.8: Trouble on the Track

Teacher Briefing

This activity uses toys to help students visualize—and calculate—the effect of mass on acceleration of objects when force is constant. While this could be done as a demonstration for the whole class, it may have more impact if each student group has the materials required to carry out the experiment.

Activity Preparation

- You will need an electronic scale or a triple beam balance.
- For each group, provide:

  Battery-operated toy truck
  Toy trailer or wheeled cart
  Rope or string (about 10 inches long)
  Cargo for the trailer (such as marbles, gravel, pennies, lead sinkers)
  Cup that will fit in the trailer
  Stopwatch
  Masking tape
  Meter stick
- Make copies of the Science Sleuth Activity Package.

First, Tell Your Students . . .

Investigators who reconstruct auto accidents have to understand basic physics. Some of the most useful laws of physics are Newton's three laws of motion. The first law of motion states that an object at rest will remain at rest unless a force acts on it. In addition, a moving object will continue moving unless a force affects it. The second law of motion says that a force is equal to the mass of an object multiplied by its acceleration. According to the third law of motion, for every action, there is an equal and opposite reaction. In this experiment, you will apply some of Newton's laws to an accident reconstruction.

Activity Procedure

1. Distribute the Science Sleuth Activity Packages.
2. If you are going to do this as a whole-class demonstration, follow the directions in the Science Sleuth Activity Package, asking various students to help. Otherwise, divide students into detective teams, and tell them to follow the directions in the activity package.

Summary and Discussion

- What supplies the force required to move the vehicle and trailer? Did that force remain constant throughout the experiment? *Answer:* The battery supplied the force needed to move the truck and trailer. Throughout the experiment, the force remained constant.
- According to the formula Force = Mass × Acceleration, when force is held constant and mass increases, what happens to acceleration? *Answer:* Acceleration decreases.
- According to your experimental results, would you expect a truck and a Volkswagen that are both stopped at a red light to be able to reach a cruising speed of fifty miles per hour in the same amount of time when the light turns green? Explain your reasoning. *Answer:* No. The truck will accelerate more slowly than the Volkswagen because the truck has more mass.

For Extra Credit

Based on your experimental results, write a rebuttal to Mr. Hickson's statement: "The weight of the freezers had no impact on my ability to drive the truck and trailer across the tracks; the truck simply stalled and left me stranded!" In your rebuttal, explain how mass affects acceleration. Apply this information to the truck and trailer.

Name ________________________ Date ________________

Science Sleuth Activity Package: Trouble on the Track

The Case

Uncle Jay may be in big trouble! According to today's newspaper, his rental truck company is being sued. One of Uncle Jay's trucks was struck by a train. Jason Hickson, the driver, had rented the truck from Uncle Jay, driven it a few blocks to a warehouse, and attached a trailer loaded with twenty-five new upright freezers. Hickson then headed for the mall to deliver the freezers to an appliance store.

According to the article, Hickson says he stopped at the railroad crossing and looked both ways. In the distance, he could see a train moving toward him. Hickson judged that he had plenty of time to make it across the track, so he proceeded. The next thing he knew, there was a loud crash. The trailer full of freezers was wrenched from his truck and pushed down the track on the nose of the train engine.

Hickson claims that since the wreck was caused by a truck malfunction, Uncle Jay, who owns the truck, owes him $55,000 in damages. The newspaper quotes Hickson as saying, "The weight of the freezers had no impact on my ability to drive the truck and trailer across the tracks; the truck simply stalled and left me stranded!"

You know that your uncle takes excellent care of his rental vehicles, so you decide to look into the matter. You suspect that Hickson misjudged the time it would take to move the truck and trailer across the railroad track.

Thank goodness, you remember Newton's second law of motion, and you think it may help prove that Hickson was lying. According to the second law, *force* equals *mass* multiplied by *acceleration.* This means that increasing the mass of an object decreases its acceleration when force is constant.

In this experiment, you will simulate the train wreck to find out how mass affects acceleration.

Activity Directions

1. Place a piece of masking tape on both ends of a meter stick. Label one end "start" and the other end "finish." Place the meter stick on the floor or a large table.
2. Use string or rope to attach the trailer to the toy truck.
3. Place the toy truck and trailer on the floor beside the meter stick with the front bumper behind the start mark.
4. Place the large cup in the trailer. Do not put anything in the cup.
5. Turn on the toy truck (set it on high), and use the stopwatch to determine how long it takes the truck and trailer to travel the length of the meter stick and cross the finish line.
6. Record the time (in seconds) in the data table at the end of this package.
7. Use the scale to weigh 250 grams of cargo. Add this cargo to the large cup in the trailer.

Name ______________________ Date ______________________

Science Sleuth Activity Package: Trouble on the Track, *Cont'd.*

8. Repeat steps 5 and 6, and record your results in the table.
9. Add another 250 grams of cargo to the large cup (for a total of 500 grams of cargo).
10. Repeat steps 5 and 6, and record your results in the table.
11. Continue in this manner until the weight is too heavy for the toy truck to pull or until you have completed the data table.

Questions for Discussion

1. What supplies the force required to move the vehicle and trailer?
2. Did that force remain constant throughout the experiment?
3. According to the formula, Force = Mass × Acceleration, when force is held constant and mass increases, what happens to acceleration?
4. According to your experimental results, would you expect a truck and a Volkswagen that are both stopped at a red light to be able to reach a cruising speed of fifty miles per hour in the same amount of time when the light turns green? Explain your reasoning.

Name ______________________ Date ______________________

Science Sleuth Activity Package: Trouble on the Track, *Cont'd.*

Data Table for Trouble on the Track

Mass of Load (grams)	Time (seconds)
0	
250	
500	
750	
1000	
1250	
1500	
1750	
2000	
2500	

Activity 4.9: Invisible Ink—Homework Assignment

Teacher Notes

Because this activity requires so many materials and a considerable amount of wait time, it's easier to do at home.

Name ______________________ Date ______________

Homework Assignment: Invisible Ink

Background

Invisible ink is not just something you read about in science fiction—there really is such a thing. If you want to send a secret message, you can write it in invisible ink.

A lot of different materials—many of them found in your kitchen—can be used for invisible ink. You'll use three of them here. In each case, you'll write a message on a piece of paper. Then you'll let the ink dry. Finally, you'll watch what happens and make a record of what you observe.

Materials You'll Need

- 4 cotton swabs
- 3 sheets of paper
- 1/4 cup milk
- 1/8 cup lemon juice
- 1/4 cup baking soda
- 1/2 cup water
- 1/4 cup grape juice concentrate
- graphite pencil
- Access to a heat source. You can use a light bulb that's turned on, a burner on the stove, or a hot plate. **Be very careful as you work with these heat sources.**

Milk Experiment

1. Pour a small amount of milk into a cup or saucer.
2. Dip the cotton swab into the milk mixture, and use it to write a message on the piece of paper.
3. Put the paper aside for a few minutes until it is dry. You can start the lemon juice experiment while you're waiting.
4. Carefully rub the side of a pencil on the paper.
5. Notice the changes that occur to the paper.
6. Record your results in the data table at the end of the package.

Name ______________________ Date ______________________

Homework Assignment: Invisible Ink, *Cont'd.*

Lemon Juice Experiment

1. Pour some lemon juice into a cup or saucer.
2. Dip the cotton swab into the juice, and use it to write a message on the piece of paper.
3. Put the paper aside for a few minutes until it is dry. While you're waiting, you can see if your paper from the milk experiment is dry.
4. Hold the lemon juice paper a couple of inches away from a heat source. Be careful not to let the paper—or your fingers—get too close to the heat.
5. Notice the changes that occur to the paper.
6. Make notes about these changes in the data table.

Baking Soda Experiment

1. Pour 1/4 cup of baking soda into 1/4 cup of water. Stir to mix.
2. Dip a cotton swab into the baking soda mixture, and use it to write a message.
3. Put the paper aside for a few minutes until it is dry.
4. Pour 1/8 cup of grape juice concentrate in 1/2 cup of water. Stir to mix.
5. Dip a cotton swab into the grape juice mixture, and "paint" over the paper with the baking soda message.
6. Notice what changes occur to the paper.
7. Make notes about these changes on your data sheet.

The Next Day

After 24 hours, check the condition of all three pieces of paper. In the last column of your data table, indicate whether you can read the message on each piece.

Name ______________________________ Date ____________________

Homework Assignment: Invisible Ink, *Cont'd.*

Data Table for Invisible Ink

	Score each of the following from 1 to 5, with 5 being the best and 1 the worst.		
Type of Invisible Ink	**Ease of Use**	**Writing Is Easy to Read**	**Message Is Still Easy to Read After 24 Hours**
Milk			
Lemon juice			
Baking soda			

Activity 4.10: Skidding to a Stop—Homework Assignment

Teacher Notes

This activity requires a bicycle and access to the outdoors, making it a good homework assignment. Besides the outdoor experiment, the assignment has an analysis component, so it might qualify as a special project.

Answer Key

1. Gravel. As the drag factor drops, friction with the road drops and length of a skid increases.
2. 73.3 feet. Students should change miles per hour to feet per second. To do so, multiply 50 mph by 5,280 feet in a mile to get feet per mile. Divide by 60 to get feet per minute, and then divide by 60 again to get feet per second.
3. 12.2 car lengths
4. One can determine how fast a vehicle was traveling.

Name ____________________ Date ____________________

Homework Assignment: Skidding to a Stop

You can tell a lot about the speed of a vehicle from the length of its skid marks. Here's an activity that shows you how.

Materials You'll Need

- Bicycle
- Bicycle helmet
- Access to a concrete or asphalt parking lot or driveway
- Access to a graveled or dirt area
- Access to an area of dirt
- Measuring tape
- Ruler
- Calculator

Background

Here is a formula for determining the speed of a vehicle based on a skid mark:

S (speed of vehicle) =
Square root of 30 × *D* (length of the skid marks in feet) × *F* (drag factor)

Drag or friction slows a vehicle. *F*, the drag factor, is a measurement that takes into account the friction of the tires against the road's surface. Drag factor varies with road conditions. The greater the drag factor, the greater the friction is between tire and road. A road with a drag factor of 0 is extremely slippery. Here are some drag factors under different driving conditions:

Driving Surface	**Drag Factor (*F*)**
Asphalt	0.75
Concrete	0.90
Gravel	0.50
Snow	0.30

In this assignment, you are going to measure skid marks and use that measurement to determine vehicle speed.

Name ______________________________ Date ______________________

Homework Assignment: Skidding to a Stop, *Cont'd.*

Activity Directions

1. Put on your bicycle helmet, and ride your bicycle down a concrete or asphalt surface for a short distance. Then put on the brakes hard. This should create a skid mark on the surface. You don't have to be going fast to make a skid mark, so be careful.
2. Measure the length of the skid mark in feet. Record the measurement in the Data Table for Skidding to a Stop.
3. Enter this measurement into the formula for determining speed:

S (speed of vehicle) =
Square root of 30 × *D* (length of the skid marks in feet) × *F* (drag factor)

4. Enter the speed into your data table.
5. Repeat steps 1 through 4 on a gravel or dirt surface and compare the results.

Data Table for Skidding to a Stop

Road Surface	**Length of Skid Mark**	**Speed**

The Case

Warren Hewlitt was driving along a rural road when he dozed off. His car flew off the road, crashed through a fence, and landed in a pasture. Highway patrol officers were dispatched to the scene of the accident. After determining that Hewitt was not harmed, officers took his statement. Next, they made a drawing of the accident scene, which they added to their accident report.

Accident Report for Skidding to a Stop

Accident Report 536-6

Date 6/20 **Time** 11:32 PM

Location Route 1, Cowpen Road, Arcadia, Texas

Name and address of Driver Warren Hewlitt, 708 Lasso Lane, Arcadia, Texas

Driver statement I was on my way home from visiting friends, and I think I dozed off. It seemed like one minute I was driving and the next minute I was crashing into a pasture full of cows. I estimate my driving speed to be about 40 miles per hour.

Road type Asphalt

Weather condition Clear and dry

Measurements of skid marks

Tire 1: 23 feet

Tire 2: 22 feet

Tire 3: 27 feet

Tire 4: 26 feet

Name ________________________________ Date ________________________

Homework Assignment: Skidding to a Stop, *Cont'd.*

Procedure

1. Examine the accident report provided by the highway patrol. Notice that there are four skid marks in the report. To determine the average length of skid marks in this accident, add the length of all four skid marks and then divide by four. This gives you the distance that the car skidded.
2. Examine the accident report to determine the drag factor involved in this accident. (Refer to the Data Table for Skidding to a Stop.)
3. Calculate the speed of Hewlitt's vehicle at the time of the accident using the formula:

   S (speed of vehicle) =
   Square root of $60 \times D$ (length of the skid marks in feet) $\times F$ (drag factor)

   ____

   ____

4. Based on the skid marks, at what speed was Hewlitt's car traveling at the time of the accident?

   ____

   ____

5. Another accident occurred on this same road last winter. It had been snowing and conditions were very slippery. The length of the skid marks in that accident were exactly the same as the length of skid marks in Hewlitt's accident. What was the speed of the car in the winter accident?

   ____

   ____

Name ______________________________ Date ______________________

Homework Assignment: Skidding to a Stop, *Cont'd.*

Questions to Answer

1. Based on the drag factors in the data table, would you expect a car to skid farther on gravel or on asphalt? Explain your answer.

___

___

___

___

2. It takes about one second for a driver to react to a change in conditions. If car A is traveling 50 mph, and car B in front of it suddenly stops, how far will car A travel before the driver reacts and applies the brakes?

___

___

3. Assume that car A is six feet long; how many car lengths does your answer to question 2 equal?

___

___

4. What information can be gained by measuring the skid marks at the scene of a vehicle accident?

___

___

___

___

Chapter Five

Using the Logical in Biological

Applying Biology to Crime Scene Investigations

Crimes involve one or more people, including the perpetrator and the victim, and a scene. Biological evidence may be transferred from one person to another or to the crime scene. Hair, saliva, blood, and semen are just a few of the biological materials that can yield information about a crime. DNA fingerprinting is one of the most important tools in positively identifying a suspect based on biological evidence. Even DNA from crimes that occurred decades ago can be analyzed with current equipment and techniques to point to a perpetrator. DNA can also be used to exonerate individuals who were convicted for crimes they did not commit. Although not as specific as DNA, hair and blood type can also help link a perpetrator to a crime.

CRIME SCENE DO NOT CROSS

Activity 5.1: Untangling a Hairy Dognapping

Teacher Briefing

In this small-group activity, students will examine human and animal hair using a magnifying glass or microscope and compare them to microscopic samples of hair from different sources. Students will record their observations, analyze data, and draw conclusions. The questions in the Summary and Discussion section could be used as an assessment device.

Activity Preparation

- Collect hairs from three humans (one blond, one redhead, and one with dark hair) and hairs from a dog and a cat. You will need a complete set of hair samples for each student group.
- Place one piece of hair from each human and from the cat in an envelope labeled "From Jake's Coat"; repeat for each student group.
- Place one piece of dog hair in a separate envelope labeled "Sarge's Hair"; repeat for each student group.
- Decide whether you are going to use a magnifying glass or a microscope, and make sure equipment is available for each student group.
- Make copies of the Science Sleuth Activity Package and the "Cross-Section of Hair Follicle and Medulla" handout at the end of the Teacher Briefing section.

First, Tell Your Students . . .

Hair is often used as evidence in solving crimes. The color, length, texture, thickness, and structure of hair can be analyzed microscopically with a magnifying glass. Microscopic viewing of hair can identify the characteristics of hair's three layers: medulla, cortex, and cuticle. Forensic scientists can also determine if hair has been colored or treated with chemicals.

Further examination can reveal if the root is attached to the hair or if it was broken off or cut. This information can often be used to implicate or exclude a suspect from the scene of a crime.

Forensic scientists must have a clear understanding of the three main layers of hair when examining hair samples. Here's a drawing that shows them. (Distribute the "Cross-Section of Hair Follicle and Medulla" handout.)

- The *cuticle,* the outermost layer, is made of overlapping scales. Humans have a different cuticle pattern from other animals, and among animals, the pattern is distinctively different from one species to another.
- The *cortex,* the layer beneath the cuticle, is made up of cells with color *pigments.* The color, distribution, and shape of the pigments can be used to differentiate races of people.

- The *medulla,* the center of the hair, can be continuous in pattern, banded, or even absent. It is also different among races of people. Both the medulla and the cuticle are thicker in animals than in humans.

Activity Procedure

1. Read "The Case" (the description of the crime) from the Science Sleuth Activity Package to the class.
2. Distribute copies of the Science Sleuth Activity Package, and divide your students into detective teams of two or three.
3. Give each student group an envelope marked "From Jake's Coat" and one marked "Sarge's Hair."
4. Have the students examine the hairs with a magnifying lens. Tell them to complete the data table in their package.
5. If you don't have microscopes available, skip to Summary and Discussion.
6. Review with your students how to use a microscope and to make a wet mount.
7. Have the students make slides of their hair samples, and examine the hairs under a microscope.

Summary and Discussion

- Ask students to use the information they have available to identify the hair samples from Jake's jacket. *Answer:* Jake's jacket contained hairs from Jake, his wife, his child, and his cat, River Lily.
- Ask students to solve the crime: Did Jake steal Sarge? *Answer:* No, there's no dog hair on Jake's coat.
- If students used a magnifying lens and a microscope, ask them to compare what they were able to see with each tool. *Answer:* Details of the medulla and cortex could not be seen with the hand lens.
- Ask students if the information in the Science Sleuth Activity Package helped them solve the crime. How? *Answer:* It provided information on the medulla and cortex of each hair.
- Describe the differences among human hair, cat hair, and dog hair. *Answer:* Human hair has a thin or fragmented medulla and a distinctive scale pattern. The medulla of cat hair is very thick, and the medulla of dog hair is intermediate between cat hair and human hair. Both dog and cat hair have distinctive cortex patterns.
- Ask students to identify the samples in "Cuticle Scales and Medulla of Human and Pet Hairs" as "human," "cat," or "dog." *Answer:* Samples A, C, and D are human. Sample B is cat, and Sample E is dog.

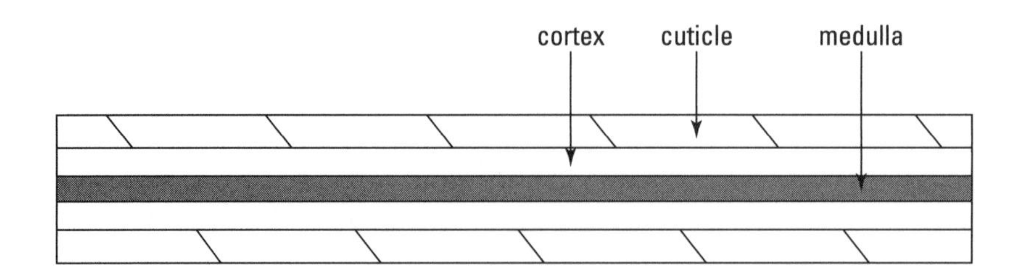

Variations in the Medulla

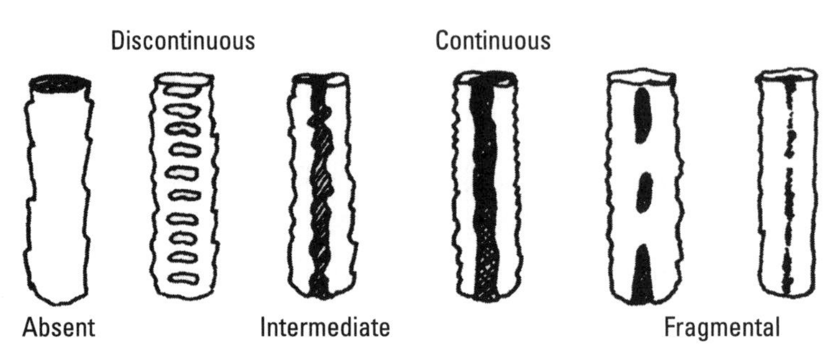

Cross-Section of Hair Follicle and Medulla

Name ______________________________ Date ____________________

Science Sleuth Activity Package: Untangling a Hairy Dognapping

The Case

At noon today, you took a stroll down Main Street on your way to the diner. Out of nowhere, an enthusiastic, golden-haired labrador retriever puppy came bounding toward you! The puppy looked just like your Aunt Alice's dog, Sarge.

A quick call to Aunt Alice revealed that Sarge was missing. You couldn't imagine how Sarge ended up so far from his home—Aunt Alice lives in a small town twenty miles from you! But Alice had a definite idea: she thinks Sarge was dognapped by her neighbor.

Yesterday Sarge just disappeared from her fenced-in backyard. Thirty minutes after she began looking for her puppy, Alice saw Jake, her neighbor, pull out of his garage and drive away. An hour later, Jake returned, removed the jacket he was wearing, dropped it in a trash bag, and threw it in the trash can. Alice was suspicious of all this activity because she knew that Jake dislikes Sarge. When Jake went inside, Alice raced to the trash can and retrieved the coat. She could see that it was covered with hair.

Alice wants you to examine the coat for any evidence that Jake may have abducted the puppy. You begin by asking Alice for a description of other people and animals Jake comes in contact with. Alice gives you the following information:

- Jake is blond.
- Jake's wife, Mary, has dark hair.
- Their son, Bo, is a redhead.
- Jake's family has a cat named River Lily.

You return Sarge to Alice and collect the jacket Jake threw away. You also take a sample of Sarge's hair. You plan to collect hairs from the coat and examine them with a magnifying lens or microscope.

Activity Directions

1. Open the envelope marked "From Jake's Coat" and the envelope marked "Sarge's Hair," and examine the hairs with a hand lens.
2. Designate the hairs from Jake's coat as Sample A, Sample B, Sample C, and Sample D.
3. Complete the data table in this package, noting the color, length in centimeters, texture, and structure of each hair. Record any other information you think may help identify the hair.
4. Look at "Kinds of Hair" and "Cuticle Scales and Medulla of Human and Pet Hair" at the end of this package. Using this information, analyze your data to reach a conclusion about whether Jake dognapped Sarge.

Name ______________________ Date ______________________

Science Sleuth Activity Package: Untangling a Hairy Dognapping, *Cont'd.*

5. Sketch a dog hair here.

6. Sketch a cat hair here.

7. Sketch a human hair here.

8. If your classroom has a microscope, use it to examine the hairs. What can you see now that you weren't able to see with the magnifying lens?

9. Based on all the information you collected in the lab, indicate the owner of each of the five hair samples found on Jake's coat.

   Sample A: ______________________ Sample D: ______________________

   Sample B: ______________________ Sample E: ______________________

   Sample C: ______________________

10. Examine the "Cuticlee Scales and Medulla of Human and Pet Hair" at the end of this package. Based on what you have learned in this lab, label each sample as "human," "cat," or "dog."

Name ______________________ Date ______________________

Science Sleuth Activity Package: Untangling a Hairy Dognapping, *Cont'd.*

Data Table for Untangling a Hairy Dognapping

	Sample A	Sample B	Sample C	Sample D	Sarge's Hair
Length of hair (cm)					
Color of hair					
Texture/structure (wavy, curly, straight)					
Was the root attached or absent					
Additional information that may help with identification					

Science Sleuth Activity Package: Untangling a Hairy Dognapping, *Cont'd.*

Kinds of Hair

Subject	Description
Caucasian human	Hair is straight, wavy, or curly. Medulla may be absent or fragmented. The width of medulla is less than one-third of the hair shaft. Pigment granules are evenly distributed.
African American human	Curly hair that has deeply pigmented, unevenly distributed granules. Medulla is fragmented or absent. Width of medulla is less than one-third of hair shaft.
Cat	Cuticle scales are evident. The medulla occupies a very large portion of the shaft.
Dog	Cuticle scales are evident. The medulla occupies over one-third the width of the shaft but not as large an area as that occupied by the medulla of a cat's hair.

Science Sleuth Activity Package: Untangling a Hairy Dognapping, *Cont'd.*

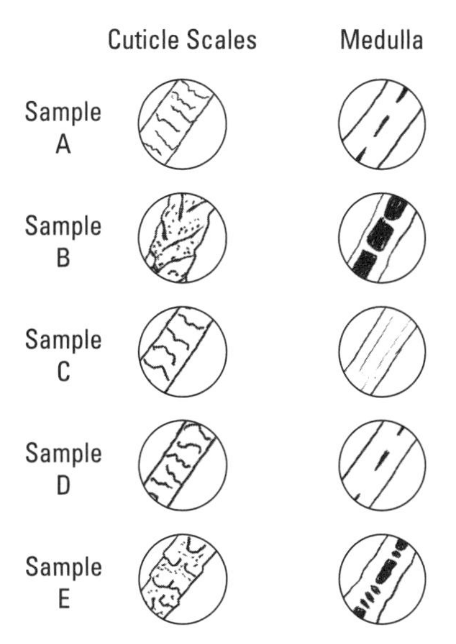

Cuticle Scales and Medulla of Human and Pet Hair

Activity 5.2: Famous Freckles

Teacher Briefing

In this activity, students create pedigrees to determine the inheritance of a sex-linked trait, based on their knowledge of genes and inherited traits. They analyze data and draw conclusions. While a brief discussion of inherited traits is included here, we assume that this activity will be used in the context of a larger curriculum on genetics and inherited traits.

Activity Preparation

- Make copies of the Science Sleuth Activity Package.

First, Tell Your Students . . .

Puppies, just like newborn babies, inherit their characteristics from their parents. Both the mother and the father pass on traits to their offspring. Traits are carried on segments of DNA called genes, which may be dominant or recessive. The presence of a dominant gene completely masks the presence of a recessive one. For this reason, recessive genes appear only when there is not a dominant gene to cover them.

Activity Procedure

1. Distribute the Science Sleuth Activity Packages.
2. Depending on the extent of students' knowledge about the inheritance of sex-linked traits, you may want them to work on this activity alone or in groups.
3. Tell them to review Ray's notes and his photo album in their package, and discuss this material with them. Cosmo II and Cosmo III carry the sex-linked, recessive trait for freckles, so they must have the gene combination X^fY.
4. Tell them to use the photo album to fill in the pedigree for Cosmo IV in their Science Sleuth Activity Package.
5. Tell them to review Laura's notes and her photo album. Discuss with students. Sweetie must have the gene combination X^fY because he has freckles.
6. Tell them to complete the pedigree for Sweetie in their Science Sleuth Activity Package.

Summary and Discussion

- Sex-linked traits, like freckles for dogs, show up more often in males than females. Why is this so? *Answer:* Sex-linked traits are carried on the X chromosome. Even if a sex-linked trait is recessive, it will show up in males because they do not have another X chromosome trait to dominate it.
- Why doesn't Cosmo IV have freckles? *Answer:* Cosmo IV's mother does not have freckles and did not pass on the trait to him.
- Could Hunter and Sugar have produced a female puppy with freckles? Explain your answer. *Answer:* No. Freckles are a recessive trait. Hunter and Sugar could not have produced a female with two recessive traits for freckles.

Here are the filled-in pedigrees:

Pedigree of Ray's Dogs

X^FY Blizzard — X^fX^f Princess

X^fY Cosmo Sr. — X^FX^F Portia

X^fY Cosmo II — X^FX^f Snowball

X^fY Cosmo III

X^FY Big Duke — X^FX^F Sunrise Rose

X^FY Little Duke — X^FX^F Chantilly Lace

X^FX^F Stella

X^fY Cosmo III — X^FX^F Stella

X^FY Cosmo IV

Pedigree of Laura's Dogs

X^FY Traveler — X^FX^f Honey

X^FY Hunter — X^FX^f Sugar

X^fY Sweetie

Name ______________________________ Date ______________________

Science Sleuth Activity Package: Famous Freckles

The Case

The new TV show *Freckles* is a hit and is going into its second season. The star of the show, Cosmo III, is a darling little black-and-white dog with distinctive freckles across his muzzle. This dog star belongs to Ray Spiffel, dog breeder and trainer.

Spiffel has spent years perfecting the breeding technique that produces black-and-white dogs with freckled faces. He knows a lot about this breed. For example, he discovered that the gene for freckling is sex linked, which means it is located on the X chromosome. He also knows that freckling is a recessive trait, so it shows up in male dogs much more often than in females.

Female dogs with the trait on just one chromosome do not have freckles; they are called *carriers.* These females may pass this recessive gene down to their offspring. To show the trait of freckling, a female must have two genes. Using the letter "f" to represent the recessive trait for freckling and the letter "F" to represent the dominant trait for no freckles, Mr. Spiffel explains the genetics of these dogs:

- A male dog with a freckled face has the gene combination X^fY.
- A male dog without a freckled face has the gene combination X^FY.
- A female dog with a freckled face has the gene combination X^fX^f.
- A female dog without a freckled face has either the gene combination X^fX^F or X^FX^F.

The producers of *Freckles* asked Ray to breed his dogs to produce puppies with freckled faces so that Cosmo III (the original Freckles) will have some help on the set. They need some identical dogs to serve as stand-ins. After carefully planning his strategy, Ray bred his dogs. He was shocked when the puppy produced from this breeding did not have freckles! What was just as shocking was the discovery that his neighbor, Laura Vanover, had a new, freckle-faced puppy.

Ray suspects that his dog did indeed have a freckle-faced puppy but that Laura stole it. Before he goes storming over to her house and makes accusations, Ray wants you to help him figure out if it is genetically possible for Laura's dog to have produced a freckle-faced offspring.

In this experiment, you will develop a pedigree for Ray's puppy and for Laura's puppy. You will use these pedigrees to explain to Ray whether Laura's dog could have had a freckle-faced puppy. You are going to develop these pedigrees by interviewing Ray and Laura to find out the history of each puppy. Below are transcripts of each interview.

Ray's Notes

The arrival of my newest puppy, Cosmo IV, was a shock. I know dog breeding, and there is no way that this puppy shouldn't have freckles! Cosmo IV's parents are Cosmo III and Stella. Cosmo III has freckles—that's why he's the leading man in the TV series. I bred him to Stella, who does not have freckles, but that doesn't matter. All of the other freckled puppies had mothers without freckles. Look at my picture album and you'll see what I mean.

Name ______________________________ Date ______________________

Science Sleuth Activity Package: Famous Freckles, *Cont'd.*

Laura's Notes

I have lived next door to Ray and his dog-breeding business for twenty years. I was completely surprised when Sweetie, my new puppy, was born with freckles. Sweetie's parents are Sugar and Hunter. Hunter was a stray, so I don't know anything about his family. I found Sugar and her mother, Honey, when the puppy was just six weeks old. After just a week at my house, Honey disappeared. Sugar does not have freckles, and neither did Honey. I suspect that Sugar's father, a dog I nicknamed Traveler, was a male that I had seen in my neighborhood for a few days. I don't know where he came from. Check out my photo album.

Activity Directions

1. Read Ray's notes and examine his photo album.
2. Use the photo album in this package to help you fill in the genotypes on the pedigree for Cosmo IV. You know that Cosmo II and Cosmo III carry the sex-linked, recessive trait for freckles, so they must have the gene combination X^fY. On the pedigree of Ray's dogs in this package, write X^fY in the spaces above Cosmo II and Cosmo III.
3. Use your knowledge of the inheritance of sex-linked traits to fill in the possible gene combinations for the other animals in this pedigree.
4. Read Laura's interview, and examine her photo album.
5. Fill in the spaces to complete the pedigree for Sweetie in this package. You know that Sweetie must have the gene combination X^fY because he has freckles. On the pedigree for Laura's dogs, write X^fY in the space above Sweetie.
6. Fill in the possible gene combinations in the spaces above the other animals in this pedigree.

Questions for Discussion

1. Sex-linked traits show up more often in males than females. In your own words, explain why this is so.
2. Why doesn't Cosmo IV have freckles?
3. Could Hunter and Sugar have produced a female puppy with freckles? Explain your answer.

Name ______________________________ Date ______________________

Science Sleuth Activity Package: Famous Freckles, *Cont'd.*

Pedigree of Ray's Dogs

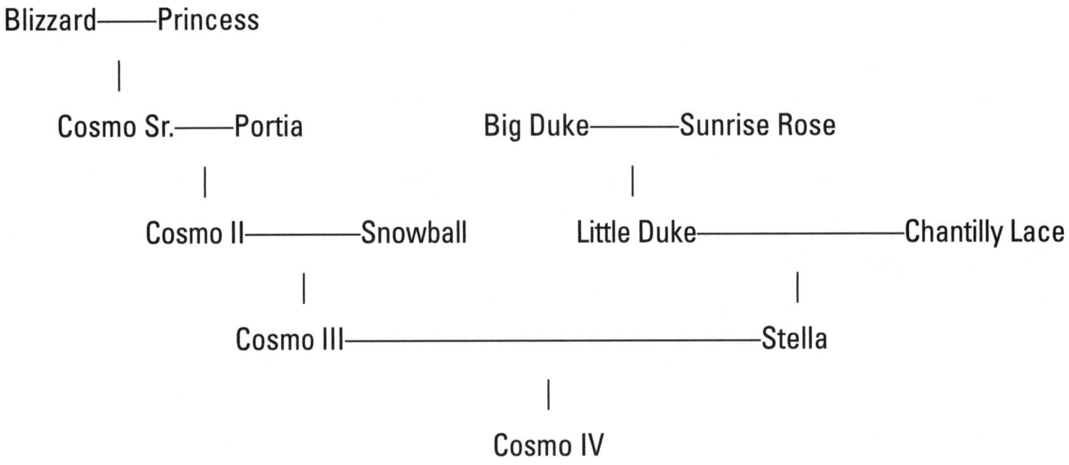

Blizzard——Princess

|

Cosmo Sr.——Portia   Big Duke———Sunrise Rose

| |

Cosmo II————Snowball   Little Duke——————Chantilly Lace

| |

Cosmo III——————————Stella

|

Cosmo IV

Pedigree of Laura's Dogs

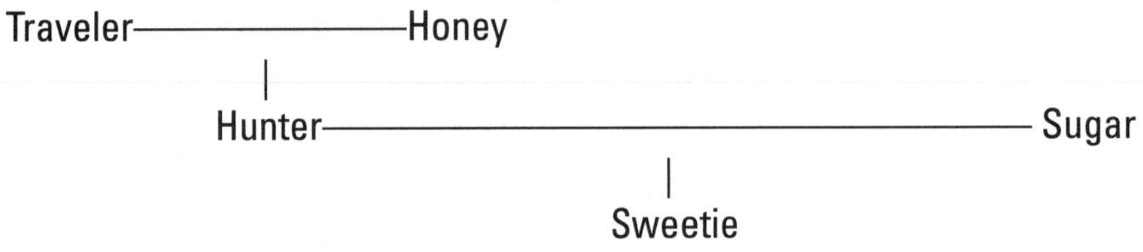

Traveler—————Honey

|

Hunter——————————Sugar

|

Sweetie

Ray's Photo Album

Laura's Photo Album

Activity 5.3: Checking It Twice

Teacher Briefing

Students carry out error analysis on DNA data. This activity is a valuable assessment and evaluation tool. Used at the beginning of a section on DNA, it can assess student background or give them an incentive to do research. Used at the end of the section, it will show students' progress in the subject.

Activity Preparation

- If you use this as an assessment device at the beginning of a section on DNA, you may want to provide some support materials for students as they review this report. These could be print or online.
- Provide colored pens or pencils.
- Make copies of the Science Sleuth Activity Package.
- If you want to simplify the activity, underline the terms and phrases that are false.

First, Tell Your Students . . .

DNA evidence is extremely powerful. It can provide a direct link between a person and a crime scene. Everyone's DNA is unique. DNA is a large molecule that is made of millions of subunits called nucleotides. In each DNA molecule, two chains of nucleotides are paired and twisted into a helical shape.

To study a sample of DNA, scientists use enzymes to break large samples into small ones. The small samples of DNA can be separated in a process called gel electrophoresis. The way that an individual's small pieces of DNA arrange themselves during gel electrophoresis produces a unique pattern called a DNA fingerprint.

Activity Procedure

1. Distribute the Science Sleuth Activity Packages.
2. Depending on how you are using this lesson, you may provide additional resources or allow students to work in pairs or teams. Following is a corrected report that will provide a key against which you can check student work.

Report on DNA Analysis

Everyone's DNA is unique, except for the DNA of identical twins. That is why the analysis of DNA can be used to identify an individual. The courts accept DNA as reliable evidence. The process of analyzing DNA is called *DNA fingerprinting*.

DNA is found in the nuclei of cells. Molecules of DNA determine the characteristics of living things. Each individual inherits DNA from his or her parents. DNA molecules are made of chains of small units called *nucleotides*. Each nucleotide is made of three parts: a sugar, a base, and a phosphate group. There are four types of nucleotides. Two of them are made of double-ring bases: adenine (A) and guanine (G). The other two are made of single-ring bases: thymine (T) and cytosine (C). These nucleotides are arranged in two long strands that are wrapped around each other to form a double helix. The strands are held together by hydrogen bonds between paired bases. Adenine pairs with thymine and guanine pairs with cytosine. The sequence of the nucleotides in a double strand of DNA makes up the genetic code.

At a crime scene, investigators try to find any biological evidence left by the perpetrator. One source of biological evidence is saliva. From a saliva sample, forensic scientists can isolate cells and extract their DNA.

In this case, there was only a small amount of saliva on the bite mark. As a result, few cells were found and very little DNA evidence was available. To solve this problem, forensic scientists amplified the DNA with a technique called *polymerase chain reaction* (PCR). This process makes a lot of DNA from just a few molecules using three basic steps—denaturing, annealing, and extending DNA:

1. The sample is warmed to cause the hydrogen bonds between the strands to break. As a result, the DNA strands separate, or denature.
2. The temperature is lowered, and primer pieces of DNA are added. *Primers* are short segments of DNA that can base-pair with the single strands. This process of pairing primers to single strands of DNA is called *annealing*.
3. The temperature is increased slightly and DNA polymerase is added. This enzyme helps extend DNA by attaching nucleotides to the ends of the primer and by helping nucleotides base pair with the existing DNA strand.

The result of PCR is that each single strand of DNA produces a new complementary strand, doubling the original amount of the DNA sample. The process can be repeated many times.

DNA fingerprinting is a technique that identifies the sequence of bases in a DNA sample. It is done in the laboratory in a procedure called *restriction fragment length polymorphisms* (RFLP). RFLP can be summarized in six basic steps:

1. DNA is removed from the cells and isolated. Almost any type of cell can provide DNA, but common sources are the skin cells in saliva, cells around the root of a hair, and white blood cells.
2. Long strands of DNA are cut into short pieces with restriction enzymes.
3. Short pieces of newly cut DNA are separated from each other by electrophoresis. In this technique, the DNA passes through a gel made from agarose, a seaweed extract. Small pieces travel through the agar gel faster than large ones. Eventually the pieces are distributed along the length of the gel and form a series of bands.

4. The pattern of bands created by the pieces of DNA is transferred from the gel to a piece of nylon. This process is called Southern Blotting. In this technique, the nylon is placed on top of the gel and allowed to soak. The DNA in the gel is carried to the nylon, where it becomes fixed.
5. Radioactive molecules called *probes* are poured on the nylon. The probes base-pair with DNA. In places where there is a lot of DNA on the nylon, thousands of tiny radioactive molecules bind to it.
6. A band of radioactive probes is invisible to the naked eye. The probes are visualized by putting a piece of photographic film on the nylon. The radioactive probes expose the photographic film, creating a dark-colored band on the film in each of the places where there is a band of DNA. The final product is a piece of photographic film that looks similar to a bar code. It is called an *autoradiograph* or a *DNA fingerprint*. No two people have exactly the same DNA fingerprint.

DNA fingerprints are used not only in forensics. They can also be used to diagnose inherited disorders. Early detection enables a child to be treated before a disease causes serious damage. Another use of DNA is in establishing paternity when one or both parents of a child are not known.

Summary and Discussion

- How do scientists amplify a small sample of DNA? *Answer:* DNA can be amplified through the PCR process.
- After a sample of DNA is amplified and cut with restriction enzymes, how are the pieces separated? *Answer:* Cut pieces of DNA are separated on a gel.
- What steps are necessary to make the bands of DNA on a gel visible? *Answer:* The bands are transferred to a piece of nylon, then visualized on photographic film with radioactive probes.
- Why is accuracy an important part of forensic work? *Answer:* DNA fingerprinting is a very exact science. Changes in procedures could produce erroneous results. (Answers will vary.)

Name ______________________ Date ______________________

Science Sleuth Activity Package: Checking It Twice

The Case

Krystal's house burned down, and she is missing. The police have arrested a suspect. At the time of arrest, he was pretty beat up, and the police hypothesize that he has been in some sort of struggle. In addition, the suspect had a bite mark on him, so detectives took a swab of dried saliva from the bite mark. They wanted to see if the saliva could be used to isolate a sample of DNA from the person who bit him. If the suspect is the kidnapper, maybe the DNA belongs to Krystal. Police also took a sample of the man's DNA for comparison.

Your partner, a rookie in forensics, has prepared a report explaining the analysis of Krystal's DNA. This report will become an important part of the file on Krystal's disappearance. Your partner asked you to read over the report to see if it is correct before she adds it to the file.

Activity Directions

1. Read the report at the end of these directions. If you find an error on the report, cross it out using your colored pen or pencil. You may write your corrections in the margins.
2. Depending on what your teacher says, you may use the Internet or reference books to make sure you are marking the report correctly.
3. When all of your corrections are made, rewrite the entire report so that it includes your changes.

Questions for Discussion

1. How do scientists amplify a small sample of DNA?
2. After a sample of DNA is amplified and cut with restriction enzymes, how are the pieces separated?
3. What steps are necessary to make the bands of DNA on an agarose gel visible?
4. Why is accuracy an important part of forensic work?

Name ______________________________ Date ______________________

Science Sleuth Activity Package: Checking It Twice, *Cont'd.*

Report on DNA Analysis

Everyone's DNA is the same, except for the DNA of brothers and sisters. That is why the analysis of DNA cannot be used to identify an individual. The courts rarely accept DNA as reliable evidence. The process of analyzing DNA is called *DNA fingerprinting*.

DNA is found in the cytoplasm of cells. Molecules of DNA determine the characteristics of living things. Each individual inherits DNA from his or her mother only. DNA molecules are made of chains of small units called ribosomes. Each ribosome is made of three parts: a sugar, a base, and a phosphate group.

There are four types of nucleotides. Two of them are made of double-ring bases: cytosine (C) and guanine (G). The other two are made of single-ring bases: thymine (T) and adenine (A). These nucleotides are arranged in two long strands that are wrapped around each other to form a double helix. The strands are held together by covalent bonds between paired bases. Adenine pairs with uracil and guanine pairs with cytosine. The size of the nucleotides in a double strand of DNA makes up the genetic code.

At a crime scene, investigators try to find any biological evidence left by the perpetrator. One source of biological evidence is saliva. From a saliva sample, forensic scientists can isolate cells and extract their DNA.

In this case, there was only a small amount of saliva on the bite mark. As a result, few cells were found and very little DNA evidence was available. To solve this problem, forensic scientists amplified the DNA with a technique called *polymerase chain reaction* (PCR). This process makes a lot of DNA from just a few molecules using three basic steps—denaturing, annealing, and extending DNA:

Name ________________________ Date ____________________

Science Sleuth Activity Package: Checking It Twice, *Cont'd.*

1. The sample is warmed to cause the hydrogen bonds between the strands to break. As a result, the DNA strands stick together, or denature.
2. The temperature is lowered, and primer pieces of DNA are added. *Primers* are short segments of DNA that can base-pair with the single strands. This process of pairing primers to single strands of DNA is called *annealing*.
3. The temperature is increased slightly and amylase is added. This enzyme helps extend DNA by attaching RNA to the ends of the primer and by helping nucleotides base pair with the existing DNA strand.

The result of PCR is that each single strand of DNA produces a new complementary strand, tripling the original amount of the DNA sample. The process can be repeated many times.

DNA fingerprinting is a technique that identifies the sequence of amino acids in a protein sample. It is done in the laboratory in a procedure called *restriction fragment length polymorphisms* (RFLP). RFLP can be summarized in six basic steps:

1. DNA is removed from the cells and isolated. Almost any type of cell can provide DNA, but common sources are the skin cells in saliva, cells around the root of a hair, and blood cells.
2. Strands of DNA are glued together with restriction enzymes to form long strands.
3. Pieces of newly cut DNA are separated from each other by electrophoresis. In this technique, the DNA passes through a gel made from tapioca, a seaweed extract.

Name ______________________ Date ______________________

Science Sleuth Activity Package: Checking It Twice, *Cont'd.*

Small pieces travel through the gel slower than large ones. Eventually, the pieces are distributed along the length of the gel and form a series of bands.

4. The pattern of bands created by the pieces of DNA is transferred from the gel to a piece of denim. This process is called Southern Blotting. In this technique, the denim is placed on top of the gel and allowed to soak. The protein in the gel is carried to the nylon, where it becomes fixed.
5. Radioactive molecules called *probes* are poured on the nylon. The probes base-pair with protein. In places where there is a lot of DNA on the denim, thousands of tiny radioactive molecules bind to it.
6. A band of radioactive probes is invisible to the naked eye. The probes are visualized by putting a piece of photographic film on the nylon. The radioactive probes expose the photographic film, creating a light-colored band on the film in each of the places where there is a band of DNA. The final product is a piece of photographic film that looks similar to a bar code. It is called an *autoradiograph* or a *DNA fingerprint.* No two people have exactly the same DNA fingerprint.

DNA fingerprints are only in forensics. They are not helpful in diagnosing inherited disorders. Early detection of disease is not helpful. In addition, DNA is not used to establish paternity when one or both parents of a child are not known.

Activity 5.4: Pointing Out the Poacher

Teacher Briefing

Students will simulate gel electrophoresis. They will analyze fictitious DNA samples and draw conclusions about their meaning. If you think your students will find this exercise difficult, you might consider letting them work in pairs or teams.

Activity Preparation

- Make copies of the Science Sleuth Activity Package.
- Provide students with scissors and tape.

First, Tell Your Students . . .

You know that DNA fingerprinting can help collar a criminal, identify a baby's father, or acquit an innocent person. What else can it be used for? To answer this question, you must understand how DNA is analyzed in the lab.

DNA is a long, double-stranded molecule. Each strand is made up of nucleotides that are attached end to end. There are only four types of nucleotides, abbreviated with the letters A, T, C, and G. Their arrangement within a strand of DNA gives that strand its unique qualities.

To make a DNA fingerprint, millions of strands of DNA are isolated from cells. These strands are cut into small pieces by chemicals called *restriction enzymes*. Restriction enzymes recognize specific sequences of DNA and make a cut within these sequences. For example, a restriction enzyme might recognize this sequence:

A-T-A-T-T-A-A-C-G-C-T-A-C-C-C-G
T-A-T-A-A-T-T-G-C-G-A-T-G-G-G-C

This enzyme might cut the sequence between the Ts to produce two fragments.

A-T-A-T T-A-A-C-G-C-T-A-C-C-C-G
T-A-T-A-A-T T-G-C-G-A-T-G-G-G-C

Each resulting fragment is called an RFLP (restriction fragment length polymorphisms).

A tiny test tube of DNA that has been cut with restriction enzymes contains millions of fragments. To analyze all of these fragments, technicians must separate them from one another. The standard separation technique is to place the fragments in a jelly-like slab called a gel and expose it to an electric current. The DNA fragments have negative charges, so they move through the gel toward the positively charged pole.

The smallest fragments move the fastest. By the time small fragments make their way across the gel, the larger ones have moved only a short distance.

Activity Procedure

1. Distribute the Science Sleuth Activity Packages, and divide students into pairs or teams if you choose.
2. Ask students to turn to the page where the DNA strands are found. Before the strand is cut, it is important to identify its origin.
3. Tell students to put the letters MJ (for Missing Jaguar) in each piece of the first strand.
4. Tell students to put the letters H1(for Hat 1) in each piece of the second strand.
5. Tell students to put the letters H2 (for Hat 2) in each piece of the third strand.
6. Tell students to put the letters H3 (for Hat 3) in each piece of the fourth strand.
7. Now they can cut the strands and put them in the gel electrophoresis chamber following the directions in the Science Sleuth Activity Package.

Summary and Discussion

- What is the role of restriction enzymes in DNA fingerprinting? *Answer:* A restriction enzyme cuts long strands of DNA into short strands. The place where it cuts a strand varies greatly among individuals.
- What do the vertical lines in the four strands of DNA represent? *Answer:* Vertical lines represent the places where restriction enzymes cut strands of DNA.
- Does the DNA from the missing jaguar match the DNA from any of the hats? If so, which one? *Answer:* Yes, Hat 3.
- How do DNA fingerprints help solve crimes? *Answer:* DNA can identify body parts from the same animal (such as pieces of hide). It can also link a person to a crime scene, identify the parents of a child, and exonerate innocent people accused of crimes.

Name ______________________________ Date ______________________

Science Sleuth Activity Package: Pointing Out the Poacher

Background

You know that DNA fingerprinting can help collar a criminal, identify a baby's father, or acquit an innocent person. But can this technique be used to prosecute an animal poacher? You hope so, because you've got a serious case on your hands.

The Case

You are part of an investigative team that is looking into wildlife poaching. Hunters may have trespassed on a local animal preserve where rare jaguars are living.

More than a year ago, one of the jaguars disappeared. Fortunately, the animal preserve had DNA on file for all the jaguars in residence. No leads were found until recently, when an informer told the investigative team that the skin of this jaguar was sold to a man in Europe who used it to make hats. Agents in Europe immediately went to the man's store and confiscated three jaguar-skin hats. DNA from the skin of each hat will be compared to the DNA of the missing jaguar. You volunteer to help with the DNA comparison.

In this lab, you will be given four paper strands that represent DNA: three from the jaguar-skin hats and one from the missing jaguar. Your job is to cut the strands with scissors at the same location a restriction enzyme would make a cut. You will arrange the fragments in order of size, from smallest to largest. Then you will compare the cut pieces of DNA from the missing jaguar to the pieces from the hats to see if you can find a match.

Activity Directions

1. Go to the "Strands of DNA" page at the end of the package.
2. Following your teacher's directions, label each piece of DNA.
3. The lines drawn through each strand represent the places where a restriction enzyme would make a cut. Use the scissors to cut the strand of missing jaguar DNA along the lines.
4. Go to the "Gel Electrophoresis Chamber" page at the end of this package.
5. Lay the missing jaguar DNA fragments in lane 1 of the gel chamber. Arrange them in order of size by placing the largest piece closest to the negative side of the gel chamber and the smallest piece nearest the positive side. Tape the fragments in place.
6. Repeat steps 3 through 5 for each of the other pieces of DNA. Place DNA from Hat 1 in lane 2, DNA from Hat 2 in lane 3, and DNA from Hat 3 in lane 4.

Questions for Discussion

1. What is the role of restriction enzymes in DNA fingerprinting?
2. What do the vertical lines in the four strands of DNA represent?
3. Does the DNA from the missing jaguar match the DNA from any of the hats? If so, which one?
4. How do DNA fingerprints help solve crimes?

Science Sleuth Activity Package: Pointing Out the Poacher, *Cont'd.*

Strands of DNA

DNA from the missing jaguar (MJ)

DNA from Hat 1 (H1)

DNA from Hat 2 (H2)

DNA from Hat 3 (H3)

Name ______________________________ Date ______________________

Science Sleuth Activity Package: Pointing Out the Poacher, *Cont'd.*

Gel Electrophoresis Chamber

Positive End		Negative End
	Lane 1	
	Lane 2	
	Lane 3	
	Lane 4	

Activity 5.5: Green Evidence

Teacher Briefing

Students create a leaf collection in this activity and use the leaves to help solve a mystery.

While you can collect the leaves required for this activity, the actual collecting provides a wonderful opportunity to get students outdoors in good weather. A school garden or nearby park will provide a great place to gather leaves. We've structured the activity as a group venture so that local plants will not be stripped bare. Of course, you will need to remind students that they need only a dozen or so samples for each group. The idea is not to have a great number but to have a great selection.

Activity Preparation

- You will need to make the usual arrangements for taking your students off the school property. Arranging to have some parent helpers is useful. If the park or garden is not on school property, you may also need to notify the park owner of your plans.
- If you prefer, you can collect the leaves yourself. Collect a dozen or so leaves from different plants, and include specimens with different edges, stem configurations, color, and size.
- For each group, you will need:

  Manila envelopes or other collecting package
  Masking tape
  Paper
  Stack of heavy books
  Glue
  Poster board
- Make copies of the Science Sleuth Activity Package.

First, Tell Your Students . . .

A good detective often sees things that others overlook. One keen-eyed investigator spotted a piece of unusual green evidence. His observation provided the missing link between a suspect and a stolen car.

A new Lexus sedan was stolen from a showroom in Phoenix, Arizona. It was later found abandoned under a palo verde tree, the state tree of Arizona. The detective who found the car also found a pager nearby that led to a suspect, Mark Brogan. To add to the case against Brogan, the detective needed some evidence that could link him to the crime scene. In a search of the suspect's home, the detective noticed something odd: a small seed pod clinging to the sleeve of the suspect's jacket. Remembering that palo verde trees produce seed pods, the detective collected the jacket and the suspicious pod. Scientific analysis of the seed pod proved that it came from the tree where the abandoned car was found. The case was solved by one detective's keen observation skills and an unusual type of seed.

Activity Procedure

1. Distribute the Science Sleuth Activity Packages, and assign students to detective teams of three or four.
2. Give them a few minutes to discuss their strategy for collecting leaves and for assigning roles.
3. Take the students to an area where there are several different kinds of plants.
4. Tell them to follow the directions in their Science Sleuth Activity Packages.
5. After students have returned to class—or the next class meeting—provide each student group with the materials to preserve their leaves.
6. Tell students to follow the directions in their activity package.
7. They can also do some research on the leaves that they have collected. For each leaf, have students locate the scientific and common names and the general characteristics.
8. For the third class session (after the leaves have dried), provide students with poster board where they can display their preserved leaves on an edited version of the data table they constructed during their collection.
9. Tell students to follow the directions in the activity package to make this album.

Summary and Discussion

After the initial excursion:

- What are some of the characteristics of leaves that help you distinguish one type from another?
- Did you see any interesting bugs or birds as you were collecting the leaves?

Later:

- Based on your leaf collection and research, what are the names of five plants that are common in your area?
- What can a preserved leaf tell you that a sketch of a leaf might miss?
- How can investigators use plant parts to help solve a crime?

Name ______________________ Date ______________________

Science Sleuth Activity Package: Green Evidence

Background

You can use your knowledge of local plants to help you solve mysteries. For example, plant material from a crime scene may be found on a suspect's clothing, linking him or her to the crime.

Plants have many more parts than just seed pods—they also have stems, leaves, and flowers. Simply learning the leaves of the local plants can be a big advantage for an investigator. In this experiment, you will create a catalogue of leaves of local plants.

Activity Directions

The activity directions are divided into three parts: collecting leaves, preserving leaves, and compiling a record.

Collecting Leaves

1. Meet with the members of your detective team, and decide on a strategy for collecting leaves. (1) Each student is responsible for collecting two leaves. In that case, make sure you go to different areas, or (2) each student plays a separate role: collecting the leaf, sketching the leaf, sketching the plant where it was found, and making notes on anything of interest in the area around the plant.
2. Go outdoors to the area where collection is to take place. Don't forget to take the data table from this Science Sleuth Activity Package so that you have a place to make notes. You'll need a pen or pencil too.
3. Collect a leaf from one plant. Put a small piece of masking tape on the back of the leaf, and write **A** on the label.
4. Next to **A** in the data table, make a sketch of the leaf.
5. In the third column of the data table, describe the plant that provided the leaf. Include information about the plant's size (estimate the height and diameter).
6. In the fourth column, describe the plant's location. Does it have flowers or seed pods? Are birds or insects present? Does it show any signs of disease?
7. Place the labeled leaf in the manila envelope.
8. If your group has divided chores, each student can fill out one column, and you can copy the information onto one master data table when you return to your classroom.
9. Make sure that your group collects ten to twelve leaves in all.

Name ______________________________ Date ______________________

Science Sleuth Activity Package: Green Evidence, *Cont'd.*

Preserving Leaves

1. When you are back indoors, remove the leaves from the manila envelope. Lay each leaf, one at a time, between two sheets of paper.
2. Stack up the paper dividers with the leaves inside. Place several heavy books on top of the stack.
3. Let the leaves remain under the books for one week.
4. Look online and in research books to learn more about the leaves you collected. For each leaf, locate the scientific and common names and the general characteristics.

Compiling a Record

1. Using your data table as a guide, draw a large data table on poster board using a colored marker.
2. Write in the notes you made during the collection, as well as any information you found out from your research.
3. Take away the books that have been weighting down your leaves, and gently separate each leaf from the paper.
4. Remove the masking tape from each leaf, and glue the leaf carefully to its proper place on your new enlarged data table.
5. Refer to your research on each leaf. Write the common name and scientific name (genus and species) of each leaf next to it.

Name ______________________ Date ______________________

Science Sleuth Activity Package: Green Evidence, *Cont'd.*

Data Table for Green Evidence

	Sketch of Leaf	Description of Plant	Plant Environment
Leaf A			
Leaf B			
Leaf C			
Leaf D			
Leaf E			
Leaf F			

Name ______________________ Date ______________________

Science Sleuth Activity Package: Green Evidence, *Cont'd.*

Data Table for Green Evidence

	Sketch of Leaf	Description of Plant	Plant Environment
Leaf G			
Leaf H			
Leaf I			
Leaf J			
Leaf K			
Leaf L			

Activity 5.6: Tell-Tale Foot

Teacher Briefing

Students determine the relationship between a person's height and the length of his or her foot. Students apply that relationship to find the height of a person who left a footprint at a crime scene.

Activity Preparation

- Make copies of the Science Sleuth Activity Package.
- Provide a tape measure (metric) for each student or student group.

First, Tell Your Students . . .

Math and science are two disciplines that often work hand in hand. Math can be used to understand the relationship between two variables in science. For example, paleontologists (scientists who study fossils and old bones) depend on math to help them predict characteristics of an organism based on limited information. A paleontologist may find one leg bone of a human skeleton, and use that bone to calculate the height of the entire skeleton. These calculations take into account a known relationship between the size of the leg bone and the size of the entire skeleton. Such calculations can be helpful in identifying the owner of the leg bone. In this lab, you will determine whether there is a relationship between the size of a foot and the height of a person.

Activity Procedure

1. Distribute the Science Sleuth Activity Packages, and divide the class into groups of about ten students each.
2. Tell students to follow the directions in their Science Sleuth Activity Packages to measure everyone's height and their foot length, recording their findings, and do the math to calculate percentage.

Summary and Discussion

- Based on student calculations, what percentage of a person's height is represented by the length of that person's foot? *Answer:* About 15 percent. This may vary slightly because the ratio between foot length and height is more accurate in adults.
- What was the height of the person who left the footprint? *Answer:* About 165 centimeters.
- A construction crew was moving dirt to begin work on a new hospital. One of the bulldozers turned up a femur. The medical examiner measured the femur and found that it was 70.4 centimeters long. How tall was this person? What would you estimate to be the length of this person's footprint? *Answer:* Height = 371.25 cm; foot length = 24.75 cm.

Name ______________________________ Date ______________________

Science Sleuth Activity Package: Tell-Tale Foot

The Case

Dr. Lenfest is your family physician and a good friend. Last night, her office was robbed. Dr. Lenfest tells you that she keeps medication in a special locked cabinet under her desk. Before this crime, the only people who knew about the cabinet were the nurses and cleaning staff who work in her office.

Based on evidence at the crime scene, the working theory is that the burglar used a tool to pry open the back window of the office, walked straight to Dr. Lenfest's hidden medicine cabinet, unlocked the cabinet, and removed all the contents. The only evidence that police have so far is a footprint outside the window.

You've been asked to help solve the case because Dr. Lenfest knows that you are a math whiz. She has asked you to determine whether there is a relationship between the length of a person's foot and that person's height. If you find a relationship, you can use it to determine the height of the person who left a footprint.

Activity Directions

1. Discuss with your group how you will measure and record each person's height and foot length.
2. Measure the length of each person's left foot in centimeters. Enter that number in the data table at the end of this package in the column titled "Foot Length."
3. Measure each person's height in centimeters. Enter that number in the data table in the column titled "Height."
4. Determine what percentage of each person's height is represented by the length of that person's foot. To do so, divide the person's foot length by height and then multiply by 100. Enter the percentage in the fourth column.
5. Calculate the average of the findings in the fourth column by adding all of the numbers in the percentage column and then dividing by the number of people in your group. This number represents the average percentage of a person's height that is equal to his or her foot length. Record this value on your data table.
6. Measure in centimeters the length of the footprint (see "Burglar's Footprint" at the end of this package).
7. Multiply the average percentage from your data table by the length of the footprint. This answer represents the height of the person who left the footprint.

Name ______________________ Date ______________________

Science Sleuth Activity Package: Tell-Tale Foot, *Cont'd.*

8. Your femur is the long bone that connects the hip joint to the knee joint. If the femur alone is used to calculate height, the following formula is used:

   Femur length × 2.38 = Height

   You can rearrange this formula to calculate the length of a femur if height is known:

   Femur length = Height/2.38

   Use the above formula to calculate the length of your femur.

9. After performing this calculation, compare it to an actual measurement of your femur (from hip joint to middle of knee). How close was your calculation to your measurement?

Questions for Discussion

1. Based on your calculations, what percentage of a person's height is represented by the length of his or her foot?
2. What was the height of the person who left the footprint?
3. A construction crew was moving dirt to begin work on a new hospital. One of the bulldozers turned up a femur. The medical examiner measured the femur and found that it was 70.4 centimeters long. How tall was this person? What would you estimate to be the length of this person's footprint?

Name ______________________ Date ______________________

Science Sleuth Activity Package: Tell-Tale Foot, *Cont'd.*

Data Table for Tell-Tale Foot

Name	**Foot Length (centimeters)**	**Height (centimeters)**	**Percentage of Height Represented by Foot Length**
Average percentage of height represented by foot length			

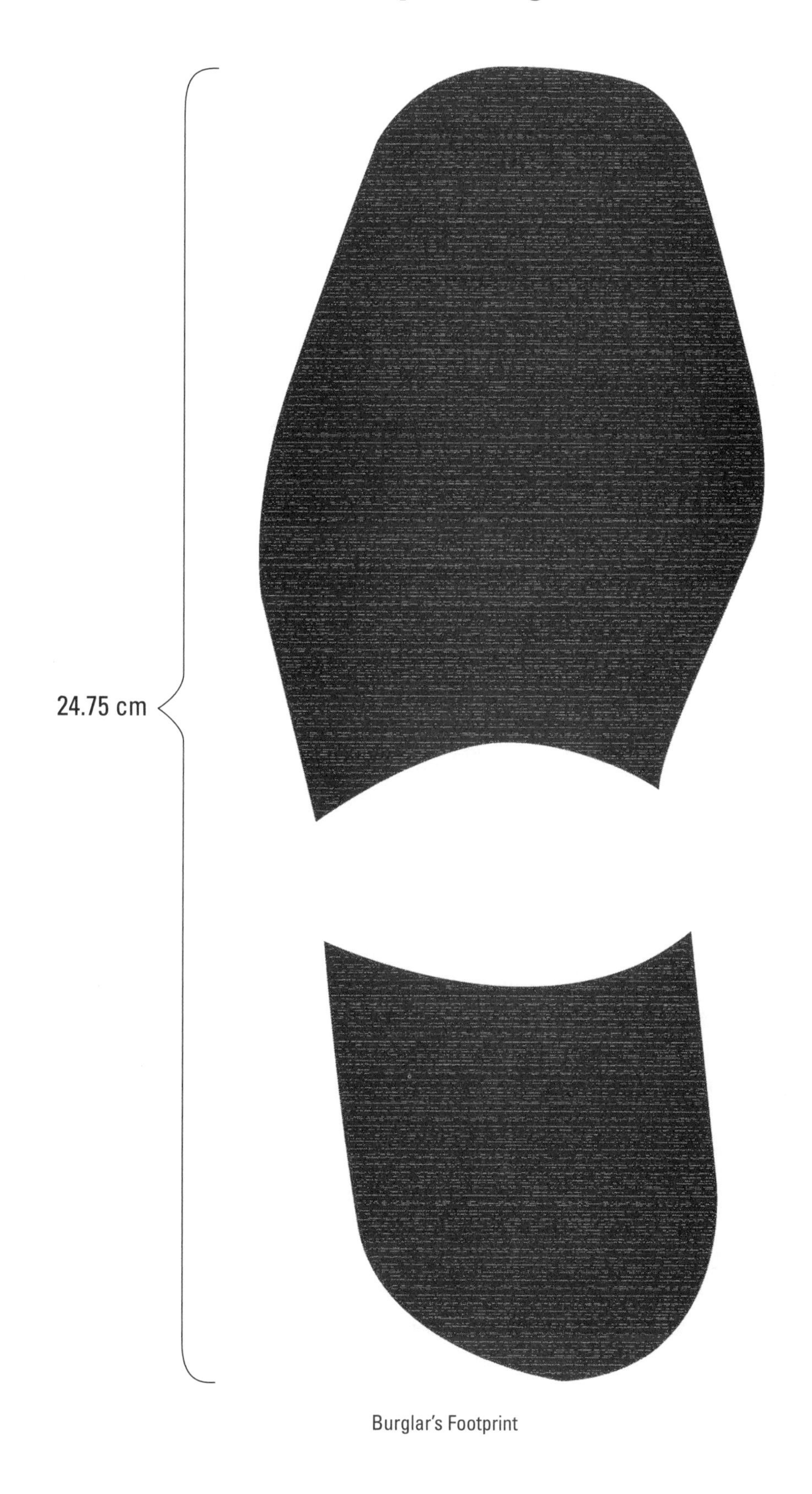

Burglar's Footprint

Activity 5.7: Detergent Deception

Teacher Briefing

Students will test samples of detergent for the presence of enzymes. They can then use their findings to draw logical conclusions.

This experiment uses gelatin, and the activity directions here assume that you will take care of providing it. If you can get enough small paper cups of gelatin, you could let each student do this experiment. Perhaps your school cafeteria would be willing to chill some small paper cups full of gelatin for the two nights this experiment requires.

Activity Preparation

- Make arrangements to obtain the required samples of gelatin for the class activity and to refrigerate them overnight.
- Obtain two kinds of detergent:

  Any detergent that lacks proteases and other enzymes. Examples are All Ultra, Ajax Ultra, Arm & Hammer Ultra, and Greenmark.

  Any detergent that contains proteases and other enzymes. Examples are Ultra Tide, Ultra Cheer, Wisk Power Scoop, ERA Liquid, and Ultra Tide with Bleach.

  You can use product labels to help make your selections.
- Put the two detergents in other containers: one labeled "Miracle Detergent" and the other labeled "Enzyme Detergent."
- For each student group, provide:

  Three small cups of gelatin per student, pair, or group
  Labels
  Marbles
- Make copies of the Science Sleuth Activity Package.

First, Tell Your Students . . .

Chemical reactions are constantly taking place in living things. Enzymes are catalysts that affect the rate of these reactions. Without enzymes, the reactions in organisms would occur too slowly to support life. Enzymes are involved in all types of chemical reactions. Many of these reactions break down one substance into two or more less complex substances.

The structures of many enzymes have been studied and are well understand. These enzymes can be manufactured and added to commercial products. One place where enzymes have been useful is in laundry detergents. Many of the stains in clothes, like those caused by food, grass, and blood, are products of living things. Enzymes can help break down these substances and make it easier to get the stains out of laundry.

In this activity, you will test materials to see if they contain enzymes. Specifically, you will find out whether some commercial laundry detergents contain enzymes that break down proteins. The protein you will use in these tests is gelatin.

Activity Procedure

1. Distribute the cups of gelatin, and divide students into pairs or groups as needed.
2. Distribute the Science Sleuth Activity Packages, and tell students to follow those directions.
3. Once the experiment has been set up, students can help you take their trays to the cafeteria, where they can be refrigerated overnight.
4. The next day, have students examine their experiment and record results in the Science Sleuth Activity Packages.

Summary and Discussion

- What does the gelatin in the cup of detergent known to contain protease look like? *Answer:* The gelatin is slightly eaten away, causing the marble to sink into it.
- Based on your experimental results, does Miracle Detergent contain protease? How do you know? *Answer:* No. The Miracle Detergent did not affect the gelatin.
- How do proteases affect proteins? *Answer:* Proteases break down proteins.
- What is the purpose of the control in this experiment? *Answer:* The control serves as a basis of comparison.

Name ______________________ Date ______________

Science Sleuth Activity Package: Detergent Deception

The Case

It's a great day for a game of pickup basketball, so you call your friend Matt Wilson and ask him to meet you at the Recreation Department. When Matt answers the phone, he's mad and in no mood for basketball. It seems that last week, a salesman for Miracle Detergent, a new company, came to Matt's house to talk business with his mom. The salesman told Ms. Wilson that his detergent is full of special enzymes called proteases. These enzymes remove protein stains like those caused by grass or blood.

Ms. Wilson owns the local laundry, so this was music to her ears! Miracle Detergent is very expensive, but Ms. Wilson was so impressed with the presentation that she purchased two dozen boxes.

Today, Ms. Wilson has been so inundated with complaints that she had to call Matt in to help her talk to customers. None of her customers are satisfied with their laundry, and some are complaining that their clothes still have stains.

Ms. Wilson got on the phone and told the Miracle Detergent salesman to come get his products because they clearly don't contain any proteases. She wants her money back. The salesman said that if Ms. Wilson wants her money back, she has to prove that the detergent does not contain enzymes.

You decide to meet Matt at the laundry and set up an experiment. You know that gelatin is a protein, and proteases break down proteins. As you head for the laundry, you work out an experiment in your head. Maybe you can use it to help Ms. Wilson get her money back.

Activity Directions

1. Label the three cups of gelatin: Miracle Detergent, Protease Detergent, and Control.
2. Gently place a marble on top of each cup of gelatin.
3. Sprinkle a teaspoon of Miracle Detergent on the gelatin in the cup labeled Miracle Detergent.
4. Sprinkle a teaspoon of detergent with a protease on the gelatin in the cup labeled Protease Detergent.
5. Put all three cups in the refrigerator.
6. The next day, retrieve the three cups, and look at them again.
7. In the data table at the end of this package, describe the position of the marble and the appearance of the gelatin in each cup.

Name ______________________ Date ______________________

Science Sleuth Activity Package: Detergent Deception, *Cont'd.*

Questions for Discussion

1. What does the gelatin in the cup of detergent known to contain protease look like?
2. Based on your experimental results, does Miracle Detergent contain protease? How do you know?
3. How do proteases affect proteins?
4. What is the purpose of the control in this experiment?

Data Table for Detergent Deception

	Miracle Detergent	**Protease Detergent**	**Control**
Position of marble			
Appearance of gelatin			

Activity 5.8: Ruined Radishes

Teacher Briefing

In this activity, students determine the impact of acid rain on the percentage of radish seeds that germinate. They do this by conducting an experiment, analyzing data, and drawing conclusions. While each student could have a set of radishes if you choose, having them do the activity in groups might be useful.

Although most of the work in this activity is done on the first day, it takes place over three days. Because the students are watching for seeds to germinate, it is important that the days should be consecutive.

Activity Preparation

- This experiment involves many materials, so you might want to set up work stations for each group with everything students will need to complete the activity:

  Soda straw
  Distilled water
  Vinegar
  pH paper and color scale
  Radish seeds
  Paper towels
  Measuring cups
  Masking tape
  Permanent marker
  Medicine dropper

- Make copies of the Science Sleuth Activity Package.

First, Tell Your Students . . .

A good friend has asked you for help with a problem that he suspects is caused by acid rain. Of course, you'll help! You try to remember what you learned on this topic in school. You learned about acid and the pH scale, which measures the acidity and alkalinity of substances. Something with a pH of 7, such as distilled water, is neutral. A material that has a pH of 1—stomach acid—is extremely acidic. You remember that acid rain has a pH of 5.6 or lower.

Normal rainfall, unaffected by environmental pollutants, has a pH above 5.6. The pH of normal rainfall is slightly acidic because the carbon dioxide in the air produces carbonic acid, a very weak acid. Acid rain is formed when fossil fuels are burned. The emissions of burned fossil fuels contain sulfuric oxide and nitric oxide. These compounds mix with water vapor to produce sulfuric acid and nitric acid. Acid rain usually has a pH of 3 or 4, but some parts of the northeastern United States have reported rainfall with a pH as low as 2, almost as strong an acid as stomach acid.

Acid rain can have adverse effects on plants. You know that it can damage plant foliage and can leach nutrients from plants. These problems can reduce plant growth rates, interfere with the production of flowers, and make plants more susceptible to diseases and insects. Can acid rain also interfere with seed germination? You decide to put this idea to the test.

Activity Procedure

1. Distribute the Science Sleuth Activity Package, and divide students into detective groups of two or three.
2. Tell the students to follow the directions in the Science Sleuth Activity Package to conduct the experiment.
3. The seed rolls will need to be tended after twenty-four hours and again after forty-eight hours.

Summary and Discussion

- Which seed roll had more seeds germinate?
- What did the liquid used in roll A represent? What did the liquid used in roll B represent? *Answers:* Normal rain and acid rain, respectively.
- Did seeds from these two cups germinate in the same way? If not, explain their differences. *Answer:* Answers may vary. Vinegar can slow seed germination.
- Will the results of your experiment help Lawton's case? Explain your answer.
- Write a letter to the mayor of the city that explains your data.

For Extra Credit

Do some research on the effects of acid rain. Write a two-page report that explains the impact of acid rain on your local environment. What are the long-term consequences of acid rain?

Name ______________________________ Date ________________________

Science Sleuth Activity Package: Ruined Radishes

The Situation

Today's mail brought bad news! You received a disturbing letter from an old friend, Lawton Gadston. The letter concerns Lawton's father, Mr. John Gadston, a farmer:

Hello,

I haven't seen you since the awards banquet. Thanks for attending that night when Dad was presented the Radish King Trophy by the Northeastern Farmers Association. We were all so proud of him!

In those days, his business was soaring, but something has gone terribly wrong since then. Dad's radish farm is on the verge of bankruptcy. During this last year, he's had trouble getting his radish seeds to germinate! I suspect the problem is linked to acid rain in our area. Several new industries have moved to our part of the state, and the air pollution has increased sharply. I'm going to ask the local officials to require all industries to install scrubbers in their smokestacks to lower pollutants. But to do that, I need some proof!

That's where you come in. Will you conduct some scientific experiments demonstrating the effects of acid rain on seed germination? I could tell them about your experimental results to give my request some clout. Please help. You may be the farmers' only hope!

Thanks,
Lawton

Activity Directions

1. Use masking tape to label one measuring cup as Cup A.
2. Fill Cup A with water.
3. Place a soda straw in the cup of water, and blow into the straw, producing bubbles, for about 1 minute. You are adding carbon dioxide to the water to form a mild carbonic acid solution.
4. Dip the pH paper into the cup of water, remove it, and note the color of the paper. Read the pH number from the bottle by comparing the color of the paper to the colors on the bottle. Record this on the data table at the end of this package.
5. Place a paper towel in the cup of water until it is saturated. Gently squeeze most of the water from the paper towel, but leave it quite damp. Spread the paper towel on a flat surface.
6. Place twenty radish seeds in a vertical column down the middle of the long side of the paper towel. Leave a little space between each seed and the next one.
7. Roll the paper towel up so it forms a cylinder that sandwiches the seeds in place. Use a permanent marker to label the seeds as Seed Group A.
8. Reserve the unused water.

Name ______________________________ Date ______________________

Science Sleuth Activity Package: Ruined Radishes, *Cont'd.*

9. Use a piece of masking tape to label the other measuring cup as Cup B.
10. Fill Cup B with vinegar.
11. Dip the pH paper into the cup of vinegar, remove it, and note the color of the paper. Read the pH number from the bottle by comparing the color of the paper to the colors on the bottle. Record this on the data table.
12. Repeat steps 7 and 8, except this time you will place the paper towel in vinegar rather than water. Label this roll of seeds Seed Group B.
13. Place both rolls in a dark location until the next day.
14. After twenty-four hours, you will need to add some more liquid to your seed rolls to keep them damp.
15. Use the medicine dropper to add water from Cup A to Seed Group A until the paper towels are damp. Replace the roll in a dark location. **Rinse out the medicine dropper.**
16. Use the medicine dropper to add vinegar from Cup B to Seed Group B until the paper towels are damp. Replace the roll in a dark location. **Rinse out the medicine dropper.**
17. After forty-eight hours, unroll Seed Group A and count the number of seeds that have germinated. Those that have germinated will have tiny white sprouts breaking through the seeds, as in the drawing here. Record the number of seeds that have germinated on the data table.

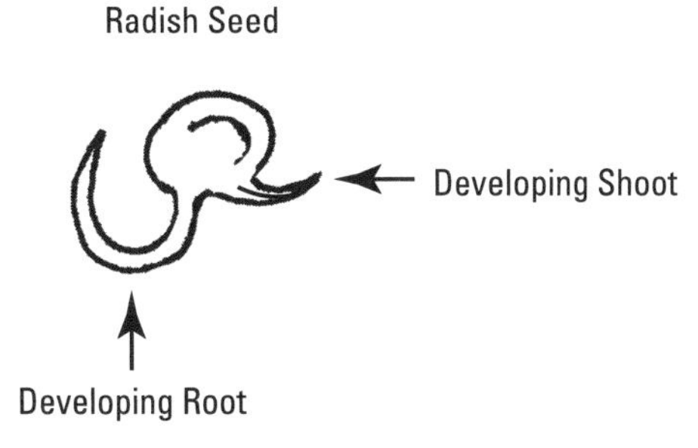

18. Do the same for Seed Group B.
19. Calculate the germination success rate (percentage of seeds that germinated) by dividing the number of seeds that germinated by 20. Then move the decimal two places to the right. Enter this percentage in the last column of the data table.

Name ______________________ Date ______________________

Science Sleuth Activity Package: Ruined Radishes, *Cont'd.*

Questions for Discussion

1. Which seed roll had more seeds germinate?
2. What did the liquid used in roll A represent? What did the liquid used in roll B represent?
3. Did seeds from these two cups germinate in the same way? If not, explain their differences.
4. Will the results of your experiment help Lawton's case? Explain your answer.
5. Write a letter to the mayor of the city that explains your data.

Data Table for Ruined Radishes

	pH of Liquid Used	**Number of Seeds That Germinated**	**Percentage of Seeds That Germinated**
Seed Group A			
Seed Group B			

Activity 5.9: The Eternal Onion—Homework Assignment

Teacher Notes

Although this activity is rather complicated, it will provide an interesting challenge for students. The materials required to complete the assignment are more readily available in a kitchen than in a classroom.

Answer Key

1. DNA is located in the nucleus of each cell.
2. DNA is released by agitation and by the action of detergent.
3. DNA is separated from cell debris by filtration. This is done in step 9.
4. Answers will vary but should include the following steps: (a) chop and blend the sample; (b) add detergent and salt solution; (c) warm; (d) cool; (e) filter; and (f) add alcohol.

Name ______________________ Date ______________________

Homework Assignment: The Eternal Onion

In this interesting experiment, you will learn how to extract DNA from an onion.

Materials You'll Need

Blender

Dishwashing detergent

Thermometer

Distilled water (about 1 cup)

Tap water

One-quart cooking pot

Stove or hot plate

Trivet or other heatproof surface

Salt (noniodized)

Large yellow onion

Knife

2 to 3 cups of ice

Funnel (large enough to hold a coffee filter)

Coffee filter

2 two-cup measuring cups

One-cup measuring cup

Narrow jar (such as a jelly jar)

Large bowl

1 tablespoon

1 teaspoon

Wooden skewer

Clock

Rubbing alcohol or denatured alcohol (the latter works better)

The Case

Your neighbor, Ms. Germaine, is a lawyer. She's busy getting ready to represent a client in a trial. Ms. Germaine's client is Dr. Allium, the creator of a unique, genetically engineered onion. Dr. Allium raises his onions on a farm in Florida. He has patented his technique and labeled the product the Eternal Onion. His onion looks a lot like any other yellow onion, but it is genetically engineered to have a very long shelf life. This means that grocery stores and consumers can keep his onions indefinitely.

Name ______________________________ Date ______________________

Homework Assignment: The Eternal Onion, *Cont'd.*

Dr. Allium knows that Karl Kantor, his longtime rival in the onion genetics business, is growing and selling onions in California. In an advertisement, Kantor claims that his products "remain fresh on your pantry shelf for six months!" Dr. Allium suspects that Kantor stole his secret. Ms. Germaine plans to compare the DNA of Kantor's onion to the DNA of the Eternal Onion and present the results at the trial.

Ms. Germaine needs your help. She wants you to explain the process of DNA extraction to the jury. To prepare yourself for this presentation, you will extract the DNA from an onion. **You will be working with a sharp knife and a hot stove during this experiment, so be very careful.**

Activity Directions

1. Use a knife to chop the onion into large pieces. Place the pieces in the blender and add enough distilled water to cover. Blend for ten seconds, or until the onion is finely chopped.
2. Make a detergent solution by mixing 1 tablespoon liquid dishwashing detergent and 1/4 teaspoon noniodized salt in a two-cup measuring cup. Add enough distilled water to make 2 cups of the detergent/salt/distilled water mixture. Stir with a spoon to mix.
3. Spoon about one cup of chopped onions into another two-cup measuring cup. Add 1/4 cup of the detergent mixture. Stir gently to mix.
4. Take the one-quart cooking pot, and add enough tap water to fill it one-quarter full. Place the pot of water on the stove or hot plate, and set the temperature on medium.
5. For thirty seconds, hold the thermometer in the pot of water on the stove or hot plate. (Don't let the thermometer touch the bottom of the pot.) When the water reaches 60°C (140°F), remove the pot from the stove and place it on a heatproof surface.
6. Set the container of onion and detergent mixture in the hot water. Let the container remain in the hot water for fifteen minutes.
7. While the onion-detergent mixture incubates, prepare a cold water bath. Put 2 to 3 cups of ice in a large bowl. Add 1/4 cup tap water to the bowl of ice.
8. After fifteen minutes of incubating in hot water, move the onion-detergent mixture to the ice bath. Allow it to stand in the ice bath until the mixture is cool. Stir the mixture occasionally to help dissipate the heat.
9. Place the coffee filter in the funnel. Stand the funnel in the jelly jar. Pour some of the onion-detergent mixture into the funnel, and fill the jelly jar about one-quarter full.
10. The liquid in the jelly jar contains DNA from the onion cells. Gently pour an equal volume of rubbing alcohol into the jelly jar.
11. The onion DNA will form a layer of thick white material between the onion liquid and the rubbing alcohol. Collect a sample of the DNA by swirling a wooden skewer through it. Gently lift the DNA from the jar.

Name ______________________ Date ______________________

Homework Assignment: The Eternal Onion, *Cont'd.*

Questions to Answer

1. Where is the DNA of an onion located?

2. What part of the procedure do you think released the DNA? Explain your reasoning.

3. In what step did you separate the DNA from cellular debris like cell walls and membranes?

4. Write a short paragraph that you can read to the jury to explain how you removed DNA from the onion. Keep your explanation simple.

Activity 5.10: Entomology Report—Homework Assignment

Teacher Notes

Be aware that the following homework assignment may not be suitable for squeamish students. However, others will learn useful information.

A completed data table should look like this ("NA" means that no answer is to be recorded in this place):

Answers for Completed Data Table

Type of Insect	Life Cycle Stage	Timing in Days	Size
Calliphora	Eggs	1	2 mm
	First instar	1–2	5 mm
	Second instar	2–3	10 mm
	Third instar	4–5	17 mm
	Prepupae	8–12	12 mm
	Pupa	18–24	9 mm
Sarcophaga	First instar	2	NA
	Second instar	3	NA
	Third instar	5	Vary from 10–22 mm
	Prepupae	8	NA
	Pupa	12	NA
Predatory rove beetle	Larvae	After 3	NA
Piophila casei	Larvae	3–6 months after death	NA

Answer Key

1. Animals move to the body of a dead vertebrate in a predictable pattern, based on their needs. Insects that lay eggs in tissue appear first. Insects that eat the eggs and larvae do not show up until those items are available. Other insects prefer to consume the body after it dries out.
2. You could assume that death occurred more than three months earlier. *Piophila casei* does not appear until three to six months after death. Bone-eating beetles do not appear until bone is exposed.
3. They feed on maggots, not rotting flesh.
4. Insects can indicate how long a body has been dead because the insects that feed on dead bodies do so at exact stages of decomposition.

Name ______________________________ Date ______________________

Homework Assignment: Entomology Report

In this activity, you will conduct research on insect life cycles and draw conclusions about the time of death based on evidence provided by insects.

The Case

Poultry is a big business in the area where you live. Prize hens and roosters are valued for their healthy offspring. For poultry farmers, buying and caring for genetically superior breeding stock is a big investment. That is why Clarence McDougal is so upset. His prize rooster, valued at $5,000, was stolen when chicken rustlers broke into his poultry farm.

After months of searching, McDougal has found one clue: the partially decomposed remains of the prize rooster. The remains are in the yard of a cabin about one mile from McDougal's farm.

The case of Mr. McDougal's dead rooster has set your brain in motion. You want to know more about the ways forensic investigators use insects to help solve cases. The odor of decay attracts certain insects in a predictable pattern. The insects either feed on the decaying carcass or on the other animals that are attracted to the carcass. Now you are ready for more details.

One important carrion-feeding type of fly is the blowfly, member of genus *Calliphoridae.* The life cycle of a blowfly (see the "Life Cycle of Blowfly" drawing) is typical of most types of flies. Adult blowflies lay eggs on a body shortly after death. The eggs hatch into small larvae called *first instars.* After a time of feeding and growing, the first instars molt, or shed their outer skins, to form second instars. These larvae feed for a time, grow, and molt into third instars. Third instars feed until they are fully grown, then form hard, dark-colored coverings called *pupa* over their bodies. Eventually the pupa open to release flies and the cycle begins again.

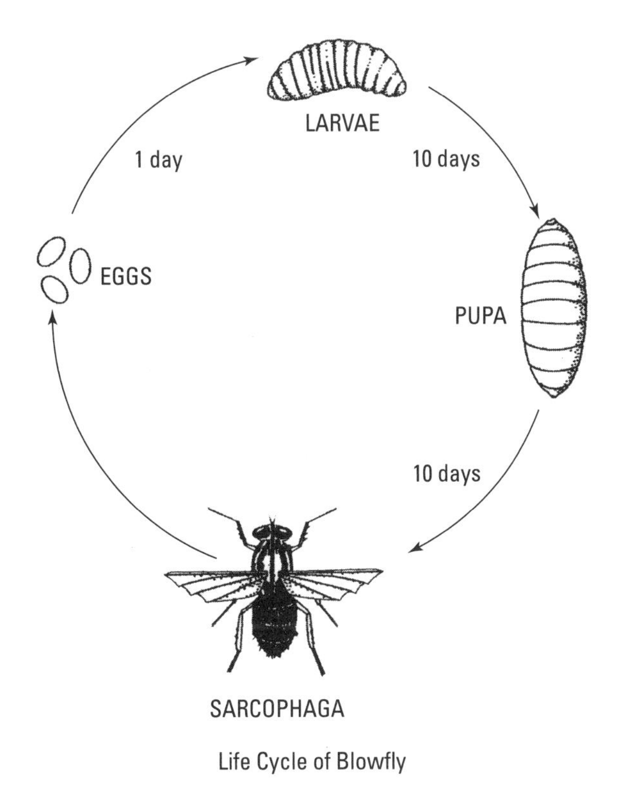

Life Cycle of Blowfly

Name ______________________________ Date ______________________

Homework Assignment: Entomology Report, *Cont'd.*

Flesh flies, members of the genus *Sarcophaga,* have similar life cycles. One difference is that flesh flies do not lay eggs. Instead, the adult female deposits first instars, so the life cycle of a flesh fly is a little shorter than the life cycle of a blowfly.

Some insects feed on fly larvae, so they do not arrive until after larvae hatch. Other insects appear on the dead body as it proceeds to decay. As the body begins to dry out, flies disappear and beetles appear. One insect that is commonly found after three months is the cheese skipper, genus *Piophila.*

In this experiment, you will learn the details of insect life cycles and find out how to use insects to determine time of death of Mr. McDougal's rooster.

Activity Directions

1. The following data table lists four kinds of insects and information about them. Some of the information has been filled in. Use the Internet or reference books to help you complete the data on the events in insect life cycles. Some portions of the table have "NA" in them. That means there is no information to be recorded in these places.

Type of Insect	Life Cycle Stage	Timing in Days	Size
Calliphora	Eggs	________	2 mm
	First instar	1–2	________
	Second instar	________	________
	________	________	17 mm
	Prepupae	8–12	________
	Pupa	________	________
Sarcophaga	First instar	2	NA
	________	3	NA
	Third instar	5	Vary from 10–22 mm
	Prepupae	8	NA
	Pupa	12	NA
Predatory rove beetles	Larvae	________	NA
Piophila casei	Larvae	________ ________	NA

Name ______________________________ Date ____________________

Homework Assignment: Entomology Report, *Cont'd.*

2. Read the following Entomology Report, case number 23112, on Mr. McDougal's rooster:

Entomology Report

Case Number: 23112

Decedent: Prize Rooster **Age:** 4

Description of Site: Wooded location one mile off of State Highway 166

Temperature: 70°F

Notes about insect activity:

1. third instar larvae of *Calliphora* plentiful

2. prepupae of *Sarcophaga* are abundant

3. 10 rove beetle larvae collected

---

3. Construct a table in which you identify all of the insects mentioned in this report, the time those insects typically arrive at a body, and what this information tells you about the time of the rooster's death:

Insect	How Soon After Death the Insect Arrives at the Body	The Clue This Information Gives About the Rooster's Time of Death

Name ______________________ Date ______________________

Homework Assignment: Entomology Report, *Cont'd.*

Questions to Answer

1. In biology, scientists refer to the gradual changes in the makeup of a community as succession. Explain how the concept of succession applies to the body of a dead vertebrate.

2. If you found *Piophila casei* and bone-eating beetles on a body, what could you say about the time of death? Explain your reasoning.

3. Why aren't larvae of rove beetles found on a body in the first day or two after death?

4. How do investigators use insects to help them establish the time of death?

Chapter Six

It Was a Dark and Stormy Night

Solving Crime Through Critical Thinking and Problem Solving

The first five chapters of this book have focused on specific skills that are components of the scientific method. In this chapter, students will apply these skills to solve cases. The case method approach to teaching can be used in many fields, but it is especially applicable to forensic science. The technique requires students to apply their skills and knowledge to solve a problem. In this process, students think critically by sorting through clues, evaluating evidence, prioritizing lines of inquiry, and observing events and materials. Solving cases gives students opportunities to see firsthand how scientific inquiry works instead of learning about the process through reading or lecture.

CRIME SCENE DO NOT CROSS

Activity 6.1: Scientific Detectives

Teacher Briefing

This activity supports your efforts to teach the scientific method. After students learn the basic elements of the scientific method, they are asked to use their new knowledge to develop an approach to solving crimes. One or more of the exercises could be used to assess students' progress. Alternatively, you could use the questions offered for class discussion as an assessment or evaluation device. Scenario 1 is the simplest and scenario 3 the most complex.

Activity Preparation

- The bare outlines of the scientific method are described here. You may want to do some independent research so that you can provide students with richer background and examples.
- Consider whether you want students to do this activity by themselves, in pairs, or in small groups. You might do the first scenario in a group, the second in pairs, and the third as an assessment tool.
- Make copies of the Science Sleuth Activity Package.
- If you decide to use one of the scenarios as an assessment tool, you may want to keep that page separate from the package and hand it out later in the class.
- If you decide to use the questions as an assessment tool, you may want to keep that page separate from the package and hand it out later in the class.

First, Tell Your Students . . .

What do detectives and scientists have in common? If you said that both depend on logical problem-solving skills to find the answers they need, you are correct. What detectives call a logical approach is very similar to what scientists call the scientific method.

Logical problem solving and the scientific method have several steps:

1. *Research and observe.* For example, a detective investigating the dognapping of the Smith family's pet dog, Rover, might notice that there are lots of fingerprints around the doghouse. Somebody sawed through the chain and took the dog, leaving fingerprints in the process. Detectives would make sure that they retrieved all fingerprints from the area.
2. *State the problem.* In this case, the problem is: *Whose fingerprints are at the crime scene?* Most crimes pose more than one problem for a detective to solve. At the same crime scene, other problems might be: *Who made the footprints nearby?* and *Who wrote the ransom note?*

3. *State your hypothesis.* A hypothesis is an educated guess about what the facts may show. In this dognapping case, the detective might hypothesize that some of the fingerprints left at the site do not belong to family members.
4. *Carry out an experiment to test your hypothesis.* You've already had some experience in developing an experiment that will provide important information. If you were investigating the dognapping, your experiment might include collecting fingerprints from family members and matching them to prints found at the scene of the dognapping.
5. *Analyze and draw conclusions.* This is an important step. First, detectives must look at the evidence. In this case, let's say that our dognapping detective finds that two sets of fingerprints do not match anyone in the family. However, in drawing conclusions, scientists and detectives have to be careful that they don't make any assumptions. If our dognapping detective concluded that a team of kidnappers stole Rover and left their prints on the doghouse, he or she might be wrong. One set of prints—or both—might belong to neighbors who attended a barbecue in the backyard or to a dog walker who takes Rover for a stroll.

In this experiment, you will spend some time thinking about how you might apply the scientific method to solve crimes.

Activity Procedure

1. Distribute the Science Sleuth Activity Package, and divide students into groups or pairs, as you have decided.
2. Tell students to look at scenario 1 and develop their investigative plan based on the scientific method.
3. As a whole class, review the scenario and how various students or groups decided to approach their investigation.
4. Repeat steps 2 and 3 for each scenario.

Summary and Discussion

- What is the scientific method? What steps make up this method? *Answer:* Steps of the scientific method: research/observe, state the problem, state a hypothesis, carry out an experiment, and analyze and draw conclusions.
- What is the difference between a problem and a hypothesis? *Answer:* The *problem* is the question to be answered. It is often stated as an open-ended question. A *hypothesis* is an idea about the answer to the problem, based on research and observation.
- Do you think that the steps of the scientific method must be followed in any particular order? Explain your reasoning. *Answer:* Answers will vary. The steps of the scientific method do not have to be carried out in the order

stated. For example, you may be aware of a problem that warrants investigation. In this case, you would not begin at the "observation" step.

- How are the jobs of detectives and scientists similar? *Answer:* Both scientists and investigators use logical procedures to find solutions to problems.

Sample Answers to Scenario 1

Research/Observe: A pry tool was used to open the kitchen window.

Problem: Whose pry tool was used to open the kitchen window?

Hypothesis: A pry tool taken from one of the suspects made the tool marks at the kitchen window.

Experiment: Investigators compare the tool mark on the kitchen window to the pry tools of the suspects to identify the pry tool used to open the window. A cast is made of the pry tool mark, and the cast is compared to the pry tools of the suspects.

Analyze and Draw Conclusions: If the cast matches any suspect's pry tool, the person who had access to that tool may be the perpetrator.

Sample Answers to Scenario 2

Research/Observe: Investigators notice footprints at the crime scene.

Problem: What can footprints reveal about the perpetrator's height?

Hypothesis: Greasy footprints leading to the car can be used to determine the perp's height.

Experiment: Measure the greasy footprints. Use the footprints to determine the height of the suspect.

Analyze and Draw Conclusions: Compare the calculated height of the perp to the height of any known suspects. If the height of the perp matches the height of any known suspects, that is a piece of evidence against that suspect.

Here are some alternative answers:

Problem: What can footprints reveal about the perpetrator's shoes?

Hypothesis: Greasy footprints leading to the car can be used to find out what size and type of shoes the perp wears.

Experiment: Make a cast of the footprints. Compare the cast from the crime scene to the sizes and shapes of shoe soles in the suspect's home.

Analyze and Draw Conclusions: Compare the shoe prints of suspects to those in the victim's home. If the shoe prints match any shoes in a suspect's possession, this information may indicate that that subject was the perpetrator.

Sample Answers to Scenario 3

Research/Observe: Fingerprints from the paint can, the tire tracks, and the down stuffing of the jacket all offer lines of investigation.

In the case of the fingerprints:

Problem: Can fingerprints on the paint be lifted and matched to known prints?

Hypothesis: Fingerprints lifted from the paint can will match known prints.

Experiment: Dust the paint can with fingerprint powder. Use tape to lift the prints, and then compare them to a set of known fingerprints.

Analyze and Draw Conclusions: Determine whether the fingerprints on the paint can match known prints. If a fingerprint match is found, the perpetrator can be identified.

In the case of the tire prints:

Problem: Can the tire prints on the lawn be matched to known tire prints?

Hypothesis: The tire prints on the lawn can be matched to known tire prints.

Experiment: A cast of tire prints is made of the prints for comparison to known prints.

Analyze and Draw Conclusions: Tire prints in the cast are matched or not matched to known prints. If tire prints in the cast match known prints, the types of tire used in the commission of the crime can be determined. This could provide a link between a suspect's car and the crime scene.

In the case of the down stuffing:

Problem: Can the down stuffing be matched to known samples of down stuffing in jackets?

Hypothesis: The down stuffing at the crime scene can be matched to known samples of down stuffing.

Experiment: The down stuffing at the crime scene is microscopically compared to known samples of down stuffing.

Analyze and Draw Conclusions: The down stuffing is matched or not matched to known samples. If the stuffing left at the crime scene is matched to a known sample, it could provide a link between a suspect's jacket or vest and the crime scene.

Name ______________________________ Date ____________________

Science Sleuth Activity Package: Scientific Detectives

Background

What do detectives and scientists have in common? If you said that both depend on logical problem-solving skills to find the answers they need, you are correct. What detectives call a logical approach is very similar to what scientists call the scientific method.

Logical problem solving and the scientific method have several steps. Make notes on each step as you listen to your teacher describe it:

1. Research and observe the scene.

____
____
____
____
____
____

2. State the problem.

____
____
____
____
____
____

3. State your hypothesis.

____
____
____
____
____
____

Name ______________________________ Date ____________________

Science Sleuth Activity Package: Scientific Detectives, *Cont'd.*

4. Conduct an experiment to test your hypothesis.

____

____

____

____

____

____

5. Analyze results and draw conclusions.

____

____

____

____

____

____

In this activity, you will spend some time thinking about how you might apply the scientific method to solve crimes.

Activity Directions

1. Look at scenario 1.
2. Decide how you would approach the investigation, using the scientific method.
3. Make notes about your plan.
4. Repeat steps 1 to 3 for each scenario.

Name ________________________________ Date ________________________

Science Sleuth Activity Package: Scientific Detectives, *Cont'd.*

Scenario 1

Christy's home has been burgled. At the crime scene you find:

- An open window in the kitchen
- Pry marks on the window

Three suspects have been identified. Each owns a pry tool. You will use the scientific method to find out which pry tool was used to open the kitchen window.

1. Research and observe.

____

____

____

____

2. State the problem.

____

____

____

____

3. State your hypothesis.

____

____

____

____

4. Carry out an experiment to test your hypothesis.

____

____

____

____

5. Analyze and draw conclusions.

____

____

____

____

Name ______________________ Date ______________________

Science Sleuth Activity Package: Scientific Detectives, *Cont'd.*

Scenario 2

Ted returned to his car to find the door open and his CD player missing. Investigators reported that:

- Greasy footprints led up to the car and were smeared on the driver's-side floor mat.
- A piece of chewing gum was recovered from the driver's-side floor mat. It was lying on top of a greasy footprint. The chewing gum has teeth marks on it.

The steps of the scientific method are listed below. Explain how each step of the scientific method can help you find out who stole Ted's CD player.

1. Research and observe.

____

____

____

2. State the problem.

____

____

____

3. State your hypothesis.

____

____

____

4. Carry out an experiment to test your hypothesis.

____

____

____

5. Analyze and draw conclusions.

____

____

____

____

Name ______________________ Date ______________________

Science Sleuth Activity Package: Scientific Detectives, *Cont'd.*

Scenario 3

The school has been vandalized. Someone has spray painted the words "Revenge is mine!" in red across the front door. At the crime scene you find:

- An empty can of red spray paint
- Fresh tire tracks on the usually well-manicured school lawn
- A fluffy pile of down stuffing, the type that is used to insulate winter coats or to make warm comforters.

Explain how each step of the scientific method can help you find out who vandalized the school.

1. Research and observe.

   ____

   ____

   ____

2. State the problem.

   ____

   ____

   ____

3. State your hypothesis.

   ____

   ____

   ____

4. Carry out an experiment to test your hypothesis.

   ____

   ____

   ____

5. Analyze and draw conclusions.

   ____

   ____

   ____

   ____

Name ______________________ Date ______________

Science Sleuth Activity Package: Scientific Detectives, *Cont'd.*

Questions to Discuss

1. What is the scientific method? What steps make up this method?
2. What is the difference between a problem and a hypothesis?
3. Do you think that the steps of the scientific method must be followed in any particular order? Explain your reasoning.
4. How are the jobs of detectives and scientists similar?

Notes

Activity 6.2: The Case of the Placido Murder

Teacher Briefing

In this activity, students can work alone or in groups to develop their observation and deductive reasoning skills to solve a crime. Alternatively, you could have students work alone and use this exercise to assess progress.

Activity Preparation

- Decide if you want to use this activity with groups or individuals and as an evaluation device or not.
- Make copies of the Science Sleuth Activity Package.

First, Tell Your Students . . .

Two of the most important skills an investigator can have may sound pretty simple: looking and thinking. Simple or not, detectives spend lots of time looking closely at a crime scene and thinking about the clues they spot.

One reason detectives do a lot of looking is that they want to find everything that isn't quite right—things that are out of place. After eyeballing clues, detectives use deductive reasoning to figure out what the clues mean. In deductive reasoning, a person looks at the clues that are available and then draws some conclusions.

Imagine you've been called in to help find the suspect in a murder. (If you choose, you could distribute the "Placido Crime Scene" drawing now.) The body of Marc Placido was found in his office. Marc, a collector of rare handguns and rifles, had obviously been murdered. Put your looking and thinking smarts to the test by solving this case.

Activity Procedure

1. Hand out the Science Sleuth Activity Package.
2. Tell your students to review the drawing and answer the questions in their package.

Summary and Discussion

If you use this activity as an assessment vehicle, postpone these questions until the next class session.

- How do you think the murderer(s) entered the office? *Answer:* The office door was kicked in.
- On what date and at what time did the struggle apparently take place? *Answer:* June 5th, 9:20 A.M.
- Do you think more than one person was involved in this break-in and murder? Why or why not? *Answer:* More than one person may have been involved; a man's watch and a woman's button were found.
- How does it seem the deceased was killed? *Answer:* He was strangled.
- Do you think the deceased was killed before or after the safe was opened? Explain your reasoning. *Answer:* After, because he is lying on top of papers from the safe.
- Who killed Marc Placido? *Answer:* Alan Thompson.
- What was the motive? *Answer:* Robbery.

Name ______________________________ Date ______________________

Science Sleuth Activity Package: The Case of the Placido Murder

Background

Two of the most important skills an investigator can have may sound pretty simple: looking and thinking. Detectives do a lot of looking because they want to find everything that isn't quite right—things that are out of place. After eyeballing clues, detectives use deductive reasoning to figure out what the clues mean. In deductive reasoning, a person looks at the clues that are available and then draws some conclusions.

Looking and thinking will help you solve the crime described in the "Placido Crime Scene" drawing at the end of this package. The body of Marc Placido was found in his office. Marc, a collector of rare handguns and rifles, had obviously been murdered. Put your looking and thinking smarts to the test by solving this case.

Activity Directions

Carefully look at the drawings of the "Placido Crime Scene" and the "Placido Murder Suspects" (both at the end of this package), searching for clues that might tell you what took place here.

Questions to Answer

1. How do you think the murderer(s) entered the office?

____

____

____

2. On what date and at what time did the struggle apparently take place?

____

____

____

3. Do you think more than one person was involved in this break-in and murder? Why or why not?

____

____

____

____

____

Name ________________________________ Date ________________________

Science Sleuth Activity Package: The Case of the Placido Murder, *Cont'd.*

4. How does it seem the deceased was killed?

____

____

____

____

5. Do you think the deceased was killed before or after the safe was opened? Explain your reasoning.

____

____

____

____

____

6. Who killed Marc Placido?

____

____

7. What was the motive?

____

____

Science Sleuth Activity Package: The Case of the Placido Murder, *Cont'd.*

Placido Crime Scene

Science Sleuth Activity Package: The Case of the Placido Murder, *Cont'd.*

Placido Murder Suspects

Activity 6.3: The Case of the Oak Street Murder

Teacher Briefing

In this activity, students learn another method of organizing information. As they carry out an experiment and collect data, they present the data in tabular form. They also plot a graph showing the dependent variable and independent variable.

This activity presupposes some knowledge of graphing. You may need to supplement the brief description here with other pieces of your curriculum.

You can use this activity as an introductory device for classes on plotting graphs, in which case you might want students to work in groups or by themselves. You could also use the activity later in your sequence as an assessment device, but it requires significant materials for each experimenter.

Activity Preparation

- For each experimenter, provide:

  Postage scale or other weighing device
  Glass of water
  Ice cube
  Clock with second hand or timer
  Graph paper
- Make copies of the Science Sleuth Activity Package.

First, Tell Your Students . . .

Detectives must be able to formulate a hypothesis, test that hypothesis, and evaluate their results to draw conclusions. In a sense, the work of a detective is very similar to that of a scientist. In this activity, you will test a hypothesis, draw a conclusion, and graph your results.

Activity Procedure

1. Distribute the Science Sleuth Activity Packages, and assign students to detective groups of two or three.
2. Tell students to follow the directions in the Science Sleuth Activity Package until they have completed their data table.
3. At this point, you may want to bring the whole class back together for a discussion of plotting graphs. In fact, the graph section of this activity could be done in a separate class session.

Summary and Discussion

- In this experiment, what is the purpose of the data table? *Answer:* The data table helps organize information gathered in the experiment.
- Based on the information in your graph, what happens to the weight of the ice cube as more time elapses? *Answer:* The weight of the ice cube decreases as time increases.
- What is the independent variable in this experiment? What is the dependent variable? *Answer:* The independent variable is the one that you are changing in the experiment. In this case, it is time. The dependent variable is the one whose changes are based on the independent variable. In this experiment, the dependent variable is the weight of the ice cube.
- Based on your experiment, how long would it take the ice cubes in a glass of tea to melt? What does this information tell you about the crime scene? *Answer:* Answers may vary.

Name ______________________ Date ______________________

Science Sleuth Activity Package: The Case of the Oak Street Murder

The Case

The Lawrence sisters—Ethel, Marilyn, and Doris—are retired school teachers who share a home on Oak Street. Since they have spent much of their lives on the precise bell schedules of schools, they have maintained a similar schedule in their retirement years.

Today when Ethel and Marilyn walked into the dining room at exactly noon, they were shocked to see Doris slumped in her chair. Doris was dead of what looked a lot like a gunshot wound! The sisters raced to the telephone and called the police. At the crime scene, police gathered information, interviewed Ethel and Marilyn, and prepared a report.

According to the report, police arrived at the crime scene at 12:20 P.M. The report also says that the table was set for lunch, and there were three glasses of tea on the table. There was no ice left in the glasses, but they were still cool to the touch. Something seems to be incorrect. You wonder if the time on the report, 12:20 P.M., is wrong since the temperature in the dining room was normal room temperature, about 72°F. If the sisters prepared the meal for exactly noon, would all of the ice melt by 12:20 P.M.? Or the time on the report might be correct, but the surviving sisters might be lying about the time they found Doris's body. You decide to do a little experimenting to learn more.

In this experiment, you will document the rate at which an ice cube in a glass of water melts at room temperature. You will create a data table to display your results and then graph those results.

Activity Directions

1. Weigh one ice cube. Record the weight of the ice cube in the data table below.
2. Place the ice cube in a glass of tap water at room temperature.
3. After five minutes, remove the ice cube. Weigh it quickly, and return the cube to the glass of water. Record the weight in your data table.
4. Repeat step 3 every five minutes until the ice cube is completely melted. Record the weight in the table.

	Weight of the Ice Cube	Time Elapsed
Time Zero		

Name ______________________________ Date ______________________

Science Sleuth Activity Package: The Case of the Oak Street Murder, *Cont'd.*

5. Use the data in the table you just completed to construct a graph. Put "Time" on the *x*-axis and "Weight of the Ice Cube" on the *y*-axis. Be sure to label your axes and title your graph.

Questions for Discussion

1. In this experiment, what is the purpose of the data table?
2. Based on the information in your graph, what happens to the weight of the ice cube as time increases?
3. What is the independent variable in this experiment? What is the dependent variable?
4. Based on your experiment, how long would it take the ice cubes in a glass of tea to melt? What does this information tell you about the crime scene?

Activity 6.4: The Case of the Missing Crown

Teacher Briefing

As we move forward in helping students to develop logical thinking skills, this activity asks them to evaluate the relative importance of facts in solving a crime. They also develop a hypothesis and revise it as new information becomes available. Students work in groups.

Activity Preparation

- Make copies of the Science Sleuth Activity Packages.
- Make copies of Clue Sheets 1 to 3. You may want to package them—for example, fold each sheet up and close it with a sticker or put it in an envelope.

First, Tell Your Students . . .

On the first day of a new investigation, detectives may have only limited information about a case. It is rare for detectives to quickly find all of the information they need to solve a case. Nevertheless, the information that a detective does possess helps him or her begin formulating some possible scenarios about what really happened. In this activity, you will find out how ideas change as more and more information is discovered.

Activity Procedure

1. Distribute the Science Sleuth Activity Packages, and assign students to groups of three or six.
2. Distribute Clue Sheet 1, and ask students to follow the directions in the Science Sleuth Activity Package. You might want to discuss the status of the investigation at this point.
3. Distribute Clue Sheet 2, and ask students to follow the directions in the activity package. You might want to discuss the status of the investigation at this point. How has the new information altered their understanding of what happened?
4. Distribute Clue Sheet 3, and ask students to follow the directions in the activity package. You might want to discuss the status of the investigation at this point.
5. Ask students how the new information has altered their understanding of what happened.

Summary and Discussion

- Look back over the three clues that you starred. Do you still feel that these are the three most important clues in solving this mystery? Explain your answer. *Answer:* Answers will vary.
- Did your hypothesis change over time? Why? *Answer:* Answers will vary. Students most likely revised their hypotheses as new information became available.
- When investigating a crime, do detectives have all of the facts they need at the beginning of the investigation? Explain your answer. *Answer:* No. As the investigation proceeds, new information becomes available.
- When you compared your hypothesis to the hypothesis of another group, did you find any differences? If so, why do you think this happened? *Answer:* Answers may vary. After the first set of clues, students may have concluded that Jane did not commit the burglary since she does not have long blond hair and that Blanche had an alibi for the time of the crime. Or students may have assumed that since Sally does not have a bag, she could not have taken the Crown of Titus out of the museum.

Clue Sheet 1

- Jane owns a clear, plastic book bag.
- Every Saturday, Jane walks by the museum on her way to her job as a lunchtime waitress at a nearby restaurant.
- Sally has long red hair.
- Blanche was seen eating lunch with a friend in the museum cafeteria at 12:30 P.M. on Saturday.

Clue Sheet 2

- Sue met Jane at the mall on 3:00 P.M. Saturday.
- Sally has a broken arm, so she doesn't carry a bag. She attaches a red change purse to her belt.
- Every morning Blanche rinses her hair in a different color. Her favorite rinse makes her hair navy blue.
- Sally spent all of Saturday with Blanche.

Clue Sheet 3

- Sue's dad works in the office at the museum, so she gets in free.
- Sally visited the museum on Saturday. Her ticket was purchased at 12:15 P.M.
- Jane has short black hair.
- Blanche has sensitive skin and cannot wear makeup.

Name ______________________________ Date ______________________

Science Sleuth Activity Package: The Case of the Missing Crown

The Case

You are a detective investigating the burglary of the Crown of Titus from the Metropolitan Museum of Art in New York City. This crown, the largest gold- and jewel-encrusted headpiece in the world, is priceless. The burglary occurred between noon and 1:00 P.M. on Saturday while the guard was at lunch.

When you arrived at the crime scene, the only clues are a strand of long blond hair and a tube of cherry-colored lipstick. Evidence seems to be pointing toward four suspects: Blanche, Jane, Sally, and Sue.

In this experiment, you will develop a hypothesis based on limited information. As new information becomes available, you will revise your hypothesis.

Activity Directions

1. Look at Clue Sheet 1, and have someone in your group read it aloud.
2. Before you discuss the clues, put a question mark next to the clue you think is most important.
3. Now discuss the clues with your group, and decide together which clue is most important. Put a star next to the clue that the group decides is important.
4. Write a hypothesis stating what may have happened based on the information available to you now.
5. Compare your hypothesis with those reached by other members of the group.
6. Look at Clue Sheet 2, and have someone in your group read it aloud.
7. Before you discuss the clues, put a question mark next to the clue you think is most important.
8. Now discuss the clues with your group, and decide together which clue is most important. Put a star next to the clue that the group decides is important.
9. Write a hypothesis stating what may have happened based on the information available to you now.
10. Compare your hypothesis with those reached by other members of the group.
11. Look at Clue Sheet 3, and have someone in your group read it aloud.
12. Before you discuss the clues, put a question mark next to the clue you think is most important.
13. Now discuss the clues with your group, and decide together which clue is most important. Put a star next to the clue that the group decides is important.

Name ______________________________ Date ______________________

Science Sleuth Activity Package: The Case of the Missing Crown, *Cont'd.*

14. Write a hypothesis stating what may have happened based on the information available to you now.
15. Compare your hypothesis with those reached by other members of the group.

Questions for Discussion

1. Look back over the three clues that you starred. Do you still feel that these are the three most important clues in solving this mystery? Explain your answer.
2. Did your hypothesis change over time? Why?
3. When investigating a crime, do detectives have all of the facts they need at the beginning of the investigation? Explain your answer.
4. When you compared your hypothesis to the hypothesis of another team member, did you find any differences? If so, why do you think this happened?

Activity 6.5: The Case of the Crushed Cameras

Teacher Briefing

Students use deductive reasoning skills to solve a problem. In this case, they have to review a picture of the Crushed Cameras Crime Scene, listen to several witnesses, and then put all of the information together, a complex task. This activity could be done in small groups, in pairs, or individually, and it could be used as an evaluation device.

Activity Preparation

- Make copies of the Science Sleuth Activity Package.
- Recruit ten students to serve as witnesses. If you are using this as an evaluation device, you may want to consider whether it's fair to ask students to perform and do the test at the same time. Perhaps another class or some colleagues could provide your acting team.
- Although you could pass this book around to performers, it might be easier to make a copy of the actor's speech that he or she could review before performing.
- Decide whether to give students written copies of the interviews as well.

Witness Scripts

Mr. Gladden, who lives in a house adjacent to the high school: "I was watching my favorite detective show last night—it had just started at 9:00—when I heard some tires squealing in the direction of the school. I had just let my dog out, so I jumped up to make sure he wasn't in the road. A car zoomed by my house. I couldn't make out much, but I was able to get part of the tag number—it started with ZNN."

Principal Tennessee Brown of AHS: "I don't know who would have destroyed those cameras. The kids all love the morning news broadcasts. Mrs. Hernandez is the teacher in charge. Her first-period communications class tapes and airs the show. Now I will tell you that Mrs. Hernandez was very angry last week when I told her that the superintendent has decided to replace her as the sponsor of the *Cougar News*. The superintendent feels that she had too many irons in the fire since she also directs the school chorus. You may want to talk to her."

Mrs. Hernandez, teacher and activity sponsor: "This is unreal! Yesterday was one of our best broadcasts here at the AHS *Cougar News*. We did a cute feature to promote the big soccer match between AHS and Lincoln High School. Our soccer coaches put on jerseys that belong to two star Lincoln players, Chris and Jimmy. We filmed the two coaches in the roles of the Lincoln players bragging about how they were going to tromp AHS in soccer next week. The campus officer came in, handcuffed both boys, then took them away in a patrol car. It was great.

"The only bad part of the day was the absence of our regular news anchors: Hosea, Mike, and Julia. I wouldn't let them participate because they've all been late to class three mornings this week. When they finally arrived late yesterday, I had no choice but to dismiss them, so I said, 'Three strikes and you're out.' They stomped out of the room and slammed the door. You better talk to them about last night. I guess you know that I didn't have anything to do with this, because I was with the chorus last night, entertaining for the Kiwanis Club. We didn't leave the Kiwanis Hall until almost 10:00 P.M."

Tabetha, weather girl for the Cougar News *team:* "Did you check on those guys we joked about in our skit, Chris and Jimmy? They play soccer for Lincoln, and the coaches made fun of them in the broadcast yesterday morning."

Hosea, member of the anchor team: "I admit that Mrs. Hernandez made me mad, but I'd never do anything like this. I was at home last night doing my homework. Mike even spent the night at my house. My mom and dad went out to dinner, and when they got in around 10:00 P.M., they stuck their heads in the door to say goodnight."

Mike, member of the anchor team: "Okay, it was a bad scene yesterday morning, but surely you don't think I'd do this as revenge. I was over at Hosea's working on some math problems. My dad dropped me off at about 6:00 P.M., and I spent the night there. My car has been in the shop for about a week, and I'm without wheels these days."

Julia, member of the anchor team: "I was tired of getting up early to do those broadcasts anyway. It was really a relief to get fired. Last night I was at the library studying until it closed at 10:00 P.M. My mom came by and picked me up. I'm getting my driver's license next week along with a new car. She won't have to cart me around anymore."

Chris, soccer player: "Sure I got mad at their stupid broadcast. It made fun of me and my friend Jimmy. Those Cougars think they are so cool. We will tear them to shreds in soccer next week. Last night, I was at home watching the videos of our previous game with AHS so I'd be ready for the next one. I hope you are not trying to pin this vandalism on me. I've never been in any kind of trouble before!"

Jimmy, soccer player: "From 8:30 to 10:00 last night I had a math tutor at my house. My parents were there too. I didn't do anything wrong. I don't like the AHS Cougars but I wouldn't break in their school."

April Fool's Day Dance sponsor: "I kept a record of everyone who bought a ticket so that next year, we can approach them again for a repeat sell. Of the suspects you listed, I see that Hosea, Julie, Chris, and Jimmy were the only ones to purchase tickets. I hope that helps you out."

First, Tell Your Students . . .

On April 2, the TV studio at Atkinson High School was vandalized. Two TV cameras used in the daily production of the AHS *Cougar News* were destroyed. Detectives collected information and evidence at the scene. You will review the information and evidence, use deductive reasoning, and draw some conclusions about what really happened at the school that night.

Activity Procedure

1. Distribute the Science Sleuth Activity Package.
2. Divide students into groups if you choose.
3. Provide the interviews conducted on the morning of April 3.
4. Introduce each witness in turn, giving a brief description of his or her relation to events—for example, "This is Mr. Gladden, who lives in a house adjacent to the high school."
5. Ask students if they want to check any facts in the witness's statement. Students should be able to check facts but not ask larger questions.
6. Tell students to use all the information they've received to solve the crime, following the guidelines in the Science Sleuth Activity Package.

Summary and Discussion

- Who had a motive to smash the cameras at AHS? *Answer:* People with motives are Mrs. Hernandez, Hosea, Mike, Julie, Chris, and Jimmy.
- Who does not have a firm alibi for 9:00 P.M. on the night of the crime? *Answer:* People with opportunity are Hosea, Mike, Julie, and Chris.
- Who do you suspect destroyed the cameras at AHS? *Answer:* Student answers will vary but most likely will be Chris.
- Can you definitely rule out your other suspects, even if evidence seems to point to one person? Explain your answer. *Answer:* No. There were no eyewitnesses to definitely put Chris at the scene.

Name ______________________________ Date ____________________

Science Sleuth Activity Package: The Case of the Crushed Cameras

The Case

On April 2, the TV studio at Atkinson High School was vandalized. Two TV cameras used in the daily production of the AHS *Cougar News* were destroyed.

The AHS school alarm was triggered at 9:02 P.M. When patrol cars arrived on the scene at 9:13 P.M., they found the point of entry to be a window in the studio; it had been pried open with some type of tool. A faint, smudged shoe print was found outside the window. Although the print was not clear, detectives measured the smudge and found it was large, but they could not pinpoint a shoe size. Found on the floor near the studio stage was a single yellow ticket stub with the words "April Fool's Dance" written on it.

The school's security camera, mounted at the end of the west wing hallway, captured two images of an intruder. At 9:02 P.M. and at 9:08 P.M., the tape showed that a single person entered and exited through the west wing window. The tape captured only the back of the intruder, who was wearing dark clothes. Shoulder-length hair could be seen sticking out from under a baseball cap.

Detectives secured the crime scene and made detailed notes, sketches, and photographs of the area around and in the school building. Now the case is in your hands. You will hear testimony from nearly a dozen people who have something to say about the crime. Use their information, the picture of the crime scene, and the skills you have acquired throughout this book to solve the case of the crushed cameras.

Activity Directions

1. Review the crime description; then study the "Crushed Cameras Crime Scene" drawing and review the detective's "Crushed Cameras Notebook" at the end of this package.
2. Listen to the witnesses, and take notes here:

Mr. Gladden, who lives in a house adjacent to the high school:

____

____

____

____

____

Principal Tennessee Brown of AHS:

____

____

____

____

____

Name ______________________________ Date ______________________

Science Sleuth Activity Package: The Case of the Crushed Cameras, *Cont'd.*

Mrs. Hernandez, teacher and activity sponsor:

____

____

____

____

____

Tabetha, weather girl for the *Cougar News* team:

____

____

____

____

____

Hosea, member of the anchor team:

____

____

____

____

____

Mike, member of the anchor team:

____

____

____

____

____

Julia, member of the anchor team:

____

____

____

____

____

Name ______________________________ Date ______________________

Science Sleuth Activity Package: The Case of the Crushed Cameras, *Cont'd.*

Chris, soccer player:

____

____

____

____

____

Jimmy, soccer player:

____

____

____

____

____

April Fool's Day Dance sponsor:

____

____

____

____

____

3. Now review all your notes and the information on each student at the end of this activity package. Each time you find a clue that links a suspect to the crime, put an X in the appropriate column of the logic table at the end of this activity.
4. When you finish the logic table, one suspect will have more Xs than the others. This person is most likely the culprit.

Questions for Discussion

1. Who had a motive to smash the cameras at AHS?
2. Who does not have a firm alibi for 9:00 P.M. on the night of the crime?
3. Who do you suspect destroyed the cameras at AHS?
4. Can you definitely rule out your other suspects, even if evidence seems to point to one person? Explain your answer.

Name ______________________________ Date ______________________

Science Sleuth Activity Package: The Case of the Crushed Cameras, *Cont'd.*

Logic Table for the Case of the Crushed Cameras

Suspects	Had an Alibi for 9:00 P.M. to 10:00 P.M.	Had a Car with ZNN on Tag	Had a Ticket Stub	Wears Large Shoes	Has Long Hair
Mrs. Hernandez					
Hosea					
Mike					
Julia					
Chris					
Jimmy					

Science Sleuth Activity Package: The Case of the Crushed Cameras, *Cont'd.*

Crushed Cameras Crime Scene

Science Sleuth Activity Package: The Case of Crushed Cameras, *Cont'd.*

Suspects:

— Mrs. Hernandez
Shoe: Ladies' 11.5
Car: Isuzu Rodeo / ZNN 32
Hair: Black - Shoulder Length

— Hosea
Shoe: Men's 11
Car: VW Beetle / PEN 400
Hair: Aburn - Crew Cut

— Mike
Shoe: Men's 12
Car: GMC Envoy / ZNN 657
Hair: Black - Spiked

— Julia
Shoe: Ladies' 5
Car: No Car - No License
Hair: Brown - Shoulder Length

— Chris
Show: Men's 11.5 D
Car: Ford Explorer / ANN 578
Hair: Blonde - Shoulder Length

— Jimmy
Shoe: Men's 10.5
Car: Ford Mustang / PEN 879
Hair: Black - Long

Crushed Cameras Notebook

Activity 6.6: The Case of *Star Trek* Art

Teacher Briefing

In this case from real life, students learn how to prioritize clues to help solve a case. There are not a great many clues, so you might consider writing them on cardboard and let the whole class decide which clues go where. However, this can also work as an individual or small group project.

Activity Preparation

- Make copies of the Science Sleuth Activity Package.
- Students will need scissors and tape.

First, Tell Your Students . . .

Many times, truth is stranger than fiction. You will read a story based on a true crime about the theft of three pieces of art. From the story and other information, you will decide which clues are important and which are not.

Activity Procedure

1. Distribute the Science Sleuth Activity Packages, and divide students into groups if you wish.
2. Pass out scissors.
3. Tell the students to cut "Clues on Statue Heist" in their activity package into separate strips and then arrange the clues in order of their importance.

Summary and Discussion

- Based on the clues, what do you think happened to Soni's artwork? *Answer:* Answers will vary. In reality, Soni's artwork was stolen in Los Angeles. In this version of the story, Cunningham was the thief. For reasons that are still not clear to detectives, Cunningham did not steal the art to sell it to art lovers (who would have paid a pretty penny for the works!). Instead, he sold the three metal artworks to metal recycling centers and was paid only for their scrap brass and copper contents. Fortunately, all three pieces were recovered by investigators before they were destroyed.
- Were all of the clues relevant to solving this case? *Answer:* Yes, in this case, but investigators do not know if the information they are gathering will be useful.
- Why might a detective collect clues that will not be useful in solving a case? *Answer:* In an effort to get all pertinent information, an investigator may gather some irrelevant material.
- Remove the two clues that you consider most instrumental in solving this case. Based on the remaining clues, could you reach the same conclusion? Why or why not? *Answer:* Answers will vary, and students will disagree. Each clue plays a vital link in understanding the event.

Name ______________________________ Date ______________________

Science Sleuth Activity Package: The Case of *Star Trek* Art

The Case

Artist Kewai Soni created the sculptures featured in the movie *Star Trek: Insurrection.* After the filming, the sculptures were stored in a studio near the artist's home. Because the statues were valued at about $30,000 each, Soni enclosed his studio in a tall, chain-link fence.

Despite his efforts to protect them, the metal artworks were stolen in three separate heists. After each robbery, the artist upgraded the security at his fenced-in studio, first adding a security system, then an extra row of barbed wire on top of the fence. Despite all of these precautions, the thief (or thieves) was still able to push the heavy pieces over the fence and load them into a truck. The only clues found at the scene were the footprints of size 12 work boots.

You have four primary suspects: Mr. Cheng, Mr. Cunningham, Ms. Fisk, and Mr. Lomas. In this activity, you will prioritize the clues and then use the clues to speculate on what might have happened to Soni's sculptures.

Clues on Statue Heist

Cheng, a professional art critic, always condemns Soni's work.

Cheng and Cunningham are both physically strong men.

Cheng drives a compact car. Cunningham drives a pickup truck. Fisk drives a utility truck. Lomas doesn't own a car; he takes the bus around town.

Cheng had a photograph of Soni's sculptures in his pocket when he was questioned by police.

When questioned by police, Cunningham had a receipt from a metal recycling dealer for $9.10.

At the time of questioning, in Fisk's coat pocket there was a map of the section of town where Soni's studio is located.

Lomas had movie ticket stubs to *Star Trek* in his pocket when police questioned him.

Fisk and Cheng, who have night jobs, were both seen at their offices by coworkers on the nights of the thefts.

Both Cunningham and Lomas are having serious financial difficulties.

Both Cunningham and Lomas own a pair of size 12 work boots.

Name ______________________________ Date ______________________

Science Sleuth Activity Package: The Case of *Star Trek* Art, *Cont'd.*

Activity Directions

1. Cut the clues in the Clues on Statue Heist into separate strips.
2. Arrange the clues in order of their importance in solving this crime.
3. Tape the prioritized clues here:

Questions for Discussion

1. Based on the clues, what do you think happened to Soni's artwork?
2. Were all of the clues relevant to solving this case?
3. Why might a detective collect clues that will not be useful in solving a case?
4. Remove the two clues that you consider most instrumental in solving this case. Based on the remaining clues, could you reach the same conclusion? Why or why not?

Activity 6.7: The Case of the Atlanta Car Thefts

Teacher Briefing

Examining evidence to detect patterns is an important skill for all the work students will do as they move forward in their education. If you can get someone to enlarge the maps, student groups will be able to work easily with them.

Activity Preparation

- Make copies of the Science Sleuth Activity Package.
- Each student or student group will need:

  Map backed on cardboard and/or enlarged
  Pushpins
  Yarn

First, Tell Your Students . . .

Over the past few months, nine expensive cars have been stolen in the Atlanta area. In each case, the car was stolen after it was left with a valet for parking. An inventory of the thefts includes more than $1 million worth of vehicles. The National Insurance Crime Bureau is investigating, and you have an opportunity to assist.

The working theory is that a ring of car thieves is moving from one part of the city to another. Once a car is valet-parked, one of the thieves slips into the parking lot, opens the car, hot-wires the ignition, and drives off. The thieves seal the cars in huge wooden boxes and ship them to Venezuela for resale. Once they reach South America, each car is given a new vehicle identification number. Unless the National Insurance Crime Bureau is able to stop the theft before shipment takes place, chances of recovering the cars are very slim.

The National Insurance Crime Bureau has asked you to see if you can find any patterns in the perpetrators' behavior that may help the bureau make an arrest.

Activity Procedure

1. Distribute the Science Sleuth Activity Packages and other materials, and divide students into working groups as you choose.
2. Instruct students to follow the directions in their activity package.

Summary and Discussion

- What pattern did you find in the occurrence of car thefts? Based on this pattern, where do you predict that the next theft will occur? *Answer:* The locations of the thefts form a star pattern. Based on this pattern, the next theft will most likely occur eleven miles southwest of Atlanta in an area two and a half miles south of Interstate 20.
- What pattern did you find in the dates of the thefts? Based on this pattern, when do you predict that the next theft will take place? *Answer:* Initially, the thefts occurred every nine or ten days. Later they were more spaced out, usually occurring every twelve to thirteen days. Based on this information, the next theft will occur on August 6 or 7.
- Is there a pattern in the types of cars stolen? If so, describe it. Is there a pattern in the colors of cars stolen? If so, describe it. What color and kind of car do you think will be stolen next? *Answer:* Every other car is a Ferrari. Red cars are stolen on the east side of town and silver cars on the west side. A silver Ferrari will probably be next.
- How can investigators use patterns to help them catch perpetrators? *Answer:* By discovering patterns in a perpetrator's behavior, an investigator may be able to predict the perpetrator's next move.

Name ______________________________ Date ______________________

Science Sleuth Activity Package: The Case of the Atlanta Car Thefts

The Case

Over the past few months, nine expensive cars have been stolen in the Atlanta area. In each case, the car was stolen after it was left with a valet for parking. An inventory of the thefts includes more than $1 million worth of vehicles (see the "Atlanta Car Thefts" list at the end of this package). The National Insurance Crime Bureau is investigating, and you have an opportunity to assist.

The working theory is that a ring of car thieves is moving from one part of the city to another. Once a car is valet-parked, one of the thieves slips into the parking lot, opens the car, hot-wires the ignition, and drives off. The thieves seal the cars in huge wooden boxes and ship them to Venezuela for resale. Once they reach South America, each car is given a new vehicle identification number. Unless the National Insurance Crime Bureau is able to stop the theft before shipment takes place, chances of recovering the cars are very slim.

The National Insurance Crime Bureau has asked you to see if you can find any patterns in the perpetrators' behavior that may help the bureau make an arrest.

Activity Directions

1. Examine the map of Atlanta at the end of this package.
2. Refer to the "Atlanta Car Thefts" list at the end of this package, to find the location of the first car theft. Mark this location on the map with a pushpin.
3. Follow the same procedure to mark the locations of the other eight car thefts on the map.
4. Tie one end of yarn around one of the pushpins (it does not matter which pin you select). Wrap the yarn around the other pushpins to help you visualize a geometrical pattern created by the locations of the thefts. If you don't see a pattern the first time you try this, unwrap the yarn and try it again. Once you discover a pattern, record it here.

   ____

Name ______________________________ Date ______________________

Science Sleuth Activity Package: The Case of the Atlanta Car Thefts, *Cont'd.*

5. In the "Atlanta Car Thefts" list, examine the dates of the thefts. Determine how many days elapsed between each theft. Record the pattern of these dates here.

____

____

____

____

6. Examine the types of the cars in the "Atlanta Car Thefts" list. Determine if there is a pattern to the types of cars stolen.

____

____

____

____

7. Examine the colors of the cars in the "Atlanta Car Thefts" list. Determine if there is a pattern to the colors of cars stolen.

____

____

____

____

Name ______________________ Date ______________________

Science Sleuth Activity Package: The Case of the Atlanta Car Thefts, *Cont'd.*

Atlanta Car Thefts

Vehicle Stolen	Date	Location
1. Porsche 911 GT2, Silver	May 2	Powder Springs—16 miles NW of downtown Atlanta
2. Ferrari 612 Scaglietti, Taupe	May 12	Hapeville—6 miles S of downtown Atlanta
3. Alfa Romeo Monza Spider, Black	May 21	Roswell—17 miles N of downtown Atlanta
4. Ferrari 575M Maranello, Red	May 31	Snellville—23 miles NE of downtown Atlanta
5. Porsche 911 Twin Turbo, Blue	June 10	An isolated region 2 miles S of Vinings; Vinings is 9 miles NW of downtown Atlanta
6. Ferrari Enzo Coup, Red	June 19	Intersection of hwy 12 and 285, 10 miles due east of downtown Atlanta
7. Rolls Royce Phantom, Red	June 31	11 miles due east of Stockbridge; Stockbridge is SE of downtown Atlanta
8. Ferrari 275 GTB/C, Red	July 12	Halfway between North Atlanta and Clarkston; these 2 towns are NE of downtown Atlanta
9. Lamborghini Murciélago, Silver	July 25	Palmetto, 23 miles SW of Atlanta

Science Sleuth Activity Package: The Case of the Atlanta Car Theft, *Cont'd.*

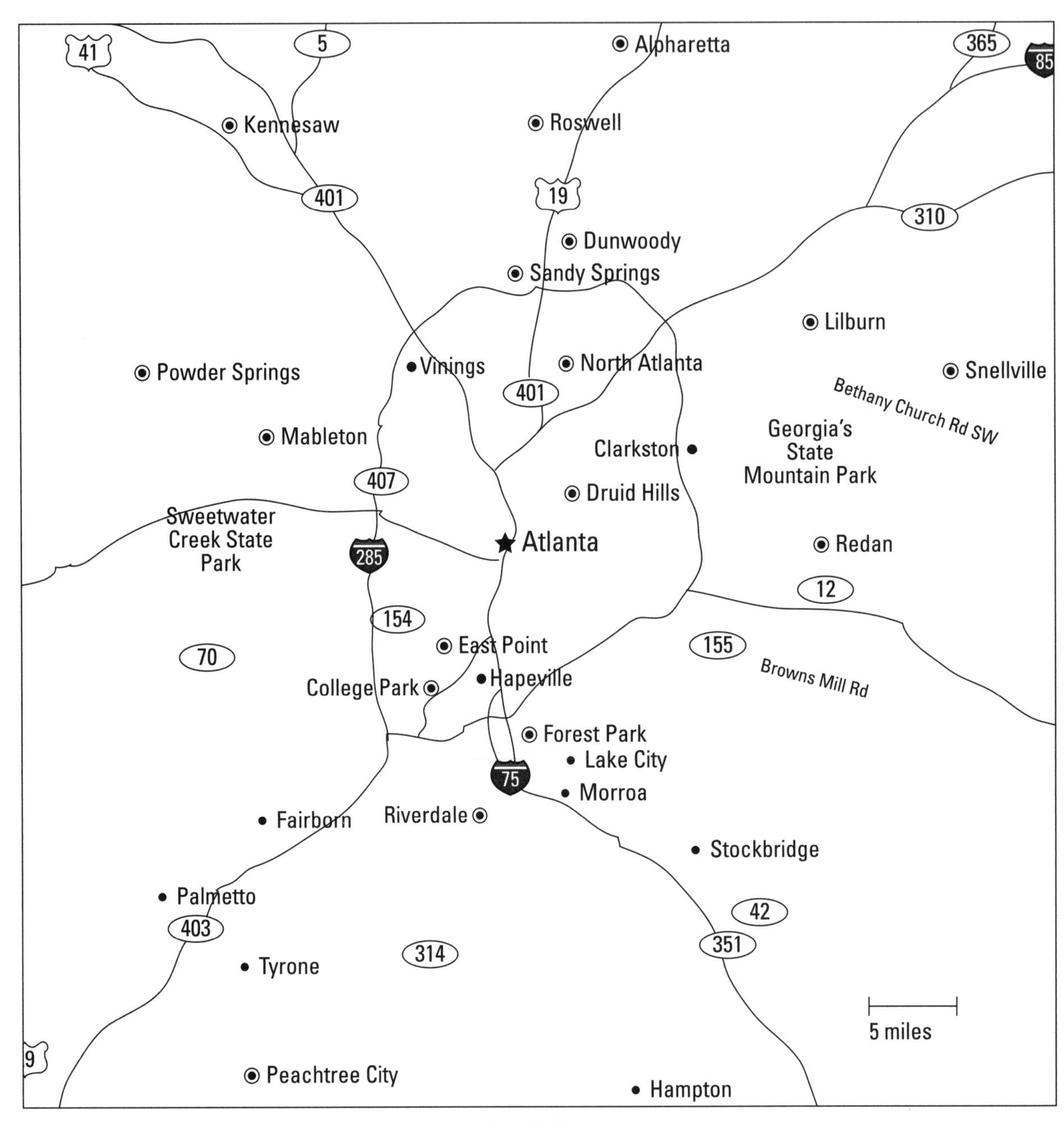

Map of Atlanta

Activity 6.8: The Budget Crunch

Teacher Briefing

This activity asks students to combine what they've learned about detective work and research with some common sense about expenses. Students make decisions on which evidence to test based on costs. This activity can easily be done in groups.

Activity Preparation

- Make copies of the Science Sleuth Activity Package.
- Students are asked to do research online or in books about the kinds of tests listed in "Costs of Investigative Procedures" in their package. You may want to do this research and make copies of it available to students, or you can make it part of your introductory remarks for this exercise.

First, Tell Your Students . . .

The good news is that you've been assigned to a new case! The bad news is that you've got to solve it with limited resources. The budget is tight, and you have been allotted only five hundred dollars to spend on tests and procedures. For this reason, you must select the tests that can provide you with the most information for your dollar.

Activity Procedure

1. Distribute the Science Sleuth Activity Packages. If you would like your students to work in groups, assign them.
2. Receive and review the student budgets.

Summary and Discussion

- What is your ideal plan for investigating this crime? *Answer:* Ideally, an investigator might want to conduct every test available.
- How is this plan affected by the budget? *Answer:* The budget limits the number of tests that can be conducted.
- How could a tight budget interfere with your ability to solve a crime? *Answer:* A tight budget could restrict the kinds of tests investigators could do, therefore limiting their information about the case.

Name ______________________________ Date ______________________

Science Sleuth Activity Package: The Budget Crunch

The Case

Sparky, a purebred border collie, has been stolen from his kennel. Sparky belongs to Frank Wilson and his mother, Sarah. While Sarah works and Frank attends school, Sparky spends the day in his kennel. As soon as Frank gets home, he unlocks the kennel and takes Sparky for a walk. The school bus drops Frank off at precisely 3:55 P.M. each day.

On Friday, the kennel door was open when Frank got home. Frank rushed to the house, where he found the back door ajar, and he called 911. Then he immediately called his mom at work to let her know what had happened and that there was no sign of Sparky.

Interviews with neighbors provide very little useful information. Mr. Dixon, who lives next door, remembers seeing a white Dodge panel truck in the Wilsons' yard when he fixed his lunch at noon. He didn't pay too much attention to the truck because the Wilsons' house is for sale, and he figured that it belonged to someone looking over the property. All other neighbors were at work.

At the crime scene, evidence is scanty. The footprints are shown in the sketch of the crime scene, "Sparky's Disappearance," at the end of this package. There was a little blood on the metal pole where the kennel door latch is located. Caught in the fence near the blood was a piece of plaid fabric, a few long black hairs, and some fur that looks as if it might belong to Sparky.

In the house, there are muddy footprints leading from the back door to the coat rack where Sparky's leash was usually hung. The back door was open, and the key that usually stays under the back door mat was missing.

Your job is to consider the best way to solve this crime, then learn about the tests and procedures that are available to you and decide which ones you can afford to use to help solve the case of Sparky's disappearance.

Activity Directions

1. Review the story of this crime and look at the drawing of the crime scene, "Sparky's Disappearance."
2. Examine the tests and procedures listed in the first column of the "Costs of Investigative Procedures." Before you begin selecting tests and procedures that you would like to have performed, you need to think about the evidence that you have and then learn what kind of information you might gain from each test. Use the Internet, reference books, or earlier activities in this book to make sure you understand the purpose of each test. For example, if you have a sample of blood, you may want to know who it belongs to. To find out, you could order a DNA analysis or a blood typing. DNA analysis provides more information than blood typing, but blood typing is less expensive.
3. Given the evidence and your knowledge about the tests and procedures, draw up a plan for investigating the case, listing each test or procedure in a separate line of the data table. Use the data table at the end of this package.

Name ______________________ Date ______________________

Science Sleuth Activity Package: The Budget Crunch, *Cont'd.*

4. Now, using the "Costs of Investigative Procedures" list at the end of this package, figure out what your plan would cost. To do so, add together the price of each test and calculate the total.
5. If the cost is under $500, you are finished. Submit the plan to your teacher for approval.
6. If the cost of your plan exceeds $500, you will need to eliminate some of the cost.
7. Remember that you cannot afford all of the tests. Decide which tests are most important so that you can keep costs in line with your budget.

Name ______________________ Date ______________________

Science Sleuth Activity Package: The Budget Crunch, *Cont'd.*

Data Table for the Budget Crunch

Plan to Solve Sparky's Disappearance	
Test or Procedure	**Cost**

Sparky's Disappearance

Name ______________________________ Date ______________________

Science Sleuth Activity Package: The Budget Crunch, *Cont'd.*

Costs of Investigative Procedures

Tests and Procedures	**Description of Test/ Procedure**	**Cost of Test/ Procedure**
DNA analysis		$250
Blood typing		$100
Analysis of blood splatter		$100
Cast made of shoe print		$ 75
Interpretation of cast by expert		$ 75
Cast made of tire print		$ 75
Interpretation of cast by expert		$ 75
Examination of fiber evidence, per fiber		$ 30
Examination of hair evidence, per hair		$ 30
Fingerprinting		$ 50
Ballistics test		$100
Gunshot residue test		$ 75
Soil analysis		$100
Drug analysis		$100
Handwriting analysis		$ 75
Paper chromatography		$100
Ultraviolet light		$ 40
Entomology report		$100
Analysis of a pedigree		$ 75

Activity 6.9: Comparing Cases—Homework Assignment

Teacher Notes

This homework assignment should follow classroom discussion of Venn diagrams.

Answer Key

1. The two cases share several characteristics:
   Murder of a man
   A man in a hat
   Outdoor setting
   Suspect fleeing toward wooded area
   Girabaldi, Turin, and Gladney
2. The two cases are unique in several ways:
   One man was stabbed; the other was shot.
   One man was lying on the ground, the other sitting on a bench.
   One murder occurred in a neighborhood, the other in a public park.
   One murder occurred at night, the other in the daytime.
3. Students may find that the victim's association with Girabaldi, Turin, and Gladney, and the sighting of a man in a green hat, link the crimes.
4. Answers will vary but might include comparing and contrasting information or data gathered in an experiment.

Name ______________________________ Date ______________________

Homework Assignment: Comparing Cases

In this activity, you will learn how to use a graphic organizer, the Venn diagram, to help you evaluate data.

Background

During an investigation, a detective accumulates a lot of information. Organizing these data helps an investigator keep track of what is known, what information is needed, and what needs to be done next. One method of organizing data is called a *Venn diagram.*

A Venn diagram is a graphic organizer that shows how much two groups are alike and how much they are different. The diagram is made of two overlapping circles, like the ones shown in the Venn diagram included in this homework package. To use a Venn diagram in detective work, in sections A and B, you write facts that are unique to each situation. In section C, you record information that is common to both situations.

In this assignment, you will examine the crime scenes and reports from two different cases. The scenes have some points in common, but in many ways they are different. You will use a Venn diagram to compare and contrast the elements of these two cases.

Activity Directions

1. Put two pieces of paper on your desk. Label one piece of paper as A and the other as B.
2. Look at the "Sketch of Crime Scene 1" at the end of this package.
3. On paper A, write down facts that you learn from looking at that drawing.
4. Then read the interview section of the "Report on the Murder of Lee Davis." Add facts about this crime that you learn from the interview to paper A.
5. Look at the "Sketch of Crime Scene 2."
6. On paper B, write down facts that you learn from your observation.
7. Read the interview section of the "Report on the Murder of Nate Brooks." Add these facts to your current list on paper B.
8. Compare the two lists of facts. On list A, circle facts that you can also find on list B.
9. On a big sheet of paper, draw a large Venn diagram. You will want extra-large paper, maybe poster board.
10. In section C of the Venn diagram, write the facts that you circled.
11. Transfer the list of facts on paper A to section A of the Venn diagram; do not transfer any facts that are circled.
12. Transfer the list of facts on paper B to section B of the Venn diagram; do not transfer any facts that are circled.

Name ______________________ Date ______________

Homework Assignment: Comparing Cases, *Cont'd.*

Questions to Answer

1. What do these two crimes have in common?

2. In what ways are the crimes different from each other?

3. After comparing and contrasting information from these two crimes, do you think that they are related in any way? Explain your reasoning.

4. How might a detective use a Venn diagram to help figure out the next steps in solving a crime?

Homework Assignment: Comparing Cases, *Cont'd.*

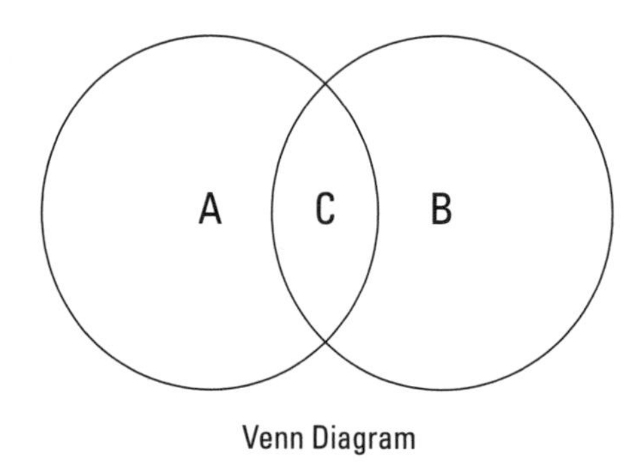

Venn Diagram

Sketch of Crime Scene 1

Homework Assignment: Comparing Cases, *Cont'd.*

Sketch of Crime Scene 2

Homework Assignment: Comparing Cases, *Cont'd.*

Report on the Murder of Lee Davis

Crime scene	Location: State Road 100, 5 miles south of Pleasantville Time: 10:01 P.M. Location of the body: 5'3" from the edge of the road, 8'9" from a tree Position of the body: Lying face up Weather: 52°F, moonless night
Description of victim	The victim was dead when police arrived at the scene. He had been stabbed in the chest with a knife that has a 3" blade. A wallet found on the victim identifies him as Alan Girabaldi, 31 years old, and a resident of Pleasantville.
Interviews at crime scene	*Nell Rockham,* neighbor of Mr. Girabaldi: "I live in that first house across the street. I was taking out the trash when I saw a man in a green hat call out to Mr. Girabaldi. Alan was walking toward that tree, and he stopped and waited for the man to catch up—I thought they were friends or something. Well, the man suddenly pulled a long knife from somewhere and stabbed it into Mr. Girabaldi's chest! I was so shocked that I screamed. The man ran toward the woods and jumped on a bicycle leaning against a tree. I dashed inside to call the police. I was afraid to stay outside with a killer on the loose."
	Felicity Strong, neighbor: "I heard a bloodcurdling scream and ran out the front door to see what was going on. That's when I saw our neighbor lying on the ground with a knife sticking out of his chest. I could see someone running toward those trees, but I don't know who it was. The person seemed to be wearing some type of hat or hood."
	Nona Girabaldi, wife: "Alan went outside for his evening walk a little before 10:00 P.M.; he's been doing this a lot lately. He rarely gets home before 7:30, and by the time we eat dinner, it's pretty late. He usually walks about 45 minutes, comes in and showers, then goes to bed. That night, he didn't come inside. The next thing I know, there's a policeman at my door telling me that Alan is dead!"
Interviews to establish background information on the victims	*Floyd Turin,* business: "I've worked with Alan Girabaldi for the last twelve years at our office, Girabaldi, Turin, and Gladney. Alan did not have any enemies; well, not true enemies. There were several clients who complained that Alan didn't save them enough money on their income taxes. And of course, there's the long-term battle between Alan and Lynette. They've been arguing for years about the way bonuses are passed out around here. Lynette feels like she is not getting her fair share of bonus earnings."
	Lynette Gladney, business partner: "Well, it's no secret. Alan and I have argued on several occasions. I've always felt like Alan did not treat Floyd and me fairly in terms of year-end bonuses. Alan refused to discuss the matter with me and told me that the decision is entirely up to him. I disagreed, but couldn't do much about it. He is, or was, the major stockholder."

Homework Assignment: Comparing Cases, *Cont'd.*

Report on the Murder of Nate Brooks

Crime scene	Location: City park, downtown Pleasantville Time: Noon Location of the body: 2′ from the sidewalk, 50′ from the entrance to the park. Position of the body: Sitting on a park bench Weather: 81°F, partly cloudy
Description of the victim	A male victim was found sitting on a park bench. He was dead when police arrived, apparently from a gunshot wound to the head. The only identification on him was a voter registration card naming him as Nate Brooks.
Interviews at crime scene	*Gus Long,* retired nurse: "When I walked by, the man on the bench was reading something. I heard two cracking sounds that sounded like gunshots, turned around, and saw a man in a green hat drop a gun and run toward those trees. I went over to the man on the bench, but he was already dead."
	Lila Salton, pet sitter: "I always walk the dogs from 11:30 A.M. to 12:30 P.M. As I approached the bench, I saw a man running toward the figure seated on the bench. That's when I knew something was wrong. When I got close, I could see that the man on the bench was bleeding and there was a gun lying on the ground. I turned around and ran in the opposite direction. I asked the first person I met to call the police!"
Interview to establish background information on the victim	*Terrence Webb,* accounting assistant: "I work at Girabaldi, Turin, and Gladney with Mr. Brooks, but I don't know him well. He works, or used to work, in the mailroom. He seemed like a nice guy."
	Lynette Gladney, business partner at Girabaldi, Turin, and Gladney: "I met Mr. Brooks at the last Christmas party, but I didn't really know him. He was pretty quiet."

Activity 6.10: The Sherlock in You—Homework Assignment

Teacher Notes

This activity involves quite a bit of work: reading a Sherlock Holmes novel and writing a new ending. It's a great assignment for creative students and is definitely in the "special project" category.

Name ____________________ Date ____________________

Homework Assignment: The Sherlock in You

Have you ever wanted to be an author? Or a detective? In this homework assignment, you get to do both.

Materials You'll Need

- Novel or story by Sir Arthur Conan Doyle
- Access to a computer *or* pen or pencil and paper

Background

Almost everyone has heard of Sherlock Holmes, ace detective. Holmes was a fictional character, a creation of Arthur Conan Doyle, an English physician. Doyle wrote his first Sherlock Holmes study, *A Study in Scarlet,* in 1887. In every novel or story that followed, Doyle featured Sherlock Holmes as a crime solver extraordinaire who used the powers of deduction and forensic science to solve his cases. In his novels, Doyle popularized the concept of investigation.

The wit and wisdom of Holmes is seen in all of his stories. In *The Sign of the Four,* Holmes explained the art of solving crimes simply: "Eliminate all other factors, and the one which remains must be the truth." In *A Scandal in Bohemia,* he pointed out that "it is a capital mistake to theorize before one has data. Insensibly one begins to twist facts to suit theories, instead of theories to suit facts." Holmes depended on logic and reasoning and in *Adventure of the Blue Carbuncle,* he admonished his sidekick, Dr. Watson, for having too few of these qualities: "On the contrary, Watson, you can see everything. You fail, however, to reason from what you see. You are too timid in drawing your inferences."

Your job is to read the first half of a Sherlock Holmes story or novel written by Sir Arthur Conan Doyle and write your own ending.

Activity Directions

1. Select one of the Sherlock Holmes novels written by Sir Arthur Conan Doyle.
2. Read only the first half of the story or book. As you read, fill in the data table at the end of this package.
3. After reading the first half of the book and completing the data table, write a two- to three-page conclusion to the novel. In your conclusion, be sure to explain the following:

   How Holmes solves the case, including what kind of forensic evidence and logical thinking he uses

   What happens to each character in the novel
4. Read the rest of the book or story.

Name ______________________ Date ______________

Homework Assignment: The Sherlock in You, *Cont'd.*

Questions to Answer

1. After reading the first half of the book, what clues or evidence did you add to complete the story?

2. After reading the entire book or story, did you draw the same conclusions as Sherlock Holmes? Explain your answer.

3. How does a good understanding of forensic science and the scientific method help an author write a convincing crime novel or story?

Name ______________________ Date ______________________

Homework Assignment: The Sherlock in You, *Cont'd.*

Data Table for the Sherlock in You

Name of the book or story you selected

Names and descriptions of characters

Mystery that Holmes is trying to solve

Glossary

CRIME SCENE DO NOT CROSS CRIME SCENE DO NOT CROSS CRIME SCENE DO NOT CROSS CRIME SCENE DO NOT CROSS CRIME SCENE DO NOT CROSS CRIME SCENE DO NOT CROSS

acceleration A change in velocity over time.

acid rain Precipitation with a pH below 5.0.

amino acid A molecule that contains an amino group and a carboxylic acid group; a subunit of a protein.

arch A fingerprint pattern in which ridges enter from one side, exit on the opposite side, and are slightly raised in the middle.

associative memory technique A method of remembering items that associates the items to be remembered with something else.

capillary action The movement of a liquid up a narrow tube against the force of gravity.

carrier An individual who carries, but does not express, a genetic trait.

cast A shape created by pouring a liquid or plastic material into an impression and allowing the material to harden.

catalyst A chemical that speeds up or slows down a chemical reaction.

cerebral cortex The outermost, folded region of the brain of a vertebrate.

chemical reaction A change in which the molecules of matter are rearranged and a new substance is formed.

chromatogram In paper chromatography, a strip of paper on which components of a mixture are dispersed.

chromatography A chemical technique for separating complex mixtures based on the mobility of the components of the mixtures.

cilia Microscopic hairlike structures on some cells.

closed question A question that has a yes or no answer.

clue Evidence that helps solve a problem.

code A system of signals or symbols used for communication.

concentric fractures Breaks in glass that form in approximately a circular pattern around the point of impact.

cones One of two types of light-sensitive cells in the retina of the eye; cones are not functional in dim light, but are sensitive to color.

cornea The transparent, dome-shaped covering on the front of the eye.

corroborate To strengthen by supplying support or evidence.

cortex The middle layer of a strand of hair located between the cuticle and medulla.

crime scene The place where an illegal act occurs and the source of evidence needed to help solve the crime.

crush mark A tool mark that compresses the ends of a material together.

cuticle The outermost layer of a strand of hair.

deductive reasoning The type of reasoning in which one draws conclusions based on known facts.

direct question A question that requires an answer.

DNA evidence Proof based on DNA, the genetic code that is unique to each person.

DNA extraction The process of removing DNA from the nuclei of cells such as those in blood and saliva.

DNA fingerprint A pattern that shows the unique DNA of an individual and can be used as identification.

dominant trait A genetic trait that masks the presence of a recessive trait.

drag A force that opposes the motion of an object.

endothermic A reaction that absorbs heat.

entomology The study of insects.

enzyme An organic molecule that slows down or speeds up chemical reactions in living things.

evidence Anything that provides proof.

exothermic A reaction that gives off heat.

experiment A set of procedures and observations that sets out to prove or disprove a hypothesis.

experimental procedure The steps of an experiment.

experimental results The raw data produced by an experiment.

eyewitness A person who has firsthand knowledge of an event.

fat A class of food whose molecules contain fatty acids.

femur The thigh bone.

fingerprint An impression made by the papillary ridges on the ends of the fingers and thumbs.

force An action that causes a mass to accelerate.

forensic scientist A person who uses several fields of science to help answer questions of interest to the legal system.

fossil fuel A fuel such as coal or oil that was made from the remains of ancient plants and animals.

friction ridges Fine lines or ridges found on the epidermis of the hands and feet that reduce friction.

gel electrophoresis A technique that separates molecules based on their size and molecular weight.

gene A section of DNA that codes for a trait.

genetics The study of inheritance of traits.

germinate To emerge from a dormant or resting state.

handwriting analysis The study of the style, lettering, content, spacing, and paper used to created a document.

handwriting sample An example of a person's handwriting that can be compared to a sample of handwriting from an unknown source.

hippocampus The section of the brain responsible for memory.

hypothesis A proposed explanation that can be tested.

impression mark An imprint or stamp in a material.

instar A developmental stage of an insect.

iris The part of the eye that regulates the amount of light that strikes the retina.

larva An immature, wormlike developmental stage of an insect.

latent prints Impressions that are not visible to the eye that are made by the fingers, hands, or feet of an individual.

leading question One that suggests a right answer or leads a person toward a particular answer.

legend An explanation of symbols on a chart or map.

lens A transparent material that can focus rays of light.

long-term memory The part of the brain that stores information for extended periods of time.

loop A fingerprint pattern in which ridges enter from one side, form a loop or swirl shape, then exit on the same side.

magnification The act of enlarging.

mass The amount of matter in an object.

medulla The innermost layer of a strand of hair.

memory The retention of information over time.

mixture Matter made up of two or more different substances.

Morse code A code made up of various dots and dashes that is used to communicate.

multistrike mark A tool mark that shows repeated movement, like the back and forth movements of a saw.

nasal mucosa The uppermost region of the nasal cavity that contains olfactory epithelium.

neuron A nerve cell; a cell that is capable of carrying an electrical stimulus.

nucleotide A molecule of DNA made up of a sugar, a base, and a phosphate group.

motion The process of a change in position of an object.

odorant A particle that can be detected by the olfactory system.

olfactory epithelium Tissue that lines the top of the nasal cavity.

olfactory system The body system that senses odors.

open question One that begins with "how," "why," "when," or some other word that permits the person to expand on his or her answer; there is no yes or no answer to this question.

optic nerve The nerve that carries visual information from the retina to the brain.

perception An awareness of the environment.

pH A measure of the acidity or alkalinity of a substance on a number scale from 0 to 14, where 7 is the neutral point.

phase of matter A state or condition of matter: solid, liquid, or gas.

physical change A change in which matter retains its chemical properties.

physical property A property of matter that can be detected through the five senses: sight, touch, sound, smell, and taste.

pigment A coloring material.

probing question A question that follows a certain line of thought to get at a fine point.

protease An enzyme that breaks down protein.

protein A molecule made of amino acids that are joined by peptide bonds.

pupa A period of development of an insect when the larval stage undergoes changes within a protective covering.

pupil The opening in the eye through which light passes to the retina.

radial fractures Breaks in glass that form straight lines extending from the point of impact.

reagent A substance used because of its chemical properties.

recessive trait A trait that is masked by the presence of a dominant trait.

restriction enzyme An enzyme that can cut a strand of DNA at a specific nucleotide sequence.

retina The region in the back of the eyeball where light-sensitive rods and cones are located.

rhetorical question A question asked for a reason other than to get an answer to the question.

rods One of two types of light-sensitive cells in the retina of the eye; rods are sensitive to dim light but are not receptive to color.

scale drawing A representation in which objects and distances are drawn to scale.

scientific method A problem-solving procedure in which a person states a problem or question, develops a plausible hypothesis, conducts an experiment to test that hypothesis, collects data from the experiment, and then draws conclusions that verify or disprove the hypothesis.

scrubbers Devices on smokestacks of factories and coal-powered electrical plants that reduce the amount of sulfur released into the atmosphere, and therefore reduce the production of acid rain.

sex-linked trait A genetic trait carried on one of the sex chromosomes, usually the X.

short-term memory The part of the brain that stores a small amount of information for thirty to forty seconds.

sizing Material used to coat paper that prevents that paper from absorbing too much ink or water.

speed The distance an object travels in a given period of time.

striated (or dynamic) mark A tool mark in which two objects move past one another and the harder object makes a mark in the softer one.

succession The change in species found in a region over time.

synthetic Man-made material.

ten code A set of code words used in police work to represent certain phrases.

tool marks Marks such as scratches or impressions left by tools and weapons.

top-of-the-letter handwriting analysis A method of analyzing handwriting that marks the top of each letter in a word or phrase for comparative purposes.

trait A characteristic of an organism.

ultraviolet (UV) light Part of the electromagnetic spectrum whose wavelength is shorter than visible light.

variable The factor that changes during an experiment.

whorl A pattern made up of a circle that does not enter or exit on either side of the fingerprint.

X chromosome Female sex chromosome.

Y chromosome Male sex chromosome.

Resources for the Classroom

Web Pages

Adventures of Cyberbee. Provides a lot of great forensic science activities such as Teeth Impressions and Foot to Height for young students. http://www.cyberbee.com/.

Archaeological Detectives. An activity on using bones to apply science techniques to solving problems. http://www.cedu.niu.edu/scied/student/2003_spring/4_blue/crime_lab_chemistry.htm.

The Case of the Burglarized Bronco Fan. A forensic activity provided by the Hughes Undergraduate Biological Science Education Initiative. http://www.colorado.edu/Outreach/BSI/pdfs/for_burglarized.pdf.

The Case of the Missing Mascot. A fun investigation that involves chromatography, fingerprinting, chemical detection, blood analysis, and physical evidence. http://educ.queensu.ca/~science/main/concept/chem/c09/C09laae0.htm.

A Case of Murder: A Forensic Science Unit. Activities for lab and class provided by teacher Thea Sinclair. http://www.accessexcellence.org/AE/ATG/data/released/0157-theasinclair/.

Case Teaching Notes for "Dem Bones: Forensic Resurrection of a Skeleton." Notes and classroom activities on forensic examination of bones by Alease Bruce at the University of Massachusetts, Lowell. http://ublib.buffalo.edu/libraries/projects/cases/bones/bones_notes.html.

Concepts/Skills Development. Simple forensic chemistry labs from Oklahoma State University. http://intro.chem.okstate.edu/ChemSource/Forensic/forechem8.htm.

DNA Fingerprinting: You Be the Judge! An Access Excellence activity on how to perform and analyze DNA fingerprinting. http://www.accessexcellence.org/AE/AEPC/WWC/1992/DNA_printing.html.

Explore More Guides to Critical Thinking. Classroom activities on critical thinking provided by Iowa Public Television. http://www3.iptv.org/exploreMore/.

Forensic Entomology. Explains how scientists use insects to help determine time of death. Established by the Brazoria County (Texas) Sheriff's Department. http://www.brazoria-county.com/sheriff/id/bugs/time_of_death.htm.

Forensic Fact Files. A teacher-friendly site on a wide range of forensic topics. http://www.nifs.com.au/FactFiles/topics.asp.

Forensic Science. Offers interesting case studies and protocols of experiments. http://www.shodor.org/succeed/forensic/.

Forensic Science Activities. Offers a variety of lesson plans based on forensic concepts. http://www.geocities.com/sseagraves/forensicscienceactivities.htm.

Handbook of Forensic Services Shoe and Tire Tread Examinations. Explains how to perform many forensic tests. Provided by the U.S. Department of Justice. http://www.fbi.gov/hq/lab/handbook/intro14.htm.

Issues of the Environment: Acid Rain. Several activities on how to investigate the effects of acid rain. http://www.necc.mass.edu/mrvis/Mr1_6/start.htm.

The Laundry Detergent Race: Investigating Genetically Engineered Enzymes. A home or classroom investigation adapted from the *American Museum of Natural History.* http://www.msichicago.org/exhibit/genetics/activity_pages/detergents.html.

Nova Teachers Guide, Forensics. Provides historical information about famous crimes that have been solved using modern forensic techniques; offers several forensic classroom activities. http://www.pbs.org/wgbh/nova/teachers/resources/subj_04_00.html.

Problem Solving: Dots, Symbols, Words, and Proteins. A great activity on logical thinking by teacher MaryLouise Sims. http://www.iit.edu/~smile/bi8715.html.

Uncovering the Evidence. A site that offers online forensic activities for students. http://www.studio2b.org/lounge/gs_stuff/ip_evidence.asp.

Who Did It? A crime scene activity that uses forensic science and laboratory skills. http://www.teachersfirst.com/lessons/forensics/tools-lab.html.

Books

Rainis, K. G. *Crime-Solving Science Projects.* Berkeley Heights, N.J.: Enslow, 2000.

Treat, L. *Crime and Puzzlement.* Boston: Godine, 1981.

Wiese, J. *Detective Science.* Hoboken, N.J.: Wiley, 1996.

Other Books of Interest

Partners in Crime

Integrating Language Arts and Forensic Science, Grades 5–8

E.K. Hein

Paper

ISBN: 0-7879-6993-1

"Hein is an innovative and entrepreneurial educator whose cross-curriculum approach paves the way for learning built on creative problem-solving and practical application of knowledge. This model exemplifies what is possible when teachers open the classroom to educational and community collaboration."

—Patricia M. Roberts, director, Institute for Educational Excellence and Entrepreneurship, College of Education, West Chester University

Partners in Crime offers middle school teachers an innovative and highly engaging resource for integrating language arts and science strategies that will challenge students while meeting standardized learning goals. With a creative approach of focusing on the practical application of critical thinking, problem solving, and prose nonfiction expression, *Partners in Crime* engages your students by asking them to solve a crime using the skills of forensic science while simultaneously teaching them key concepts in language arts. As flexible as it is creative, *Partners in Crime* can be used for a variety of classroom settings whether as a single activity, weekly lesson, full unit, or school and community project.

The activities in *Partners in Crime* can also help you build teamwork by tapping into your school community, resources, and technology. Throughout the book, your students are encouraged to conduct original research and challenged to draw conclusions based upon their ability to weigh evidence. *Partners in Crime* also contains suggestions for helping you and your students make connections with local law enforcement that will provide support for deeper understanding of the exercises. The book is filled with ideas for encouraging students to create written reports, presentations, films, and videos. The book also includes activities and guidelines for benchmarking student performance during and after each unit.

E.K. Hein is a middle school language arts teacher in the suburbs of Philadelphia, Pennsylvania. He has taught language arts and English skills to students for eight years. In 2002 his "Investigating Crime Scenes in Literature" was featured in *The Wall Street Journal* as a model for innovative, engaging curriculum.

Other Books of Interest

Family Science

Activities, Projects, and Games That Get Everyone Excited About Science!

Sandra Markle

Paper

ISBN: 0-471-65197-4

Why should your kids have all the fun? In *Family Science*, award-winning author and science educator Sandra Markle presents more than 200 safe, easy-to-do science activities for entire families to enjoy together.

Divided into lively, thematic chapters that arrange the activities by age level, this step-by-step guide lets you mentor your children as they discover the world around them and practice key problem-solving skills. From biology and chemistry to earth science and physics, you'll tackle investigations, experiments, expeditions, and competitions guaranteed to get your family's creative juices flowing and bring out everyone's inner scientist. You'll also help your kids learn how to apply scientific concepts to real-life situations. Best of all, each activity can be completed with everyday items found around the house, so you can get started right away!

Complete with "Brain Boosters," "That's Amazing" facts, and tasty recipes, *Family Science* is the best way to learn while having fun with your family!

Sandra Markle is the award-winning author of over seventy science books for children and educators. She's developed science TV specials for CNN and PBS, developed a science education Web site for the National Science Foundation, and written for many magazines, including Disney's *FamilyFun*. Markle is also a nationally known science education consultant who frequently speaks at workshops and conventions and visits schools presenting hands-on science programs for children.

Other Books of Interest

Hands-On Life Science Activities for Grades K–6, Second Edition

Marvin N. Tolman

Paper
ISBN: 0-7879-7865-5

"The Hands-On books are an awesome resource that has enhanced my science units. Every activity has easy step-by-step instructions, a materials list, and teacher information. My students and I love the activities."

—Patti W. Seeholzer, third-grade teacher, River Heights Elementary School, Utah, and winner of the 2002 Presidential Award for Excellence in Science Teaching

This second edition of Marvin N. Tolman's best-selling book *Hands-On Life Science Activities for Grades K–6* offers compelling activities that help teach students thinking and reasoning skills along with basic science concepts and facts. The book's activities follow the discovery/inquiry approach and encourage students to analyze, synthesize, and infer based on their own hands-on experiences. This new edition includes an expanded "Teacher Information" section, and increased emphasis on collaboration, shared observations, and writing. It includes inquiry-based models and cooperative learning projects using materials easily found in the classroom or around the home. Many of the activities can easily become great science fair ideas, and lessons and activities are correlated with national science standards.

Designed to be user friendly, the book is organized into seven sections and printed in a lay-flat format.

- Living Through Adaptation
- Animals
- Growing and Changing
- Plants and Seeds
- Body Systems
- The Five Senses
- Health and Nutrition

Marvin N. Tolman, Ed.D., is a popular presenter at national meetings of science teachers, contributes to academic journals, reviews science education materials, and edits textbook and journal series. Currently, he is professor of teacher education at Brigham Young University and author of the popular *Hands-On Science* series from Jossey-Bass.

Other Books of Interest

Hands-On Earth Science Activities for Grades K–6, Second Edition

Marvin N. Tolman

Paper
ISBN: 0-7879-7866-3

"The Hands-On books are an awesome resource that has enhanced my science units. Every activity has easy step-by-step instructions, a materials list, and teacher information. My students and I love the activities."

—Patti W. Seeholzer, third-grade teacher, River Heights Elementary School, Utah, and winner of the 2002 Presidential Award for Excellence in Science Teaching

This second edition of Marvin N. Tolman's best-selling book *Hands-On Earth Science Activities for Grades K–6* offers compelling activities that help teach students thinking and reasoning skills along with basic science concepts and facts. The book's activities follow the discovery/inquiry approach and encourage students to analyze, synthesize, and infer based on their own hands-on experiences. This new edition includes an expanded "Teacher Information" section, and increased emphasis on collaboration, shared observations, and writing. It includes inquiry-based models and cooperative learning projects using materials easily found in the classroom or around the home. Many of the activities can easily become great science fair ideas, and lessons and activities are correlated with national science standards.

Designed to be user friendly, the book is organized into eight sections and printed in a lay-flat format.

- Air
- Water
- Weather
- The Earth
- Ecology
- Above the Earth
- Beyond the Earth
- Current Electricity

Marvin N. Tolman, Ed.D., is a popular presenter at national meetings of science teachers, contributes to academic journals, reviews science education materials, and edits textbook and journal series. Currently, he is professor of teacher education at Brigham Young University and author of the popular *Hands-On Science* series from Jossey-Bass.

Other Books of Interest

Hands-On Physical Science Activities for Grades K–6, Second Edition

Marvin N. Tolman

Paper
ISBN: 0-7879-7867-1

"A great resource for all prospective and practicing elementary teachers."

—David T. Crowther, associate professor, science education, University of Nevada, Reno

This second edition of Marvin N. Tolman's best-selling book *Hands-On Physical Science Activities for Grades K–6* offers compelling activities that help teach students thinking and reasoning skills along with basic science concepts and facts. The book's activities follow the discovery/inquiry approach and encourage students to analyze, synthesize, and infer based on their own hands-on experiences. This new edition includes an expanded "Teacher Information" section, and increased emphasis on collaboration, shared observations, and writing. It includes inquiry-based models and cooperative learning projects using materials easily found in the classroom or around the home. Many of the activities can easily become great science fair ideas, and lessons and activities are correlated with national science standards.

Designed to be user friendly, the book is organized into eight sections and printed in a lay-flat format.

- Nature of Matter
- Energy
- Light
- Sound
- Simple Machines
- Magnetism
- Static Electricity
- Current Electricity

Marvin N. Tolman, Ed.D., is a popular presenter at national meetings of science teachers, contributes to academic journals, reviews science education materials, and edits textbook and journal series. Currently, he is professor of teacher education at Brigham Young University and author of the popular *Hands-On Science* series from Jossey-Bass.

Other Books of Interest

Crime Scene Investigations

Real-Life Science Labs for Grades 6–12

Pam Walker and Elaine Wood

Paper

ISBN: 0-7879-6630-4

Turn your students into super sleuths with the 68 exciting lessons and labs in this unique resource! All provide complete teacher background information and reproducible worksheets that challenge students to observe carefully, think critically, conduct lab tests, document results, and try to meet the burden of proof to solve crimes ranging from check forgery to murder.

For easy use the labs are organized into four sections that will:

- Reinforce skills of observation, experimentation, and logical thinking
- Help students identify unknown substances, recognize patterns, and determine the chain of events
- Teach principles of inheritance, DNA analysis, and skeletal structure
- Demonstrate how reconstruction of past events can influence the outcome of a criminal investigation

All lessons and activities include complete background information with step-by-step procedures for the teacher and reproducible student worksheets.

Critical Thinking: Reinforce skills of observation, experimentation, and logical thinking.

Physical Science: Apply the principles of chemistry and physics to identify unknown substances, recognize patterns, and determine the chain of events.

Life Science: Focus on evidence left at crime scenes by living things and teach principles of inheritance, DNA analysis, skeletal structure, and characteristics of hair and skin.

Earth Science, Archaeology, and Anthropology: Consider unidentified remains, mummies, skeletons, and more to demonstrate how reconstruction of past events can influence the outcome of a criminal investigation.